Magic and Superstition in Europe

Critical Issues in History

Consulting Editor: Donald T. Critchlow

Magic and Superstition in Europe

A Concise History from Antiquity to the Present

Michael D. Bailey

ROWMAN & LITTLEFIELD PUBLISHERS, INC.
Lanham • Boulder • New York • Toronto • Plymouth, UK

ROWMAN & LITTLEFIELD PUBLISHERS, INC.

Published in the United States of America
by Rowman & Littlefield Publishers, Inc.
A wholly owned subsidary of The Rowman & Littlefield Publishing Group, Inc.
4501 Forbes Boulevard, Suite 200, Lanham, Maryland 20706
www.rowmanlittlefield.com

Estover Road
Plymouth PL6 7PY
United Kingdom

British Library Cataloguing in Publication Information Available

Library of Congress Cataloging-in-Publication Data

Bailey, Michael David, 1971-
    Magic and superstition in Europe : a concise history from antiquity to the present /
Michael D. Bailey.
        p.   cm.— (Critical issues in history)
    Includes bibliographical references and index.
    ISBN-13: 978-0-7425-3386-8 (cloth : alk. paper)
    ISBN-10: 0-7425-3386-7 (cloth : alk. paper)
    ISBN-13: 978-0-7425-3387-5 (pbk. : alk. paper)
    ISBN-10: 0-7425-3387-5 (pbk. : alk. paper)
    1. Magic—Europe—History.   2. Superstition—Europe—History.   I. Title.
BF1589.B35   2007
133.4'3094—dc22

                                                        2006022247

Printed in the United States of America

♾ ™ The paper used in this publication meets the minimum requirements of American
National Standard for Information Sciences—Permanence of Paper for Printed Library
Materials, ANSI/NISO Z39.48-1992.

To my teachers and my students

Contents

Acknowledgments

This book owes its genesis to Donald Critchlow, who suggested that I write for what was then his series. My thanks go to him for his invitation, and to the editors and staff at Rowman and Littlefield for seeing the project through to completion. I was eager to write this book, since I had been teaching the history of European magic and witchcraft for several years, trying to develop a coherent general narrative that would make sense of the long history of magic and also trying to situate the development of magical beliefs and conceptions of superstition within the broader course of European history. For serving as unwitting preliminary audiences for many of my thoughts on these matters, I thank the students who took my seminars at the University of Cincinnati, Saint Louis University, the University of Pennsylvania, and Iowa State University. I began to write the book at the University of Pennsylvania, where I was a Mellon Fellow at the Penn Humanities Forum, and I largely completed the project with the help of a summer fellowship from the Center for Excellence in the Arts and Humanities at Iowa State University.

In the course of my work, a number of people have assisted me, directly or indirectly, and I must thank several former teachers, present colleagues, and friends. Richard Kieckhefer and William Monter will find many of their ideas about the history of magic and witchcraft reflected here, not simply because they taught me so well in my impressionable youth, but because a decade later, in my possibly more judicious middle age, I continue to find their arguments compelling. Bill also generously read large sections of the work in draft, which his comments and occasional corrections greatly improved. Robert Lerner helped shape my thought on superstition. More basically, he helped make me a historian, and my larger notions of the course of Western history owe much to him (even when my interpretations may differ from his). Edward Muir has also taught me a great deal, especially through his work on ritual. I am grateful for stimulating conversations with Ann Moyer and especially Edward Peters at the University of Pennsylvania. At Iowa State, my colleagues David Hollander, John Monroe, and Matt Stanley provided invaluable help by looking over sections of the manuscript that fell within their chronological areas of expertise.

Like most authors, I am fascinated by my subject. I am also fortunate enough to have in my life some dear friends who gently remind me that matters of magic and superstition can seem a bit esoteric. They were often in my thoughts as I completed this book intended to convey the historical scope and importance of magic to a broad audience. To whatever extent I have succeeded in achieving that goal, it is at least partly because of their inspiration.

Introduction

At the beginning of one of the most famous literary depictions of magic and magicians in Western culture, Johann Wolfgang von Goethe's (1749–1832) brilliantly driven and dissatisfied Faust laments that he has thoroughly studied all the major areas of learning as categorized in his day—philosophy, jurisprudence, medicine, and theology. Yet he declares himself, for all his effort, to be "only so wise as I was before," not having achieved any of the deep knowledge he desires. For this, he will turn to magic, summoning the demonic spirit Mephistopheles and demanding that he reveal the secret truths of the world. The arrogant Faust wagers his soul that his full desire will never be satisfied. Two centuries earlier, Christopher Marlowe (1564–1593) had presented his *Dr. Faustus* as lusting not just after knowledge but also after power. In the "lines, circles, scenes, letters, and characters" of necromantic texts he believes he can find such magics that "All things that move between the quiet poles / Shall be at my command." Even kings and emperors will lack the power, indeed the "omnipotence," that he will wield.[1]

Based on an actual historical figure (who will be mentioned briefly in chapter 6), the legendary character of Faust serves to illustrate how for centuries, indeed for most of European history, magic could be a serious subject for serious men (Goethe, admittedly, was writing after this time had largely passed). Although it stood outside all accepted avenues of inquiry and behavior, it promised knowledge and power greater than any other human pursuit might provide. Magic was often considered dark and sinister, indeed demonic; yet it was also intriguing and alluring. Learned authorities, even when they did not pursue magical practices themselves, sought to understand their operations. Philosophers debated whether occult magical properties existed in nature, and if so, how and to what ends these could be exploited.

Physicians considered magical causes for disease. And, particularly during the era of the great European witch hunts, judicial authorities put suspected magicians to death because theologians told them that magic almost always involved terrible pacts made with the devil.

Magic continues to fascinate modern minds, and it remains the object of considerable academic and scholarly investigation. Those drawn to study the subject today typically no longer regard magic as a fearful threat to society, nor do they intend their works to be used as weapons in a war aimed at extirpating perceived magical practices and those who might perform them. Nevertheless, just as authorities in the past, modern scholars seek to understand and explain magic and superstition—topics that have always been regarded as inherently mysterious, murky, and in all senses occult—in ways that will be clear, meaningful, and enlightening to their contemporaries. This, certainly, is the goal of the present book. My approach is not philosophical (that is, theoretical) or scientific; still less is it legal or theological. Rather, it is historical, seeking to trace the development of magic and superstition in Europe from antiquity to the present. Covering such a long span of time, especially in a brief book, carries limitations, risks, and unavoidable detriments, but it also affords the opportunity to present the full historical trajectory of magic, albeit synoptically, at least in the West. This picture might then prove useful as a basis for further, more detailed investigation.

Any general inquiry into the realm of magic must begin with the fundamental question: what is magic, exactly? For much of European history, educated authorities defined magic mainly in terms of human invocation of demonic powers in opposition to divine will and directed against the stability and proper order of Christian society. In the modern world, such a definition no longer suffices, but magic is still often conceived in contrast (if no longer in direct opposition) to religion. That is, rites or actions that seek to access and manipulate supernatural powers—spirits, demons, cosmic forces—but that are not contained within some established and widely recognized modern religious system might be described as magic. Another opposition, perhaps even more essential for the modern world, exists between magic and science. Any attempt to control or affect the physical world or the human psyche that does not conform to modern scientific principles or operate through scientifically understood chains of causation can be described as magic. If one does not believe that such actions will produce any real or direct effects, they can also be termed superstitious.

These modern distinctions are generally not applicable in a historical context, however—certainly not in Europe before the Scientific Revolution and Enlightenment of the seventeenth and eighteenth centuries. This is not because premodern people did not distinguish between religion and magic or between science and magic, although the manner in which they understood these categories could be quite different from those common in the modern West. Rather, it is most basically because the premodern world distinguished much less clearly between religion and science. By this I mean that no absolute boundaries were believed to exist between the supernatural and the natural; indeed, the natural world was conceived as a direct manifestation of supernatural order. Spiritual forces, divine or demonic, infused material creation and were active in the operations of the physical world. Thus human attempts to control or affect events in the world could proceed along what most modern Westerners would regard as purely natural lines, along purely spiritual ones, or, as was often the case, could combine elements of both, since contemporaries recognized no fundamental disjuncture between these approaches. The sharp separation of the spiritual world and religious belief from the physical world and scientific rationalism, which is such a fundamental feature of modern Western culture, is a relatively recent product of Europe's movement toward modernity. It is in fact a cornerstone of what is perceived as "modernity," although an absolute separation between these spheres of reality is by no means universally accepted even in the West today.

While medieval and early modern Europeans did not understand religion or science in fully the same way as modern Westerners typically do, educated authorities did distinguish *magia* (magic) from *scientia* and certainly from proper *religio* or *fides* (faith), although of course still not in ways precisely identical to those most common in the modern West. The situation is similar with *superstitio* (superstition). Magic and superstition have never been identical categories, yet they often overlap. A superstition need not entail belief in or attempted recourse to magic, but many magical practices can be regarded as superstitious. This has been equally true, although for very different reasons, in both the modern and premodern eras. In modern parlance, superstition is most often set in stark opposition to science and scientific rationalism. A superstitious belief is one held without proper scientific grounding, and in the scientific worldview superstitious acts produce no real effects, although credulous minds yearn to believe that they do. Religious systems themselves may be regarded as superstitious by those who do not hold any faith in them. In medieval and early modern Europe, on the contrary, superstition was the direct opposite of proper religion. All superstitious actions, authorities held, were grounded in some sort of basic error in belief or ritual action. They were not, however, necessarily regarded as irrational or inefficacious. For example, a magical incantation would be regarded as superstitious if it was deemed to draw on the power of demons rather than on the virtuous power of Christ or his saints. It might still produce a very real effect, however, since demons were believed to have real power in the world, and educated authorities could explain their abilities in systematic, rational, and—in the understanding of that period—entirely scientific ways.

This is not to say that medieval and early modern people, even learned authorities, had absolutely clear or stable ideas about the precise boundaries of magic or superstition. These categories were always somewhat vague and their connotations could change significantly over time. Precisely because they were so bound up with a multitude of ways in which premodern people interacted with, understood, and attempted to shape their world—ways that modern Western culture might label as either religion or science—magic and superstition were often hotly contested categories. As terms, they almost always carried a negative connotation, set in contrast to officially approved knowledge or belief, or legitimate rites or actions. Few people in any premodern era would ever have labeled their own actions magical or superstitious. Rather, magic and superstition were almost always what other people did and believed in, whether those others were from a foreign culture or from another social or perceived intellectual level within a given society. Yet the definition of otherness is an essential element of the definition of one's own self and society, as well as of gradations and divisions within a society. Even when certain groups—be they elite, learned Renaissance mages, or modern neopagan Wiccans—have declared that some of what they do is indeed magic, it has usually been part of an attempt to separate themselves from the established intellectual and cultural norms of their times and to add their voices to a redefinition of certain aspects of their society.

Magic and superstition, then, far from being exotic or marginal issues in European history, have always been integral aspects of Western societies and cultures. Their greatest importance lies precisely in their deployment as categories of anything from mild condescension to virulent condemnation intended to define the limits of acceptable belief or action in any number of areas—health and healing, the achievement of good fortune and success, the attainment of love or friendship, control over one's personal destiny, or the acquisition of wealth and power, to name just a few. This book traces the history of that deployment, exploring how magic and superstition were understood and used over the course of European history. Rather than defining magic and superstition as theoretical abstractions and then looking to see whether and to what degree these existed in the past, I approach the development and use of these categories as important historical phenomena. My most basic criterion for determining what beliefs and practices to include in my exploration is whether a society or some significant segment within it—usually but not necessarily intellectually or judicially powerful elites bent on condemning—would have considered a given set of beliefs or practices to be magical or superstitious. Since authorities often disagreed on the exact limits of these categories, however, and since more popular understandings could be extremely fluid, I am fairly capacious in my conception of the topic.

Applying contemporary, historical definitions of magic and superstition will not resolve all problems of categorization, as such definitions have always been sharply contested, and just as often ignored, by various groups at various times. In antiquity, for example, a multiplicity of cultures, and above all a multiplicity of religious cults, created exceptionally slippery concepts of magic and superstition. What one society considered wholly legitimate cultic rites, their neighbors would explicitly label "magic." In medieval Europe, as Christianity became hegemonic, theoretical definitions of magic and super-stition could become more stable and uniform. Christian theology clearly separated demonic from divine power, and magic, for the most part, was con-ceived as drawing on the former. Yet in practice, whether a given healing or protective rite, or even a harmful curse, invoked the power of demons or of the deity could be terribly difficult to determine. In the absence of clear, authoritative pronouncements on the provenance of some particular act (and often even after such pronouncements were made), many people continued to engage in traditional rites. It is unlikely that they considered their own actions to be "magic." Yet others considered them so, and for the purpose of this study, such practices cannot be ignored.

Although this book treats magic and superstition broadly across an extended period of time, nevertheless it aims to provide a concise overview of this enormous topic. Brevity in all areas will be the cost, as will the neces-sary imposition of certain limitations of scope. The first of these will involve the scope of "Europe" itself, which here will almost always mean western or west-central Europe. As a geographical entity, Europe is easily enough defined as the landmass north of the Mediterranean and Black seas and west of the Ural Mountains. Throughout most of history, however, these bound-aries have had little political or cultural meaning. In antiquity, Greek and Roman civilization occupied certain areas of the European landmass, but these cultures were essentially Mediterranean, sharing far more in common with North Africa and the Near East than with the Celtic and Germanic peoples who also inhabited much of the European continent. Each of these cultures' conceptions of magic and superstition, as well as those of ancient Jewish culture, will be treated here as providing essential foundations for later European understandings of magic.

The main focus of this book will extend from the political, intellectual, and cultural ascendancy of Christianity in the fourth and fifth centuries to the eighteenth-century Enlightenment, when concerted efforts were undertaken to excise Christian religion from other areas of European thought and political life. Since throughout this period magic and superstition were defined primarily by Christian authorities and within an essentially Christian culture, Europe itself will be defined largely as Western Christendom, the boundaries of which fluctuated but generally centered on western Europe. Much will be lost by this definition. Medieval Byzantium and the whole rich culture of Eastern Christianity, including its traditions of magic and condemnations of superstition, will be excluded. Islamic traditions of magic will be considered only insofar as they influenced Western Christian ones, despite the fact that Muslims ruled over most of the Iberian peninsula for centuries during the Middle Ages and over most of the Balkans during the early modern period. Likewise, Orthodox Russia will be discussed only briefly to present a contrast to Western patterns of witch hunting. Within Western Christendom, Jewish magical traditions will not be given the independent attention that, in a longer treatment, they would certainly deserve. Rather, as with Islam, Judaism will be examined mainly for its influence on the overall historical development of magic in Europe.

Magic and superstition occupy a very different place in the modern Western culture that Europe has spawned than they have in any previous society. The German sociologist Max Weber argued at the beginning of the twentieth century that a central facet of modern Western culture was its "disenchantment" (*Entzauberung*, literally, "removal of magic"). This had largely occurred, he thought, during the Protestant Reformation and its break from medieval Catholic "superstition." Later scholars, recognizing that the world of Reformation Europe was still profoundly concerned with magic—the sixteenth and seventeenth centuries were the era of the major European witch hunts, after all—pushed disenchantment back to the Scientific Revolution and then to the Enlightenment, when magic and superstition, along with much of religion itself, were excluded from a modern worldview that would now be grounded in scientific rationalism. Of course, this disenchantment never took full hold, and so the history of magic hardly ends in the seventeenth or eighteenth centuries. Magical traditions persist in the modern

West and continue to draw, sometimes in historically very inaccurate ways, on medieval and early modern roots. Moreover, magic continues to play its historical function as a category through which, by defining otherness, essential aspects of modern society and Western culture—above all the very notion of "modernity" itself—can be defined or challenged.

Ever since the Enlightenment, when progressive philosophes produced diatribes against "medieval superstition" (by which they meant organized churches and religious ritual as much as magic), the history of magic has had a place in Western thought. In the last decades of the twentieth century the subject became a truly burgeoning field. A survey such as this would not be possible without a wealth of detailed studies on which to draw, at least for most of the areas covered. Above all, the topic of early modern witchcraft and witch hunting has been examined extensively, indeed, far out of proportion to other areas of magic and superstition, and one of the goals of this work will be to set the phenomenon of diabolical witchcraft more appropriately in its larger context. The tendency to focus only on a single period, or subperiod, and often only on a single aspect of magic within the long stretch of Western history is certainly understandable and indeed necessary, given the historical complexity and cultural specificity of the issues involved. Nevertheless, I hope that a concise and coherent overview of European magic and superstition generally, with all the necessary limitations and omissions, will prove useful for both students and scholars, not only those interested in some specific aspect of magic covered here, but also those concerned with understanding magic itself as a vital aspect of larger European history. Beyond this, I hope that an account of the development and deployment of concepts of magic and superstition across European history may help inform scholars working in fields other than history and studying cultures other than those of Europe. Above all, I hope that this book will provide access to anyone—professional academic, student, or general reader—who wants to know more about magic as a vital and perennial aspect of human society, human culture, and human nature itself.

Note

1. Johann Wolfgang von Goethe, *Faust, Part I*, lines 354–59; Christopher Marlowe, *Dr. Faustus*, lines 50–56.

CHAPTER ONE

Roots in the Ancient World

Sometime in the later fourth century C.E., a well-educated young man living in the cosmopolitan Roman city of Carthage (located on the southern shore of the Mediterranean, near what is now Tunis) discovered that a spoon was missing and could not be found anywhere in his household. Since the spoon was apparently of some value, he asked his friend Licentius to consult a certain Albicerius, who was a famous local diviner. Licentius, accompanied by a slave, sought out this man, who, for his part, immediately and correctly identified the location of the lost spoon. He then provided an additional service, telling Licentius that the slave who accompanied him had secretly pilfered some of the money that he was carrying to pay the diviner. This, Licentius reported, Albicerius did before he had even seen the money or knew how much had been brought to pay him.

Such magical and divinatory practices were common in the ancient world. Thus this story is largely unremarkable, and similar tales probably played out fairly often in teeming Carthage. Yet one fact sets this story apart. The man who had lost the spoon and sent Licentius on his errand was Augustine, future bishop of Hippo, saint, and the most important and influential of all the Latin fathers of the Christian church. In numerous writings, including his famous *De civitate dei* (City of God) and equally important (for the subjects dealt with here) *De divinatione daemonum* (On the Divination of Demons), Augustine established virtually all the essential elements of Christian conceptions of magic and superstition that later authorities would follow throughout the European Middle Ages and early modern period. This story, however, reveals a younger Augustine, not yet the church father, but a worldly Roman living in a culture thoroughly permeated with what, in modern vocabulary, would be called magical practices.

The account above comes from one of Augustine's lesser works, a treatise called *Contra academicos* (Against the Academics). Augustine offered a perhaps even more telling example of the pervasiveness of magic in his day in his far more famous *Confessiones* (Confessions), in which he recounted how he had once decided to enter a public contest in poetry recitation as a test of his oratory and rhetorical skills. On this occasion, a certain magician (Augustine claimed not to remember the man's name) approached him and asked what he would be willing to pay in order to be assured of victory. Augustine rebuffed the man, telling him that he abhorred his "filthy rites." Apparently Augustine knew that such magic would involve the ritual killing of an animal, and he refused to allow even a fly to be slain to ensure his victory in the contest. Writing in the *Confessions* after his complete conversion to Christianity, Augustine explained that animals were slain in such magical rites as sacrifices to demons. He lamented that at the time this encounter actually took place, he had rejected the magical assistance only out of revulsion at the blood-rites involved and not out of pious devotion to God and rejection of any demonic ceremonies.

These two examples reveal much about the nature of magic and its place in the late imperial Roman world. First, magical services were readily accessible, and supernatural aid could be employed for even the most mundane ends, such as locating a lost utensil. Second, practitioners of such arts might be well-known professionals, earning their livelihood by their skills in this craft, although amateur practice surely also abounded. Finally, however common magical practices were in the ancient world and however openly professional magicians might practice their art, there was something vaguely disreputable and distasteful about their acts, such that a not-yet-particularly-pious young Augustine might send a friend to seek out the services of a magician but would turn away in disgust when approached by one himself.

These stories serve another purpose, as well. They link the coming Christian world of medieval and early modern Europe and the beliefs and concerns about magic, witchcraft, and superstition that prevailed there to the older cultures of the ancient West and their understandings of such beliefs and practices. Before Augustine was a foundational figure in the early history of Christianity, he was a Roman intellectual, fully educated in the rich classical tradition. As Christianity grew within the Roman world, eventually emerging as the official religion of the empire in the fourth century, it adopted and adapted much of that tradition, such that later European conceptions of magic and superstition (the very words, as we shall see, are of Greek and Roman origin, respectively) rest on classical foundations. This chapter, therefore, surveys that foundation of magical concepts, beliefs, and practices in antiquity.

Rites of Power in the Ancient West

Although the ancient Greeks invented the name "Europe" (*Europa*) to distinguish the lands west of the Aegean Sea and the Hellespont from Asia to the east, none of the cultures or civilizations of the classical era can really be described as European. The late Roman Empire in which Augustine lived his life included within its borders a good portion of the lands that would come to be Christian Europe, but the center of the Roman world was the Mediterranean Sea. Although Augustine was born on the southern shores of those waters and was thus an African, he certainly would not have felt that he crossed any great cultural divide when, for example, he went north to Rome and then Milan in 383 to find employment as a teacher of rhetoric, to pursue Neoplatonic studies, and ultimately to undergo a full and final conversion to Christianity. In its cosmopolitan culture, as in its basic geography, the Roman world was Mediterranean, and at its eastern end, the empire incorporated most of those lands that had given rise to earlier civilizations of the ancient West—Greece, Egypt, and even for a brief time Mesopotamia. It was to the Hellenized east, where a remarkable synthesis of these cultures had long since occurred, that Rome looked for its heritage. It was also from the east that magic was believed to have come. But the very concept of magic, how it arose and what it entailed in the ancient world, is a complex subject that must be explored in detail.

The category of magic is often vague and its boundaries can be quite fluid. Seemingly clear enough in a very general sense—everyone knows more or less what is meant by "magic" or "magical," after all—the term proves terribly difficult to define coherently and satisfactorily for all the contexts in which it can be used. This has been true historically as well as in the modern world. Moreover, while beliefs and practices that can be categorized as magical have been present in every human culture known to history, what has been meant or just as often merely connoted by specific terms for magic has changed significantly over the millennia. For example, medieval Christian Europe, drawing on doctrines established in no small part by Augustine, struck upon a fairly definite means of defining magic, as a method of invoking or employing supernatural spiritual forces as well as occult natural powers, in opposition to religious ritual and ceremony. Religion drew on divine power, asserted generation after generation of clerical authorities, while magic functioned mainly by invoking the power of demons. In theory, this distinction was clear enough. In practice, the boundary demarcating divine from demonic forces proved terribly difficult to distinguish in many cases, and uncertainty in such matters was a constant element in European thought on magic. Yet even this problematic distinction cannot be applied to the pre-Christian cultures of the ancient world.

Most ancient peoples did not conceive of a single divine force animating the entire universe. Rather, they believed in numerous deities, both their own gods and also those of other peoples, which were usually held to be real and powerful, albeit foreign, entities. In addition to deities, most ancient cultures also believed in a wide range of lesser spiritual beings inhabiting the world. The Greeks referred to such spirits generally as *daimones*, which for the Romans became *daemones*. Early Christian authorities, writing in both Greek and Latin, conceived of these creatures as demons, inherently evil beings and ultimately fallen angels assailing humanity at the command of their prince, Satan. Yet for the ancients, such creatures were not necessarily evil or hostile to humanity. Instead, they were a part of a vast, often morally ambiguous realm of spiritual powers, including the gods themselves, which could prove dangerous, harmful, or destructive, but which could also be accessed by humans for aid and protection through ritualized acts, verbal formulae, or ceremonies.

The cultures of the ancient West developed a range of terms—often vague, but sometimes quite precise—to designate, describe, and occasionally condemn these practices, and these categories are rarely translated adequately by modern terms such as "magic" or "witchcraft." Moreover, there is no reason to assume that the ancients necessarily saw all such practices as inherently similar to one another or would have understood the propriety of grouping them under broad labels. Yet, aside from highly focused studies, there is no way for modern scholars to disentangle themselves fully from modern categories, and the best we can do (certainly the best that can be attempted in a very general survey such as this) is to be aware of the difficulties and dangers these categories present. If we accept the very basic definition that magic is any attempt to manipulate supernatural or natural forces by anything other than direct, physical means, we will recognize that religion itself (another term difficult to disassociate from its often historically inapplicable modern connotations), or at least much religious ritual and ceremony, is not in any clear way separable from magic. In fact, religion may better be conceived as a subcategory of magic itself. Such an approach would not be entirely alien to ancient thought, for ancient societies typically regarded the religious rites of foreign peoples as magical practices, and certainly the earliest Christian authorities explicitly categorized all pagan religious rites as superstitious and magical.

This is not to say that ancient peoples drew no distinctions between what in modern terms might be described as "the religious" and "the magical." To claim that a Babylonian priest regarded the cultic rituals he performed as being akin to the charms employed by a rustic healer or the spells of some maleficent sorcerer would surely be false. Yet the ancient situation is so complex, and so distinct in many ways from any modern categories, that at least initially even the public, cultic rituals of early cultures (their "religion," that is) must be presented, so that the full spectrum of ancient rites of power can be appreciated. Within that spectrum, we will begin to see how ancient peoples understood and distinguished between various types of rites, and we will explore some of the terms ("magic" and "superstition" among them) that they developed to demarcate different kinds of practice. These distinctions and demarcations were, however, never absolutely clear within any ancient culture. Moreover, as this chapter examines several cultures spanning at least a millennium, I cannot always employ culturally or historically specific terminology. In drawing general conclusions, I often employ a generalized concept of magic that, as will be shown, was almost certainly alien to the ancient world. Yet I also try to clarify ancient conceptions of the practices dealt with here, insofar as they were clear at the time.

The earliest evidence for powerful rites intended to affect the physical or spiritual world in some way comes from the very earliest Western civilizations to leave written records. Curse tablets and spells have been found among the cuneiform writing of the great Mesopotamian city-states. The production of this fragmentary evidence was obviously limited to the small, literate class of priestly scribes that dominated these cities, and these sources must mask a much larger and now doubtless unrecoverable world of common or popular spells, charms, and other rites. This evidence is also, however, indicative of the place that such rites occupied in these civilizations. That is, what to modern minds could appear as magic was not in any way marginal, but was a central part of the social structure of these cultures. The Mesopotamian city-states were not simply physical territories united under a ruler; they were not purely human political units. Rather, they were essentially divine or supernatural (again, the modern terms fail to catch the full and real meaning). Amid the numerous deities recognized and worshiped by the ancient Mesopotamians, each city was typically linked to a particular patron god and his or her cult. Each was centered physically around a great temple complex in which resided the scribe-priests who represented a political and social as well as a spiritual elite. Each was ruled by a priest-king who derived his authority from the god he represented. Marduk, for example, was supreme in Babylon; Assyria was the land of the god Assur.

This connection between the physical and spiritual realms—between the mundane and the supernatural—was essential to all aspects of human life, so much so that even to imply a boundary between them would doubtless have made little sense to ancient peoples. All variety of success or misfortune, whether of a society or an individual, depended on the maintenance of proper harmony with the gods and other forces that shaped the world. Victory or defeat in war, the healthy growth or withering of crops, the fertility of animals as well as of human beings, and individual health and good fortune or their opposites all derived from an individual's or a society's relationship with powerful spiritual entities. Many rites and ceremonies existed to generate and solidify harmony. These included the civic rituals for which kings and priestly castes were mainly responsible, but also extended to many individual rites of prayer and purification. Taboos were numerous, and the violation of any of them, knowingly or not, would disrupt the essential harmony on which the world depended. Thus practices arose to undo damage or to ameliorate the violation of a taboo. In addition, there were harmful forces that actively sought to disrupt an individual's or a city's relationship with the gods. Such means of assault on persons and on the body politic were held to be as serious, in many cases far more serious, than any physical crime. Legislation was passed against such acts, and protective and curative rites were developed to combat them. Indeed, much of our knowledge of the harmful spells and the wicked spell-casters believed to exist in ancient Mesopotamia comes not from preserved records of evil practices or rituals themselves, but from legislation, proscriptive literature, and counter-ceremonies.

The Mesopotamian cities can serve as a brief introduction to the earliest conceptions of spells, curses, blessings, and other rites of power in Western culture. Other civilizations were similar in many respects. In ancient Egypt too, for example, all of human society and the entire natural world were regulated by relationships of harmony or disharmony with divine or spiritual forces. Egypt also had a small priestly class at the tip of its social pyramid whose primary function was to maintain proper relationships with the gods on behalf of all the people. And Egypt's rulers, the pharaohs, were held to be not merely earthly representatives of the gods, like Mesopotamian kings, but rather to be gods themselves. In Egypt too the violation of numerous taboos or the failure to observe properly any number of rites could have disastrous results, for either groups or individuals. As in Mesopotamia, counter-spells, purification rites, and protective rituals abounded.

The best-known Egyptian protective rites, surviving the millennia to remain firmly fixed in the popular imagination of the modern world, are the various rituals and ceremonies, to say nothing of potential curses, surrounding mummification and funerary practices. Ensuring the proper repose of the dead and their easy entry into the other world was critical for Mesopotamian cultures too, and so complex funerary rites certainly also developed there, as well as protective spells to ward off the angry dead if these rites were improperly followed. But the awesome evidence of Egyptian funerary practices, at least those performed for the wealthiest members of Egyptian society, has left an indelible mark on the psyche of all later Western cultures. A ritually inscribed gem from the Hellenistic period, for example, depicted a mummy surrounded by writing that enjoined the child of a certain woman to sleep as the mummy does, that is, to die. The notion of Egypt as the land of magic par excellence, often old, secret, and sinister magic, remained vibrant throughout the Roman period and well after.

The classical civilizations of Greece and Rome were not so very different in their essential conceptions of supernatural forces from the earlier cultures of Egypt and the Near East. Greek and Roman societies too were largely structured around ceremonies and rites that allowed human beings to affect or control these forces, or to protect themselves from them. Despite the classical world's being typically associated in the modern imagination with the birth of philosophy, democracy, and rational thought and organization of society, we must remember that Greek city-states were customarily centered around great temple complexes, just as the earliest Mesopotamian cities had been. Civic cults were at the core of Greek political life. The Capitoline Hill in Rome was likewise surmounted with temples. The establishment of a city and the marking of its boundaries were as much religious as political acts. And at the individual level, every Roman family venerated its own household gods and ancestral spirits. One need only recall the famous image from Virgil's *Aeneid* in which, as Troy burns, the hero Aeneas carries both his father and the carved icons of his household gods down to the sea, where they embark on the quest that culminates in the foundation of Rome.

Magic and Superstition in Greece and Rome

Although in their general understanding and practice of numerous rites and ceremonies that could be labeled as magical the Greeks and Romans were not radically different from other early Western cultures, they certainly stand as the most direct and important sources of influence from the ancient world on later European civilization. While it is extremely difficult to measure the degree to which actual antique rites survived to influence common beliefs and practices in later European societies, the writings of Greek and Roman authorities profoundly influenced all later thought about magic and superstition, from the Middle Ages until the Scientific Revolution and Enlightenment of the seventeenth and eighteenth centuries. The very words with which such subjects were discussed and debated were frequently of Greek and Roman origin. *Magic* derives from the Greek *mageia*, whence the Latin *magia*. *Superstition* is an even younger word, of exclusively Roman origin (*superstitio*), although some of the same connotations seem to have been carried by the Greek word *deisidaimonia* (literally, excessive fear of spiritual powers or *daimones*).

The term *mageia* came into Greek from the east. Its definition was initially fairly precise, although not in any sense that relates directly to modern notions of magic, and certainly not to the modern desire to separate the magical from the religious. *Mageia* referred simply to rites and ceremonies performed by a *magos*. The *magoi* (plural of *magos*) were the priestly caste of the Persian Empire, the political and cultural nemesis of the independent Greek city-states through much of the fifth and fourth centuries B.C.E. As mentioned already, ancient cultures commonly believed the deities of other peoples to be real and to have real power over the world. The rites of foreign cults, therefore, were generally held to be effective. Nevertheless, they were usually looked upon with a certain amount of disdain, precisely because they were foreign, and were seen as strange and often sinister, in contrast to the entirely wholesome character of domestic civic cults. The Greeks were no exceptions, and so from its very inception the term *mageia* carried some negative connotation.

In his *Historia* (Histories), an account of the conflict between Greece and Persia, the historian Herodotus (ca. 484–425 B.C.E.) describes the *magoi* as officiates at sacrifices and funeral rites, and also as interpreters of dreams. He attributed other powers to them as well. When, for example, a storm was wrecking the fleet of the Persian king Xerxes, the *magoi* engaged in certain ceremonies, and the storm ended after four days (although Herodotus allowed himself to wonder whether the storm might simply have abated naturally). The slightly later historian Xenophon (ca. 430–355 B.C.E.) regarded the *magoi* as experts in all things having to do with the gods and divine cults. There was a dark side to their activities, though. Herodotus relates how the *magoi*, unlike the priests of other foreign cults—for example, those of Egypt—engaged in animal sacrifices. With their own hands they killed all manner of living creatures, he claims, excepting only humans and dogs. Moreover, they did this not purely out of duty to their gods, but also because they clearly enjoyed it. Nevertheless, since this was the custom in their land, Herodotus withheld any judgment or explicit condemnation.

For the Persians themselves, the *magoi* were not always benevolent figures. Herodotus describes the brief usurpation of the Persian throne by a *magos* just prior to the reign of Darius the Great (522–486 B.C.E.); this is essentially confirmed by a Persian source. The Behistun inscription, a long historical text carved into a cliff face in the Zagros mountains along a road that, in antiquity, connected the city of Babylon with the Persian capital of Ecbatana in Media (now central Iran), describes how Darius overcame the usurper Gaumâta, who is termed a *magos*, although there is no direct indication, either here or in Herodotus, that he used his powers to facilitate his usurpation.

Negative depictions of the *magoi* among Greek authors are not hard to find. One of the earliest such references may have come from the writings of the philosopher Heraclitus of Ephesus (ca. 535–475 B.C.E.). His original text is not known to have survived, but according to later sources, he linked the *magoi* to wild, nighttime wanderers and believed that they practiced wicked and impious rites. In his play *Oedipos tyrannos* (Oedipus the King), Sophocles (ca. 495–406 B.C.E.) used the term *magos* to describe the prophet Tiresias—by no means in a positive light. Tiresias was regarded as a respected seer whose powers came from the (Greek) gods. When he made a prediction unfavorable to Oedipus, however, the king became enraged and accused him of being a *magos* and an *agyrtēs*, that is, an itinerant and disreputable beggar. Shortly thereafter, he labeled him a *mantis*, a term for a less-than-respectable diviner.

The case of Tiresias allows us to see that the Greeks themselves had their own versions of the *magoi*, that is, priests and experts in religious/magical ceremonies who also functioned as soothsayers and diviners, interpreters of dreams, and so forth. Many such people served at the temples that dotted the Greek landscape, both in cities and in the countryside. As professional priests attached to specific and publicly supported cults, their official status was fairly secure. There were other figures, however, who claimed similar powers and expertise, although they had no official appointments and were not attached to any permanent and respectable institutions. These people were not necessarily regarded as charlatans. Tiresias is one such figure—

albeit a legendary one—who was highly regarded. But many sorcerers and diviners, who were often itinerant and clearly made a living by a combination of begging and peddling their skills, were looked upon as disreputable and potentially sinister. Plato (427–347 B.C.E.), in his *Politeia* (Republic), criticized the *agyrtai* and *manteis*, who would go door to door claiming to have healing or protective powers, for offering to harm or curse anyone their clients might designate.

Already in the fifth century B.C.E. the terms *magos* and *mageia* were coming to be associated with such people and their practices. Some of these people may actually have been Persian *magoi* who had crossed into Greece and continued to practice their craft. Their strange language and foreign association would certainly have added a secretive and sinister cast to their actions. More central to the negative reputation that accrued around most practitioners of magical arts—whether actual *magoi* or homegrown *agyrtai, manteis*, or those called by other appellations—was the notion that their actions were private and secretive, as opposed to open and public. The civic cults of the Greek city-states operated to preserve public welfare by maintaining proper relationships with the gods. The actions of private agents, even when they benefited those who had contracted with them, might serve to upset the overall harmony of the cosmos and thus the proper ordering of society. Ultimately, there seems to have been a clear sense in the ancient world that such power was inherently dangerous in the hands of individuals who were unregulated and unsupervised by any official structures or institutions.

Although notions of and about the *magoi* intertwined with other conceptions of powerful ritual practices in the Greek world, the term *mageia* never became a catchall category. Instead, it was the Romans who turned *magia* (the Latinized form of *mageia*) into a more generalized concept, but this transformation occurred very slowly. The word begins to appear in Latin in the first century B.C.E., in the works of Cicero (106–43) and Catullus (84–54). Yet here the word retained its narrowest Greek meaning, that is, the arts of the Persian *magoi* (now *magi* in Latin). This is not to say that the Romans had no notion of disreputable or illicit rites of power before this time. The earliest known code of Roman law, the Twelve Tables, usually dated to around 450 B.C.E., referred to harmful spells or incantations (*carmina*). Other Roman legislation referred to the practice of *veneficium*, literally meaning poisoning, which was regarded as similar to causing harm through spells or curses. The Greeks also had this notion, expressed in their word *pharmakon*. Unlike *pharmakon*, however, which always remained narrow in meaning, the Latin *veneficium* seems to have become a somewhat more generalized term, covering various forms of harmful spells and curses in addition to cases of poisoning per se.

The first appearance of a truly general concept of "magic" in Roman usage is found only late in the century. In his *Eclogues*, written in the fourth decade B.C.E., the poet Virgil (70–19) used the adjective *magicus* in a fairly generalized sense. Only in the first century C.E., however, with the writings of Pliny the Elder (23–79), did a term for magic as a general category really appear. In his *Naturalis historia* (Natural History), Pliny discussed *magicae vanitates*, or magical vanities. These comprised a wide array of arts covering most of those practices in the ancient world that moderns would see as magical. They arose first in Persia, Pliny explains, where they were developed and used by the Persian *magi*. He equates them above all with false medical practices, that is, spells or other rites used for healing or for causing physical harm. Yet he also includes notions of false astrology (*artes mathematicae*) and divinatory rites in his discussions. Pliny equated many of these magical vanities with false or improper religion, and here his conception of magic comes close to another term of purely Latin derivation—superstition.

Roman usage of "superstition," like the use of the borrowed Greek word for magic, has a long and interesting history. The noun form, *superstitio*, was of relatively late origin, appearing only in the work of Cicero in the first century B.C.E.. The adjectival form *superstitiosus*, however, can be found as early as the works of Plautus (ca. 254–184 B.C.E.). The original usage seems to have connoted divination or prophecy. Such practices were central elements of Roman religion, that is, of the public, civic cults of the Roman Republic and later empire. Few ancient cultures had as clear a sense of possessing a divinely appointed destiny as did the Romans, and discerning that destiny in advance was very important to them. Superstitious divination, however, typically referred to non-Roman rites or personalized prophecy rather than the public rituals designed to determine and ensure the overall destiny of Rome. Such divinatory practices seem to have been on the rise in the wake of the Second Punic War (218–201 B.C.E.). Although Rome had emerged victorious from war, Roman society was undergoing rapid change, and the republic's future course seemed very much in doubt. Concern over potentially antisocial ritual practices increased apace. For example, in 186 B.C.E. authorities severely repressed certain rites performed to Bacchus that were deemed dangerous to the Roman state. Likewise, personalized prophecy was regarded as presenting a significant public danger for the Roman people. Since so much of Rome's identity was caught up in a sense of its own trajectory toward its future greatness, private revelations (assumedly false or at least misleading ones) that might contradict or call into question Rome's public destiny could corrupt the will of the citizenry.

In this sense, Cicero strongly condemned *superstitio* in his work *De divinatione* (On Divination). Yet the meaning of superstition was becoming broader. Perhaps because divinatory practices were so central to the Roman public cults, *superstitio* gradually came to imply all forms of false or non-Roman rites. It could be applied to foreign cults, which Roman authorities typically tolerated, although they also feared that these cults would somehow sap the virtue of Roman citizens. The cult of the Egyptian goddess Isis was particularly popular in Rome around this time, for example, and was consequently also often held up for particular censure. In addition, *superstitio* could be applied to the improper observance of Roman cultic practices. In particular, it implied excessive observance, such as the obsessive devotions that some parents apparently paid in order to ensure that their children would not suffer untimely deaths. The Greeks, especially certain Greek philosophers, had also castigated excessive rites performed out of unwarranted fear of spiritual powers, *daimones*, which they described as *deisidaimonia*, a term often translated as "superstition."

This sense of superstition as improper, misinformed religion would come to be very important for later Christian Europe. Insofar as it was a foreign cult, Christianity was labeled superstitious by some Roman authorities. Responding in kind, early Christian writers declared that all Roman cults, since they were directed at false gods, were misguided and superstitious. Superstition then became a general term applied to all the pagan religions that Christianity would encounter as it spread across the Roman world and into northern Europe. Since all the supposed deities of the pagan pantheons were, for church authorities, actually Christian demons in disguise, and since Christianity came to posit that most magical practices drew on the power of demons, almost all forms of magic became forms of superstition.

The Uses of Magic in the Ancient World

Ancient magical rites, whether or not labeled *mageia*, took a wide variety of forms and could be used for almost any purpose, from the spectacular and even cosmic to the most mundane. Literary depictions of magicians and sorcerers have them controlling all the forces of the natural world and playing with the very fabric of the human mind and body. In Book 4 of his *Aeneid*, the Roman poet Virgil vividly describes one such figure as being able to stop the flow of rivers and reverse the course of the stars in the night sky. She could summon the spirits of the dead from the underworld, make the earth groan beneath her feet, and cause trees to uproot themselves and march down from the mountains. As mentioned already, according to the Greek historian Herodotus, the Persian *magoi* may have quelled a storm that was wrecking the fleet of King Xerxes during his invasion of Greece. From one of the earliest pieces of Western literature from the Greek archaic age, Homer's *Odyssey* (written probably in the eighth century B.C.E.), comes the famous account of the sorceress Circe transforming Odysseus's men into swine. And the hero of the Roman writer Apuleius's (ca. 124–170 C.E.) pseudo-autobiography *Metamorphoses*, or *The Golden Ass*, a love-struck young man named Lucius, suffers most of that work's comic misadventures having been transformed into a donkey. Such spectacular displays of power abound in classical literature and may indicate the extreme effects that ancient people thought spells, potions, and powerful rites could have. But certainly the streets of neither Athens nor Rome were thick, on a daily basis, with sad young men transformed into donkeys. For the most part, magical rites were performed for more practical, though no less awesome, ends.

One of the most essential purposes of magical rites in the ancient world was divination. Such practices could take many forms, and which (if any) to categorize as "magical" poses a difficult problem, since, as already noted, divination was an important function of many wholly approved public cults in antiquity. The Persian *magoi* functioned as interpreters of dreams, and they were also learned astrologers, prognosticating by the course of the stars. Astrological prediction was a major element of most ancient cultures. The priests of Babylon and other Mesopotamian city-states were famous for their knowledge of the stars, and these skills were passed on and diffused throughout the ancient world. In an example so commonly known in the West that it often escapes notice, the *magi* whom the Gospels describe coming to visit the infant Christ were, of course, following the sign of a new star that they had observed in the heavens and interpreted as heralding the birth of a great king. Divination was also a major aspect of the communal rites of the Egyptians and Greeks and was a central element of Roman cultic practices.

Although these rites would be entirely approved within their own culture, their status became less certain in other societies. The rites of the Persian *magoi* were literally "magic" in Greece; Egyptian ceremonies became "superstitious" in Rome. Moreover, predictions of the future could be attempted in many ways aside from elaborate cultic rites, and all of these practices carried different levels of respectability and social legitimacy. Priests—but also ordinary people—observed the flights of birds and the entrails of animals. They

hearkened to celestial signs, such as the course of the stars, the flight of comets, and eclipses of the sun and moon. They might attempt to see the future
in polished mirrors, or in placid, reflective water, or in the bones of animals.
One very common form of divination was to cast lots (Latin, *sortes*). At least
in later Latin sources, this practice came to be called *sortilegium*, which would
eventually become a more general term for other magical practices as well.
It provided the root of the later French *sorcellerie* (thirteenth century),
whence the English *sorcery*.

Another very common category of practice that might be classified as
"magical" consisted of love spells, which attempted to instill, or in some
cases repress, passionate feelings. Such practices seem to have been evident
across the entire social spectrum of the ancient world. In the *Aeneid*, Virgil
recounts the tragic love of the Carthaginian queen Dido for the hero Aeneas.
Fleeing the destruction of Troy by the Greeks, he refused to abandon his
destiny, which was to found the city of Rome, in order to live in contentment
and pleasure with Dido in Carthage. In her frustration and grief, the queen
turned for aid to a priestess/magician (that is, a priestess to the Carthaginians
but a sorceress to the Romans) who sought to snare Aeneas in a powerful
love spell. The hero's fate was too strong to overcome, however, and the
abandoned Dido committed suicide.

At the other end of the social spectrum, love magic was often found in
brothels. The Roman poet Lucan (39–65 C.E.) mentions a prostitute who
was rather deficient in physical charms and therefore employed a love potion
to steal the regular customer of another woman in the same brothel. Such
practices persisted throughout the Roman period. The legend of the Christian saint Hilarion (ca. 291–371) tells of a young woman living in the
Roman Empire who had dedicated her life to Christ. A frustrated suitor spent
an entire year learning magical practices at the temple of Asclepius (Amenhotep) in the Egyptian city of Memphis. He was then able to cast a spell so
powerful that the woman lost all control over herself and was ready to abandon her chastity. Only the power of the saint was able to free her.

We need not turn to literature only for examples of the ubiquity of this
type of magic. There is ample evidence from legal sources and from archeological finds that testifies to such practices. Potions or philters (that is,
potions made in conjunction with other rites or rituals of power) were a very
common way of bewitching someone to fall into or out of love. Another
method was to use a practice quite common, and somewhat unique, in the
classical world—to perform a binding spell (*katadesmos* in Greek, from *kata-
deisthai*, "to bind"; commonly referred to as *defixiones* in Latin, from *defigere*,

"to fix" or "bind"). This was a spell that aimed to restrain or control the will or actions of a particular person. Arousing love or passionate desire was a very typical use. The frustrated suitor in the legend of Saint Hilarion used such a spell. In fact, however, this type of practice could be employed for almost any purpose that could loosely be related to binding or compelling someone or something. People could be made to fall in love, or passion could be quelled between a loving couple, but another common use was to bind witnesses in court so that they would be compelled to deliver testimony of a certain kind. Other binding spells might seek to harm a person physically or even kill. Or they could be used to inflict economic damage. Spells were used to bind craftsmen's tools or otherwise make people unproductive. In perhaps the broadest sense, spiritual forces—*daimones*—could be bound to perform almost any function.

The essence of a binding spell was a verbal formula, spoken or written, designed to command or compel someone or something. Very typically these formulae were inscribed on gems or other items, often specially made curse tablets composed of thin pieces of lead (see figure 1.1). The conniving suitor from the legend of Saint Hilarion brought such an item back with him from Egypt and cast his spell by burying it under the threshold of the Christian woman's house. The unlucky hero of Apuleius's *Metamorphoses*, himself a curious but bungling amateur in the world of spells and enchantments, discovered the workshop of a sorceress fully equipped to make such magical objects. These tablets or other items were inscribed with a spell, normally with the names of the persons to be affected and sometimes with images as well. In a particularly physical display of binding or transfixing, one or more nails might be driven through the tablet. The items were then often buried in a location believed to augment their potency. This might be someplace in proximity to the intended victim, or a graveyard might be used, especially if the binding was directed at the spirit of a deceased person or aimed to use the powers of the dead to accomplish its purpose. In a similar way, tablets were often buried at crossroads, near springs, or cast down wells—anywhere spiritual forces were believed to be present, or where contact with chthonic powers might be had. A number of tablets have been recovered from within and around the great hippodromes of the Roman world. Seeking to ensure victory for one team, people inscribed tablets with injunctions to bind the limbs of opposing teams' horses or quell the desire for victory in opposing charioteers or, on occasion, simply to knock out their eyes.

Aside from curse tablets, the ancient world also used what have been called in some modern scholarship voodoo dolls. Although in no way directly

Figure 1.1   Roman curse tablet (*defixio*) with nail holes.

Source: © Copyright the Trustees of the British Museum.

connected to the beliefs or practices of modern voodoo (or more properly Vodoun, now a fully established religion in Haiti and elsewhere in the Caribbean), the term is conveniently descriptive and gives an immediate sense of these items. Quite simply, a doll-like form would be crafted, ritually identified with the intended victim in some way, and then used as part of a binding rite. Rather more brutally, the carcasses of small animals could also be used, their bodies twisted or bound in some way to symbolically or sympathetically evoke the intended magical binding. Animals as large as cats (a creature that itself always had magical connections) might be twisted or contorted, their limbs or backs broken. A creature's mouth might be bent around, for example, and stuffed with its own tail or paw in order to symbolize compelling someone to silence or perhaps something more violent. Such practices were widespread in the ancient West. They seem to have been common in most cultures, and they evidence a fair degree of cultural borrowing and appropriation. For example, binding formulas cut into curse tablets often included invocations not only of gods indigenous to the location in which they were made but of foreign deities as well: a Greek spell might invoke a Babylonian god; a Roman could call upon the Hebrew deity or an Egyptian god.

As this discussion of binding spells indicates, a very common purpose of magical rites in the ancient world was to strike out at real or perceived enemies to cause them physical or other harm. There were other means of harming, aside from binding curses. The Romans believed in spells that had the power to transfer crops from one field to another, and throughout the ancient world poisons were generally regarded as very much like other magical potions (love potions, for example), and poisoning was treated as a form of assault akin to cursing or causing injury by other ritual means. Against such dangers, of course, people developed remedies and means of protection. Among the most common were amulets or talismans, which might be seen as the opposite of curse tablets. They were small objects—perhaps a gem or a figure—held to have protective power or inscribed with some sort of protective formula and carried about the person. In addition, people who felt themselves to be under magical assault could seek a more specific counter-spell, either to undo the magic that had been used against them or to strike back against the person who cast the original spell. To attain relief, victims might turn to the gods and very public rituals, or they might seek the private services of a professional practitioner of magic. Healing and harming were typically thought to be opposite sides of the same coin, and those who had the knowledge and power to bring about the one were usually believed to be able to accomplish the other as well.

The Users of Magic in the Ancient World

Just as magical practices were ubiquitous and varied in the ancient world, the sorts of persons, or beings, who might employ these rites were equally numerous. As with the uses of magic, we may begin with the most spectacular and cosmic. Given that modern scholars see no essential distinction between religious rites and magical ones in most ancient cultures, aside from contemporary cultural perceptions, it should come as little surprise that the gods themselves might be described as using what can appear to be magic. That is, sometimes gods were depicted exercising supernatural or spiritual power that seems somehow innate. In other instances, however, gods used spells, incantations, or other rituals, just as any human priest or magician might do. For example, in one of the foundational myths of ancient Egyptian culture, the god Osiris was murdered and dismembered by his brother. The goddess Isis, his wife, then sought the pieces of his body throughout the world, and when she had assembled them, knitted them back together and restored Osiris to life by means of certain rituals. Among the Greeks, the smith-god Hephestus (Vulcan to the Romans) was often described as incorporating spells or charms into his craft—there being as little clear distinction between magic and technology in the ancient world as between magic and religious rite.

The situation becomes even blurrier when one turns from the major gods of any of the ancient pantheons to the enormous hosts of lesser spirits, deities, and demigods believed to populate the world. The Greeks, for example, told of a race of magician-smiths, the Telchines, who were not unlike Hephestus. They were the original inhabitants of the island of Rhodes, which supposedly rose out of the sea. In addition to their metallurgical powers, they could also change shape at will, and they could control the weather. The most obvious example of this sort, however, was Circe, a goddess or at least a demigod. When the wandering Odysseus came to her island, she transformed his men into swine, not absolutely through inherent power, it would seem, but by using a magical potion that she brewed. Odysseus was able to protect himself from her enchantment by using the power of a certain herb. Although of divine origin, Circe, as described by Homer in the *Odyssey*, became one of the classic literary archetypes of harmful human sorceresses or witches, not only for the ancient world but also for the whole of the later West. The figure of Medea was in many ways similar to Circe, and even further highlights the possible connection between deity and magician. When the hero Jason and his crew of Argonauts traveled to the distant land of Colchis to retrieve the Golden Fleece, they encountered Medea, who, if not a goddess herself, certainly had divine ancestry and who was also a priestess in this foreign land (not unlike the Persian *magoi*). Like Circe, she too became an important literary archetype of the sorceress in the ancient world and thereafter.

Aside from the blurry distinction between at least low-level deities and human magicians, there were in the ancient pantheons certain specific deities who were especially associated with spells, potions, or the powers of binding rites and to whom human magicians often had a special devotion or from whom they learned their arcane knowledge and ritual skills. In some of the earliest cultures, the most important figure of this type was the central mother goddess, representing reproduction and fertility. This type included the Sumerian goddess Inanna, Babylonian and Assyrian Ishtar, Egyptian Isis, and Phoenician and Syrian Astarte. In addition to being general fertility goddesses, all these deities had some connection to the moon, which in its waxing and waning could imply the cycles of death and regeneration, as well as some connection to the underworld, and most basically to mysterious, nocturnal activities. In Greek and Roman myths, the various functions of these mother-goddesses were broken up and distributed over several deities. Associations with magic clung most strongly to those goddesses connected to the moon. The Roman goddess Diana (Greek Artemis), associated with the moon as well as the hunt, was linked to magic. As will be seen in later chapters, even more than in the ancient world, Diana became linked to the practice of magic, superstition, and above all, witchcraft by Christian authorities in medieval and early modern Europe.

In the classical world, the moon-goddess most associated with magic was Hecate. A lunar deity often placed in a sort of triumvirate with Diana and the goddess Selene, Hecate was also closely associated with the underworld and was very much a figure of malevolence and terror. She was imagined as a three-faced spirit who roamed the night and haunted crossroads, visible only to dogs. The howl of dogs at night was believed to be a sign that Hecate was approaching. She was a patron of magic and magicians. The Greek poet Theocritus (ca. 310–250 B.C.E.) composed a poem appropriately entitled *The Sorceresses* (*Pharmakeutriai*) in which a young woman named Simaitha attempted to rekindle the passion of her lover by magical means. She gathered various ingredients and implements and performed a ritual on a moonlit night that summoned Hecate. She then used the goddess's power in a binding spell of the sort described above.

Any god who offered knowledge or skills to humankind could also be associated with magical practices. The Egyptian Thoth, a god of knowledge and writing, was seen as a patron of magic, as was the Greek Apollo, a god of knowledge, science, and especially medicine. Demigods too played a role, such as Asclepius, the son of Apollo, who became a great physician and was eventually elevated to godhood, worshiped by the Greeks from the fourth century B.C.E. and also later by the Romans. Then there was the remarkable figure of the Egyptian Amenhotep, chief magistrate, scribe, and engineer of the Pharaoh Amenhotep III around 1400 B.C.E.. An actual historical figure, quite likely considered a magician in his day, he became a legendary figure and was finally deified over a millennium later during Egypt's Ptolemaic period.

Also from Egypt came the purely literary figure of Hermes Trismegistus, or Thrice-Great Hermes. In the second and third centuries C.E. a large body of anonymous astrological and magical works were produced, most likely in the cosmopolitan city of Alexandria, that came to be attributed to this invented figure, a mix of the Egyptian Thoth and Greek Hermes, or associated with his supposed teachings. The Hermetic Corpus, as these works came to be known, became extremely important to the later history of magic during the European Renaissance of the fifteenth and sixteenth centuries, when they were recovered by scholars and held to be sources of ancient wisdom.

Returning somewhat from the realms of pure legend and fantasy to the more day-to-day world of ancient life, any of the priests who served in the cults of these various deities might be seen as magicians, or certainly as students of magical practices. Indeed, all ancient priests would have performed rites and rituals that could be regarded as magical. Doubtless the people of any given community would not have regarded their own civic priests as being in any way similar to, say, the jilted sorceress of Theocritus, crouching beneath the moon and summoning Hecate. Nevertheless, some essential affinity between their rituals would have to be acknowledged. Moreover, as already discussed, ancient peoples commonly considered the priests of foreign cults to be magicians. Aside from official priests associated with specific temples and set cults, there were also itinerant prophets, seers, and soothsayers throughout the ancient world who claimed special access to the powers or knowledge of the gods. Such people were always held in lower regard and were often viewed with suspicion. We have seen how in Greece they came to be associated with the practice of *mageia*. These wandering seers made their living either by begging or by charging for their services, and ancient societies seem never to have lacked people offering magical services for a price. When Augustine lost his spoon, for example, he knew precisely where to turn for magical aid because Albicerius was famous in Carthage. A number of magical texts exist from the ancient world clearly written by experts who had, or at least considered themselves to have, special training and skills in spell-casting or divination to which ordinary people did not have access.

On the other hand, however, there was clearly a great deal of amateur magical activity in ancient times. Curse tablets, for example, could be purchased from a professional, but they seem just as often to have been fashioned directly by the person who sought to work the curse, who assumedly would not have been specially skilled or trained in such arts. And doubtless ancient peoples also employed a vast array of minor, everyday sorts of spells, charms, or blessings that were simply part of the common culture and required no special or secret knowledge. Such quotidian practices often escape historical detection precisely because they were so common that they aroused no special notice at the time and so left no historical record. One could ask whether, simply by virtue of their wide acceptance, they are rightly considered to be "magic" in the general sense I have employed here, namely practices that were mysterious or foreign, antisocial, or at least vaguely disreputable. Just as no ancient person would have considered his or her own city's priests to be magicians, probably few people regarded any simple rites they performed to be magic. Yet others, at least on occasion, certainly did, above all authorities (either legal or intellectual), who sometimes derided many common practices as superstitious at least. Whatever imprecision arises, common spells and charms cannot be excised from a general consideration of magic in the ancient world (or, as we shall see in later chapters, in the medieval or early modern worlds either).

As obscured as it is to historical detection by its vary ubiquity, some glimpse into this common world of the mundanely magical can be gained especially from literary sources. These often contain references to simple people, frequently women, who possessed no special knowledge or ritual power but who knew a few simple spells or had some expertise in herb-lore. There was in ancient Greece, for example, a defined category of professional, or at least semiprofessional, root-cutters, who had great knowledge of plants and other natural elements, and who could fashion medicines and potions from them. Homer, in the *Iliad*, described the woman Agamede, who possessed special knowledge of all the plants in the world. This sort of person could be well respected and valued for her medical expertise, but there was certainly also a danger in claiming such knowledge or such skills, for those who could heal were also believed to be able to harm. Someone accused of being a poisoner, a *pharmakeus* in Greek or *veneficus* in Latin, was probably most often a person such as this.

In medieval and early modern Europe, authorities sometimes used the term *veneficium* to designate witchcraft. Can we also speak of witchcraft and witches in the ancient world? The answer, as with so much else about the history of magic, depends on the meanings and connotations given to the various words involved. In later Christian Europe, and especially in the fifteenth, sixteenth, and seventeenth centuries—the era of the major witch hunts—the various terms for "witch" usually connoted an evil person who worked harmful magic and who did so in the direct service of the devil, having made an explicit pact with Satan. In the narrowest sense, this thoroughly Christian idea of witchcraft cannot be applied to the ancient world. Yet ancient cultures did conceive of (usually female) practitioners of negative or harmful magic who were in some way defined as inherently evil and who acted in association with dark or nefarious supernatural entities. Witches in this sense, although difficult to discern directly, were clearly believed to exist in ancient Mesopotamia. Most of our information about profoundly negative magic comes from curative or defensive rites, and these sources often provide scant information about the people or entities thought to cast harmful spells, but a major defensive ceremony known as *Maqlû* (literally "burning"), which was common in Babylonia and Assyria, gives a sense of the perceived menace. The long ceremony begins with this formula:

> I have called upon you Gods of the Night:
> With you I have called to Night, the veiled bride;
> I have called upon Twilight, Midnight, and Dawn.
> Because a witch has bewitched me,
> A deceitful woman has accused me,
> Has (thereby) caused my god and goddess to be estranged from me (and)
> I have become sickening in the sight of those who behold me,
> I am therefore unable to rest day or night,
> And a gag continually filling my mouth
> Has kept food distant from my mouth and
> Has diminished the water which passes through my drinking organ,
> My song of joy has become wailing and my rejoicing mourning.[1]

What is important here is the general nature of the magical assault being described. The "witch" (*kaššaptu*) has not merely performed a single injurious or criminal act, but has brought pervasive evil. *Maqlû* itself was a long and complex ritual that centered on the destruction by fire of images made to represent the threatening witches. The ceremony was not meant to be practiced by individuals who felt themselves to be the victim of evil magic but was performed at predetermined times by a king for the protection of all the people, again indicating that the witches were not individuals committing specific crimes by magical means (against which there was extensive legislation) but inherently evil beings intent on corrupting all of society.

Classical Greek and Roman literature contains many descriptions of women using harmful magic as well as descriptions of more profoundly malevolent creatures. Though of divine origin, Circe is often considered to be a witch. Certainly she used harmful magic against Odysseus and his men, and there seems no real motivation for her actions other than some inherent malice toward humanity. The character of Medea can be seen as even more profoundly malevolent. Depicted in numerous pieces of classical literature, she has somewhat different attributes, according to which version of the myth is followed. She is often said to have killed her own brother and dismembered his body to perform a spell to protect her lover Jason as he fled with her from the land of Colchis. Later, when Jason fell in love with another princess, Medea gave her a robe that engulfed her in flames when she put it on. After this, to punish Jason, she killed her own children by him and fled in a chariot drawn by dragons. She was considered to be a priestess of the terrible goddess Hecate and in league with various forces of the underworld, and like Circe she became a major archetype for witchcraft in later medieval and early modern Europe.

A connection to Hecate was a definite sign of witchcraft in ancient Greece and Rome. Theocritus's *Pharmakeutriai*, mentioned above, can be translated as *The Sorceresses*, or *The Witches*. The poem opens with the love-lorn Simaitha summoning Hecate as part of a ceremony to create a love spell. Although involved with very dark forces, Simaitha was not a particularly horrible figure, but other literary witches were far more terrible. The Roman poet Horace (65–8 B.C.E.) created the character of Canidia. Interestingly, this literary figure may have been based on a real woman—an herbalist, root cutter, and perfume maker named Grattidia. In his first *Satire*, Horace presents Canidia, along with other witches, haunting a graveyard in order to dig up the dead and harvest their organs for various magical potions. In a slightly later work, he reintroduces her, again along with other witches, kidnapping a young boy and burying him in sand up to his neck. Their purpose was to torture him to death by dehydration and then cut out his liver for use in a love potion.

Certainly the most terrible and terrifying witch presented in ancient liter-

ature was Erictho, as described in the Roman poet Lucan's *Pharsalia*, an epic
account of the civil war fought between Julius Caesar and Pompey. This war
was conducted mainly in Greece, and Erictho was made to be an inhabitant
of Thessaly, a region with a reputation for dark magic and sinister supernatural powers in the ancient world. She was a truly horrible, semidemonic figure
who lived in tombs and, like Canidia, frequented graveyards, collecting bodies and pieces of bodies that she kept for various magical purposes. She was
herself an image of death, and where she walked, plants would wither and
the air would become poisonous. After a great battle, the son of Pompey
needed the services of a powerful diviner, and he was sent to Erictho. To
work her spell, she scoured the battlefield looking for an appropriate corpse,
which she then dragged to a dark forest glade. There, crowned with snakes,
she performed a complex and terrible ceremony to revive the corpse and
make it speak to her, bringing knowledge out of the underworld. When the
spirit of the dead man resisted her summons, she threatened the gods themselves if they did not compel the spirit to obey her.

The practices of Canidia and Erictho, amplified to a terrifying degree for
literary effect, nevertheless give some sense of who might actually have been
considered a witch in the ancient world. Early in Greek history, a particular
type of ritual expert developed, known as a *goēs*, a sort of seer or medium
who could act as an intermediary between the living and the newly dead.
The name derived from *goos*, a ritual lament over the dead, and *goētes* were
specialists in funerary rites and other aspects of the treatment of the dead. In
their ceremonies they often invoked Hecate, as a goddess of the underworld.
Their expertise relating to the spirits of the dead gradually expanded, until
they were thought to have special powers over all spirits or *daimones*, through
whom they could work a great deal of magic. Although initially they seem
to have served a useful social function, they were increasingly regarded as
malevolent figures, and the rites that they performed were usually believed to
be wicked or harmful. The name for their practices, *goēteia*, became a general
term for malevolent magic and is often translated as "witchcraft."

In ancient literature, witches were almost always depicted as female. This
holds true from the use of the feminine *kaššaptu* in the Babylonian *Maqlû*
ceremony through Homer's account of the seductive but terrible Circe to
Lucan's vicious and abominable hag Erictho. The antique world seems
clearly to have associated harmful magical forces principally with women, at
least in its literary imagination. There appears, however, to have been little
reality behind this association. That is, when information is derived solely
from nonliterary sources—court cases centering on accusations of magic, the

physical remains of curse tablets, the inscriptions which sometimes indicated the person performing the spell, or other sources—all admittedly sketchy for most of the vast span of ancient history—men appear to have been the practitioners of magic as much as, if not significantly more than, women. One immediately obvious possible explanation for this discrepancy is that the literate authors of history and legend were all men and so naturally used female images to depict the absolutely strange and sinisterly other. Yet the history of magic is incredibly complex, and the associations drawn between gender and magic are perhaps the most complicated aspect of that history. The multifaceted and by no means thoroughly explored connections between gender and magic in the ancient world can stand as the first signal of that complexity in this survey.

Not identical to human witches, but certainly akin to them insofar as they were feminized images of evil, were a host of monstrous creatures that haunted the ancient night. The most familiar forms these creatures took, influential on the later European imagination, were the *strix* and *lamia*, both figures of Greco-Roman belief. The *strix* (literally "screech owl" in Latin) was thought to be an evil monster that flew through the night, preying on sleeping children by devouring them or sucking their blood in vampiric fashion. The *lamia* was a similar monster, originally a legendary queen of Libya who slept with the god Zeus and was in turn punished by Hera, his jealous wife, who murdered her children. Lamia then became a night-wandering creature doomed to prey on the children of other women. The ancient Sumerians had also believed in a similar terrible spirit named *Ardat Lili* or *Lilitu*, a winged and taloned creature that roamed the night preying on humans, and ancient Hebrews believed in *Lilith*, the apocryphal first wife of Adam who refused to accept the authority God had given him over her and became a fearful night-stalking monster (see figure 1.2).

Such images informed many, if not all, literary depictions of human witches. Lucan's Erictho, for example, appears far closer to these supernatural monsters than to any human practitioner of magic. In medieval and early modern Europe, these images would continue to resonate, and the words *strix* and *lamia* would eventually come to mean "witch," especially in Mediterranean lands. In their original context they might serve to argue somewhat against the notion that ancient concepts of witchcraft were based primarily on some direct and inherent connection drawn between women and the practice of magic per se. Rather, even more unattractively, they seem to indicate a basic linkage between women and certain notions of sinister, nocturnal, somewhat sexualized threat embodied in female monsters. These images

Figure 1.2 Ancient Mesopotamian relief depicting the "Queen of the Night," likely the demon Lilitu.

were then imported into the arena of magical practices and practitioners, carrying with them their particular associations with gender and female sexuality. This amalgam supported much of the linkage between women and harmful and horrific magical rites in ancient culture, or at least in ancient literature, rather than any real-world association of women with magic, and clearly fed into later understandings of witches and witchcraft.

The Condemnation of Magic and Superstition

The topic of witchcraft leads obviously to a discussion of the degree to which magical practices were condemned, legally or otherwise, in the ancient world. Given the wide variety of rites, rituals, and actions that could be described as magical, there is no sense in which any blanket statement can be made. Certainly many practices were condemned, and many more were held in ill repute. Even if disdained by some, however, many practices were still widely tolerated. Nevertheless, given that all ancient societies believed in the real effectiveness and power of various magical practices, any of these practices that aimed to commit a crime, such as murder or theft, was proscribed by law. The famous Code of Hammurabi, compiled around 1750 B.C.E. and one of the earliest legal codes known to have existed, contained sections directed against magical crimes. Likewise, the Twelve Tables, the first important Roman law code, proscribed enchanting someone (*incantare*) with an evil spell (*malum carmen*). Ancient law usually focused on the effects of magic, rather then on magical acts themselves. So long as no crime was committed or clear harm done, there were no laws against magical practices per se. This was quite different from what would come to be the case in Christian Europe. By the time of the witch hunts of the sixteenth and seventeenth centuries, for example, in many jurisdictions a witch could be executed even if she performed no witchcraft, that is, even if she did not work any harm or commit any crime by magical means, because the category of "witch" had itself become criminalized.

This is not to say that the ancient world regarded, or treated, magical crime just like any other type of offense. The categories of magical practices, and the terms used to describe them, were, as we have often seen already in this chapter, frustratingly vague and shifting, making legal analysis difficult. Yet because so many kinds of ritual practice in the ancient world touched upon the vital relationship between humans and the gods, behind whatever physical or material harm magic might cause there always lurked the danger of moral transgression and corrupting taboo. In the Greek world, for example, drugs and potions of all kinds were categorized as *pharmaka*, but this term also very often meant specifically poisons. In some cases, laws were passed only against the use of specifically harmful *pharmaka*; in others, though, *pharmaka* were proscribed generally—they were all, by implication, potentially harmful. In classical Athens, a man who felt himself or his family to have been injured by *pharmaka* could bring a suit in court centering on the wrongful harm that had been done to him. He could also, however, bring a suit that focused on the impiety of the person who had supposedly employed the *pharmaka*. Legal actions for impious acts were common in Athens, because any form of impiety could threaten the harmonious relationship between the community and the gods and thus threaten the entire city. The penalties, needless to say, could be just as severe as any handed down for committing an actual, physical injury or material crime.

In the Roman world, *veneficium* retained its first meaning of the act of poisoning, but it also became a more general term for harmful acts performed by any magical means. Later Roman historians reported that in the second century B.C.E. there were mass executions for what they at least referred to as *veneficium*. Magistrates ordered such executions in 184, 180/79, and 153 B.C.E., both in the immediate vicinity of Rome and elsewhere on the Italian peninsula; the numbers of those sentenced to death were in the thousands. Such extreme responses imply that authorities were not acting to punish individual offenders or singular criminal acts but rather to curb a substantial perceived threat to society as a whole. These actions may have been connected at least in some general way to the Roman Senate's bloody repression of rites to Bacchus in 186 B.C.E. Yet the *Lex Cornelia*, enacted in 81 B.C.E., still legislated in its section *De sicariis et veneficis* only narrowly against using a harmful drug (*venenum malum*) against someone. Cases often had to contend with questions of what constituted a harmful drug or poison, as opposed to a beneficial drug, or a drug intended to be beneficial but that had an unexpected harmful effect.

The Roman category of superstition also presented problems. Insofar as *superstitio* meant the practice of improper, excessive, or foreign rites, the danger was not that harmful acts might be committed, but that the essential character of the Roman state and the virtue of its citizens might be corrupted. Yet *superstitio* was in many ways a very vague term. Indeed, there is evidence that the term was left deliberately vague in legal and other official contexts. This allowed Roman society, which was often quite tolerant and accepting of foreign rites, to condemn whatever was commonly judged to be unwholesome at a particular time or in a particular context, without being locked into strict categories of what was and was not legal. During the late imperial period, for example, as Christianity was gaining strength and becoming the majority cult in many areas of the empire, this ambiguity allowed the same term of reprobation to be directed at whatever practices local societies found strange or unacceptable—in some cases Christian rites were superstitious, while in other cases pagan ones were. Added to all this was the fact that a perceived general connection between superstition and harmful magic was emerging. The connection was first spelled out in a legal code of 297 c.e., in which *superstitio* was linked to *maleficium*, by this time the most common Latin term for harmful, criminal magic.

Despite this slight, and late, linkage, most of the condemnation directed against superstition was not legal but moral. In this sense Cicero wrote about superstition as a general corrupting presence in society. Much the same was true of other aspects of magic. As we have seen, from at least the fifth century b.c.e., the Greeks were attaching the term *magos* to various more or less unsavory characters. Magic was foreign, strange, secretive, often harmful, and always performed by individuals for personal reasons, or by professional experts of questionable morality who took money for their services. All this stood in contrast to the rites and rituals of official, public cults, which were indigenous, or at least believed to be so, and were seen as essential to the character of any community. Public cults were beneficial and protective, not just for individuals but for society as a whole, and priests were respected people of the highest social standing. While there was no sharp line dividing the "magical" from the "religious" in the ancient world, still different rites could occupy very different places on most people's moral spectrum.

In addition to legal and moral sanctions, there was also the possibility of intellectual condemnation being directed against magic and superstition. Educated people in positions of intellectual authority might deride certain magical or superstitious rites as false or fake, arguing that they were devoid of real power and were practiced only by fools or charlatans. Greek philosophers condemned *deisidaimonia* because they felt that common people practiced such "superstition" due to a lack of understanding about how *daimones* actually operated in the universe. Yet these condemnations were always nuanced and limited to some degree. Certainly many authorities did argue that some specific rites or practices were empty or meaningless and that some people who claimed esoteric knowledge or skills were frauds, either simply delusional or, more likely, intent on bilking honest people out of money by claiming to perform various magical services. Plato held many magical rites and their practitioners in very low esteem. Pliny the Elder, in his extensive descriptions of magical activities in his *Naturalis historia*, often made clear that he placed no credence in the rites he described. Still, he gathered all this knowledge together, and not exclusively as a catalog of errors. He noted, moreover, that even well-educated people, not entirely without reason, feared the power of harmful spells. The physician Galen (ca. 130–200 C.E.) ridiculed many medicinal magical practices as ineffective and derided the simple people who performed them as lacking in understanding. Nevertheless, he recommended that certain rites and rituals should always be observed when gathering medicinal herbs and preparing medicines.

So thoroughly was belief in the real power of rites and ritual actions, verbal formulae and invocations, natural elements and spiritual forces engrained in the ancient world that no one sought to deny the efficacy of all such things categorically. These ideas were absolutely essential to the way in which ancient peoples viewed their world and were fully incorporated into their intellectual systems, whether we label those systems as religious, scientific, or magical. There was as little ground separating medicine from magical healing as there was separating astronomy from astrology. While some intellectuals might be more skeptical of a greater number of practices than others, some imbued their philosophical systems with a great deal of what modern minds might call magic. The philosopher Plotinus (ca. 205–270 C.E.), for example, the founder of the school of Neoplatonic thought, believed that there were natural bonds of sympathetic force connecting all things in the universe, material and spiritual, terrestrial and celestial. Through philosophical training and contemplation, people could learn to manipulate these forces for their own purposes. Not only were these theories important in the ancient world, they formed the basis of a great deal of highly intellectual, learned magical practice in the Renaissance of the fifteenth and sixteenth centuries, when Neoplatonism experienced a major revival in Italy and elsewhere in Europe.

Magic and Witchcraft in Hebrew Scripture

A fairly marginal force in the ancient world compared to the cultural dominance Greece achieved during the Hellenistic period or to Rome's world-spanning empire, Hebrew culture nevertheless obviously exerted tremendous influence on later Christianity and thus on the entire history of Christian Europe in the medieval and early modern periods. During the major witch hunts in Europe, for example, a principal justification for the execution of witches was the injunction in Exodus 22:18, perhaps most famously rendered into English as "Thou shalt not suffer a witch to live."[2] Thus the depictions of magical practices contained in Hebrew scripture, and the judgments rendered by Hebrew culture on these practices, became essential foundations for the later history of magic in Europe.

The place of magic, or rather of various rites of power, spells, and ritual practices in Hebrew culture, was little different from the place of such practices in other ancient societies. Rites could vary widely in their performance and purpose. Moreover, no absolute distinction existed between religious and magical practices. Magic, for the Hebrews as for Greeks, Romans, and other ancient peoples, was what the priests of other cultures did. Within Hebrew society, any rites or practices designed to invoke or compel supernatural forces or to manipulate natural forces or elements in nonphysical ways but which were not under the control or supervision of the official priestly caste might also be considered magical. The implications and connotations of various rites could be just as indistinct and mutable in Hebrew culture as in any other ancient society. Unlike most other ancient peoples, however, the ancient Hebrews were, or became, monotheists. Thus, while the Greeks or Romans could explain the workings of magical rites by the power of any number of deities or lesser spirits that inhabited the universe, whether their own or those of other cultures, the Hebrews needed to explain such things in a universe presided over by their one god.

There is much highly charged debate about when the ancient Hebrews became fully monotheist—believing that their god was the only divine entity in the universe, responsible for the whole of creation, and governing the fates of all peoples. One theory holds that prior to the sixth century B.C.E., the Hebrews were monolatrists, but not monotheists. They worshiped only one god themselves, but, like other ancient peoples, they did not deny the reality of the gods of other cultures. In the sixth century, mainly as a result of the Babylonian Captivity (586–538 B.C.E.), in which the temple in Jerusalem was destroyed by Babylonian forces and large numbers of captives were taken to Babylon, Hebrew belief became more fully monotheistic. Separation from a cultic center, in this case the temple in Jerusalem, was more traumatic for ancient people than it would be for practitioners of most modern religions because of the much more profound connections believed to exist between physical place, divine force, and community in the ancient world. Positing a single god who governed the entire world and who, while not recognized by other peoples, was equally present among all nations would be a possible response to what could otherwise be a catastrophic separation of a people from their particular cultic site.

Without entering any further into the debate surrounding this issue, we can see the possible effects of such developments in terms of perceptions about the functioning of various rituals in two of the most famous scriptural accounts concerning the operation of rites of power: the contest between Moses and the priests of Pharaoh in Exodus 7:8–13, and the contest between the prophet Elijah and the priests of Baal in 1 Kings 18:17–40. In the first of these episodes, the Lord commanded Moses and Aaron to go before Pharaoh and perform a wonder, so that the Egyptian king would see the power of the Hebrew god and release his people from captivity. When Aaron threw down his rod before Pharaoh, it became a snake. The priests of Pharaoh were able to replicate this feat, however, by their own "secret arts." Aaron's serpent devoured the Egyptian ones, thereby demonstrating the superiority of the Hebrew god, but there was no intimation that the powers of the Egyptian priests, drawing on their own gods, were not real. The situation was quite different in the later account of Elijah confronting the priests of Baal, who had been seducing the Israelite people into idolatry. At the command of the king of Israel, Ahab, the entire nation assembled to observe the contest. Elijah faced four hundred fifty priests of Baal. He asked them to build an altar, select a bull for sacrifice, and pray to their god to send fire to consume the offering. Although the priests labored at their rites until midday passed, they produced no effects. Then Elijah constructed an altar to the Hebrew god. He too selected a bull, and ordered that the sacrifice should be drenched in water, just for good measure. He then invoked the Lord, and immediately fire descended from heaven, consuming the bull, the altar, and boiling away the water. The clear implication was that there existed only one divine force in the universe, and the rites of other gods were not simply foreign to the people of Israel and improper to them, but were, in fact, utterly empty.

Perhaps because the religious singularity of the Hebrews, be it monolatry or full monotheism, allowed for a somewhat sharper distinction to develop between "religion" and "magic," Hebrew culture might have been somewhat more sweeping in its condemnation of magical practices than many other ancient traditions. There is, after all, the stark statement of Exodus 22:18, "Thou shalt not suffer a witch to live." This passage, however, must be clarified. The Hebrew word for a magical practitioner, so often later rendered in English as "witch," is kešeph, which connotes someone who performs secretive and harmful magic and poisoning and is cognate to kaššaptu, the term used in the Code of Hammurabi and Babylonian Maqlû ceremony. As discussed above, legal prohibitions of specific forms of harmful magic such as this were not meant as blanket condemnations of all practices that might be considered to be magical. Moreover, there is debate about whether the original intent of this passage was that sorcerers should be put to death or merely exiled, that is, not tolerated to live within a given community.

An example of multifaceted Hebrew attitudes toward magical practices can be found in the famous account of the "witch" of Endor. The first king of the Israelites, Saul, had exiled all sorcerers and diviners from his kingdom. He then found himself in need of prognostication on the eve of a great battle. The Lord would not speak to Saul, however; that is, official religious rites to divine the future had failed him, and he needed to seek help elsewhere. His servants informed him that a diviner or seer (there is no indication that she was involved in harmful magic or witchcraft of any kind) could be found in Endor. Saul went to her, and she summoned the spirit of the dead prophet Samuel to speak with him. Saul violated his own law here, and his actions were condemned by the shade of Samuel, but nevertheless he received information about the coming battle, which he was to lose. In medieval Europe, when the woman in this story was coming to be regarded as a witch in the later Christian sense, that is, as someone in league with the devil, arguments were made that the supposed spirit of Samuel must have been a demon in disguise. Yet in the original passage, there is nothing to indicate that the woman's powers were anything other than they seemed, and the divination she provided was effective and accurate, albeit illicit both legally and, it would seem, socially.

The seemingly most thorough condemnation of magical practices in Hebrew scripture comes in Deuteronomy 18:9–11: "When you come into the land that the Lord your God is giving to you, you must not learn to imitate the abhorrent practices of those nations. No one shall be found among you who makes a son or daughter pass through fire, or who practices divination, or is a soothsayer, or an augur, or a sorcerer, or one who casts spells, or who consults ghosts or spirits, or who seeks oracles from the dead." This passage covers many of the forms that magical practices could take in antiquity and appears to offer a fairly unambiguous condemnation. Yet attention should be given to the opening of the passage, in which all the categories that follow are described as the abhorrent practices of other nations, that is, foreign rites and rituals. The context here was purportedly the entry of the Hebrews into the promised land of Canaan, and the injunction was that they should not become corrupted by the foreign cults they were going to find there. This meaning is further highlighted by the fact that the material in Deuteronomy, as other early books of Hebrew scripture, developed out of long oral tradition but was probably only written down after the Babylonian exile, when consciousness of the danger of corruption by foreign nations and foreign practices was doubtless at a fever pitch. Several of the practices proscribed in this passage, in fact, do not seem to have been common in pre-exilic Hebrew or Canaanite culture, but were common in Babylonia.

In sum, the Hebrews were like other ancient peoples in that one of the principal distinctions they drew was not between religion and magic in a modern sense, but between their own cultic rites and those of foreign peoples. For complex reasons due to the nature of Hebrew belief in a single god and the experience of exile in other lands, they perhaps did construct a stricter separation between religion and magic, in this ancient sense, than was the case in other antique cultures. This is no small point, as Christianity would take up these features of Hebrew faith and use them to shape its own categories of magic, which would of course become the principal categories shaping European thought down to the Enlightenment of the eighteenth century.

Notes

1. From Tzvi Abusch, "The Demonic Image of the Witch in Standard Babylonian Literature: The Reworking of Popular Concepts by Learned Exorcists," in *Religion, Science, and Magic: In Concert and in Conflict*, ed. Jacob Neusner, Ernest S. Frerichs, and Paul Virgil McCracken Flesher (Oxford: Oxford University Press, 1989), 32–33; reprinted in Abusch, *Mesopotamian Witchcraft: Toward a History and Understanding of Babylonian Witchcraft Beliefs and Literature* (Leiden: Brill Styx, 2002), 8.

2. Here from the King James Version; all other biblical quotes are taken from the New Revised Standard Version.

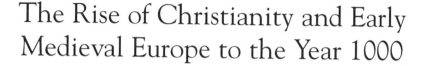

CHAPTER TWO

The Rise of Christianity and Early Medieval Europe to the Year 1000

While Rome ruled the ancient West, accommodating within its cosmopolitan culture the many cultic rites and magical practices of the Mediterranean world, a new system of belief arose. A small Judean sect slowly grew and spread through the empire until it encompassed most of the West, inheriting more than a little of Rome's imperial structure and ambition. Christianity established basic theological and philosophical doctrines, shaped quotidian beliefs and practices, and strongly influenced social and political structures throughout medieval and early modern European history. Its effect on the history of magic was profound. Because essentially distinct categories of "magic" and "religion" cannot accurately be applied to any period of premodern history, Christian belief and practice necessarily pervaded all aspects of magic in Europe until at least the eighteenth century. While Christian authorities drew heavily on ancient thought, however, in some respects their conceptions of magic and attitudes toward its practice differed significantly from those widely held in antiquity. The rise of Christianity can, in fact, been seen as marking an important step toward more sharply differentiated conceptions of religion and magic, because Christianity, from its earliest days, posited a more fundamental distinction between what we might label as magic and religion (church authorities more commonly distinguished between superstition and religion) than had yet been imagined in the ancient world.

As outlined in the previous chapter, a general category of magic emerged only gradually, and never completely, in the ancient West. Rather than using a single broad term to encompass a range of acts, ancient people more often distinguished between various forms of specific rites and practices, all designed to allow humans to access and manipulate supernatural or occult natural forces. They divided these practices into separate categories, based not so much on conceived differences in the essential nature of their operations, but rather on whether they involved indigenous or foreign rites, whether the rites were properly or improperly performed, or performed to excess, and above all whether the rites were performed by official, communally sanctioned priests or by others for individualized gain or profit. Christian authorities continued to observe these distinctions in certain ways, but because of Christianity's unique beliefs and place in ancient society, Christians could not employ these categories entirely as pagan Roman authorities had done. Moreover, Christianity developed a single, broad criterion for categorizing practices based on the essential nature of the power that they were designed to invoke, or that authorities deemed that they invoked.

Christian authorities sharply distinguished what they regarded as manifestations of divine versus demonic power. All rites directed toward the Christian god were deemed legitimate and proper. Any practices that sought to invoke demonic forces were rejected and condemned, and into this category authorities ultimately lumped all non-Christian rites, as well as any Christian observances deemed to be carried out improperly. Needless to say, this category encompassed most forms of magical practice. Authorities also distinguished between the supposed effects of various practices. Drawing on divine power, the more "religious" activities of prayer and devotion could produce miracles, while magical operations might only result in "wonders" (*mira* as opposed to *miracula* in ecclesiastical Latin). This strict dichotomy did not always suffice. Throughout the Christian era, for example, educated men raised arguments about the existence of a category of natural magic that drew on forces inherent in the universe that might be hidden or occult but were neither demonic nor divine. Such powers, including the natural forces that the stars were supposed to exert over earthly bodies, which were legitimated by almost all systems of ancient thought, were very difficult for Christian authorities to deny, and so ideas of natural magic took their place somewhat uneasily in Christian systems of thought. Such cases aside, however, the essential and stark Christian distinction between divine and demonic power had profound effects on how magical practices were perceived and how magic as a general category developed.

By linking magic strongly to conceptions of the demonic, Christian thinkers separated anything touching upon the divine cult from the realm of the magical. Such a move was not wholly unprecedented in ancient distinctions between approved civic cults and other private practices, but it was even more thoroughgoing. Those practices that Christian authorities continued to regard as magical were severely condemned. This too was not wholly different from ancient conventions. As we have seen, while official civic rites enjoyed full approval, ancient peoples often looked askance at other magical practices. Yet such moral censure was rarely absolute, and in legal terms, ancient societies usually only condemned magic that was directly harmful. Under Christianity, since most magic was linked to the power of demons, which were held to be utterly evil, moral censure against magic became far more complete. Moreover, while Christian kings and other lay authorities, at least in the early medieval period, generally continued to legislate only against magic used to harm or commit criminal acts, over the course of centuries the medieval church also became a powerful political and legal institution, and it directed its considerable energies toward the eradication of moral and spiritual deviance—in this case, entanglement with demonic powers—rather than solely against antisocial actions like murder and theft.

The firm distinctions that Christian authorities created regarding magic, and upon which they sought to act, were clear in theory but proved difficult to determine reliably in practice. Divine as well as demonic power were prevalent and active in the Christian world, and humans could access divine power through numerous, seemingly automatically effective ritual means, leading some modern scholars to ignore basic medieval distinctions and speak of the "magic" of the medieval church. In practice, the attempt to categorize certain practices as magical or superstitious was an important part of the long process by which Christianity sought to define its own nature. For essentially the first thousand years of Christian history, this process played out in the arena of Christian encounters with paganism. Early Christianity developed in a world dominated by the pagan cults of Rome and other ancient Mediterranean cultures. Later, as the Roman Empire slowly disintegrated, Germanic peoples moved into Christianized lands, and Christianity eventually spread beyond former Roman boundaries into pagan northern Europe. Moreover, for centuries many Christian authorities were deeply concerned about supposed residual paganism believed to persist in various regions of Europe long after official Christianization. It is this period that this chapter explores, from the time of Christ to roughly the year 1000, when Christian conceptions of magic and superstition and concerns over these developing categories took shape very much as part of the formation of Christendom itself.

Magic and Superstition in Early Christianity

Jesus of Nazareth, identified by some as Christ (the "anointed one," or the messiah) already during his lifetime, was born during the reign of Herod the Great (37–4 B.C.E.) and was executed during Pontius Pilate's term as Roman prefect of Judea (26–36 C.E.). According to the Acts of the Apostles, his followers were first identified as a distinct sect—as Christians—in the city of Antioch in 42 (Acts 11:26). The Acts were written perhaps as early as 62, and the Gospel accounts of Christ's life were all written between 70 and 100. While these sources can hardly be taken as unbiased accounts of Christianity's earliest history, they do represent early Christians' constructions of their own story—a story into which magic and magicians figure from the very beginning. The three magi who, in Gospel accounts, traveled to see the infant Jesus were, of course, Persian *magoi*, wise men and astrologers following the sign of a new star they had seen in the heavens. Later Christian authorities interpreted this story as signifying the place of magic itself in the new world ushered in by Christ's birth. In pagan antiquity, they asserted, some magical practices had been permissible. After all, no ancient people had full and proper access to divine truth and power, not even the Jews, and to Christians all ancient cults were superstitious and magical. With the coming of Christ, however, and the spread of his teachings, recourse to magic became unnecessary, since the true way was now revealed. The magi recognized this, and by bringing gifts to the infant Jesus and acknowledging him as king they symbolized the abandonment of their old practices and their submission to the new Christian system of ritual and power.

While for Christians the coming of Christ represented the overthrow of the magicians, for non-Christians Jesus himself seemed very much like a *magos*. He wielded tremendous power that, sometimes at least, he exercised through ritualistic performances. For example, the Gospel of Mark describes the case of a deaf-mute brought before Jesus. He put his fingers in the man's ears and spat on his tongue while commanding "ephphatha," or "be opened," and the man was cured (Mark 7:33–34). Even more dramatically, the Gospel of John describes how Christ once healed a blind man. He spat on the ground so as to make mud and spread this over the man's eyes. He then had him go and wash in a pool, after which the man could see (John 9:6–7). Much of the time Jesus did not use such elaborate means to exert power, simply touching people or speaking words of command to them such as "be healed" or "rise up." Nor did he typically use his power as other magicians did, for personal gain or to earn money. Yet the similarities are evident.

Throughout the Gospels, Christ was described as commanding and casting out demons, which to ancient non-Christians would have naturally suggested the interaction between *magoi* and the *daimones* they invoked and commanded. Upon seeing Jesus's mastery over powerful spirits, the Bible recounts, the Pharisees accused him of being in league with these creatures, declaring: "By the ruler of demons he casts out demons" (Matt. 9:34, also Matt. 12:24, Mark 3:22, Luke 11:15). For Christians, this was a terrible slander against Christ's true nature, but to most pagan observers such a charge would not have appeared out of place or unreasonable.

Christ bequeathed his power over demons to his disciples and ultimately to all Christians, who could then exorcise evil spirits in his name (e.g., Mark 3:15, Luke 9:1). The followers of Christ thus also seemed like magicians to many in the ancient world, for they supposedly wielded amazing powers. The Acts of the Apostles, in particular, recounts many marvelous deeds attributed to the disciples. People carried the sick into the street simply so that Peter's shadow might pass over them as he walked by, for even this indirect contact could heal them (Acts 5:15). Paul bestowed a similar healing power on pieces of cloth. People sought to touch him with handkerchiefs and aprons so that they could then use these to cure the sick (Acts 19:11–12). Even non-Christians attempted to use the power Christianity seemed to offer. For example, seeing Paul's abilities, the sons of a Jewish priest tried to exorcise an evil spirit in the name of Christ. The demon merely replied to them, "Jesus I know, and Paul I know, but who are you?" When the people of the city of Ephesus, where this occurred, saw how Paul's power totally surpassed that of all other ritual practices, they supposedly burned all their books of magic (Acts 19:13–19). Not all Christian power was benign. At the city of Salamis on Cyprus, the disciples Paul and Barnabas encountered a Jewish magician called Bar-Jesus or Elymas, who actively opposed their preaching. Paul invoked the power of the Holy Spirit to blind the man, albeit only for a time, so that others would realize the superiority of Christian power and therefore of Christian teachings (see figure 2.1).

The most famous encounter between a disciple of Jesus and a magician, however, was that between Peter and Simon of Samaria, also known as Simon Magus (that is, Simon the Magician), related in Acts 8:9–24. In the biblical account, Simon practiced magic openly and held the people of Samaria in thrall until the disciple Philip came and preached about Christ. Even Simon was convinced and converted to Christianity. Then Peter and John also came to Samaria, and when Simon saw the extent of their power, he reverted to his magician's way of thinking and offered Peter money to

Figure 2.1   Saints Simon and Jude confronting three magicians.

teach him his secrets. Peter rebuked him, and the account ends with Simon repenting. As early as the second century, however, Christian authors, in commenting and expanding on this story, were painting Simon Magus much more as an unrepentant foe of Peter. The apocryphal text known as the Acts of Peter describes far more extensive contests of power between them, with Peter, of course, always the victor. For example, Simon sought to convince people that he could raise the dead by causing a corpse to twitch and move, but Peter was able to restore the dead person fully to life. Simon then declared that he would fly up to heaven and began to rise into the air. Peter, however, was able to bring him crashing back to earth. Later commentary on this passage argued that, since Simon was clearly in league with demonic forces, he must have been borne aloft by demons. Peter merely had to exorcise these to cause Simon to fall.

When the apostles of Christ or other early Christians competed with practitioners of magic and won believers by demonstrating the superiority of their power, they were little different from the priests of any other cult in the ancient world, all of whom set themselves up as superior to base magicians. Yet of all the cults of the ancient world, Christianity was in a particularly precarious position in regard to accusations of magic. Roman authors such as Tacitus (ca. 55–117) and Suetonius (ca. 69–140) derided Christian practices as superstitions. Based in Judaism, but having failed to find acceptance among the vast majority of Jews, Christianity had difficulty presenting itself to skeptics as anything other than a new and improper (i.e., superstitious) offshoot of an established cult. Moreover, the figure of Christ himself presented problems. Christians recognized him as a god—indeed, as God—invoked him in their rites, and claimed to wield power in his name. Yet Christians also maintained that Christ was human. To the casual observer in antiquity, then, here was a man, an itinerant beggar, who claimed considerable prophetic, healing, and other powers, and who worked wonders to attract a following. This was the very image of the *magos*.

The charge that Christ was in fact a magician troubled Christianity for several hundred years. Already in the late second century, the Roman author Celsus (even approximate dates for his life are unknown) argued that the young Jesus had studied magical arts in Egypt, the land of occult knowledge par excellence in the Roman mind. Christians themselves maintained that the holy family had spent time in Egypt shortly after Christ's birth, fleeing the persecution of Herod, so the argument seemed plausible and the early Christian writer Origen (ca. 185–254) had to respond forcefully against this claim. A century later, Eusebius of Caesaria (ca. 263–340) refuted similar suggestions that Christ was a magician, as did the church father Augustine of Hippo (354–430) almost a century after that. In addition, the major symbol that came to be associated with Christ, the cross, was for the Roman world not an icon of resurrection and salvation but a horrifying image of death, and one often associated with malevolent magic. Sorcerers and witches in the classical world were supposed to frequent graveyards, and they often used the bodies or the body parts of crucified or otherwise executed criminals in their spells. Thus when Christians employed the sign of the cross as a symbol of power, often to command or drive off demonic presences, suspicions of the darkest sort of magic were raised in non-Christian minds.

Most basically, of course, Christianity aroused opposition from Roman authorities because Christians refused to recognize the validity of Roman cultic practices. Already in a letter to the Christian community at Corinth, written in the late 50s, Paul had denounced all pagan rites as the worship of demons (1 Corinthians 10:20). As Roman authors continued to categorize Christian practices as superstitions, more or less inimical to the well-being of the empire, Christian authorities expanded on Paul's basic point and labeled all pagan rites and practices as superstitious and essentially magical. Conceptions of magic, and the category of magic, came to take a central place in Christianity's efforts to separate itself from the larger pagan world in which it initially developed. The importance of magic in Christianity's construction of its own identity can be seen in the writings of the early authority Irenaeus (ca. 130–200). In his treatise *Adversus haereses* (Against Heresies), he portrayed Simon Magus, the magician, as a chief fomenter of heresy, using his powers to simulate divine miracles and draw people away from true faith in Christ. Here magic was presented as essentially opposed to Christianity and a main source for the corruption of the faith.

Other early writers made use of magic to distinguish or solidify the boundaries between the Christian and pagan worlds. Irenaeus's near contemporary Tertullian (ca. 160–225) focused on the difficulties magic, or the perception of magic, might create for Christians at a more practical level, living in a still largely pagan world. Christian women, he warned, should avoid marrying pagan men. These men would naturally see their brides' prayers, use of the sign of the cross, and other Christian acts as signs of magic, and would be critical or try to dissuade the women from their practices. Conversely, he noted that Christian women who would never think to engage in openly pagan practices should also be careful to avoid making use of any pagan herb-lore, for the knowledge of such arts derived ultimately from demons. Nearly two centuries later, John Chrysostom (ca. 347–407) raised a similar point by criticizing Christian women who, when their children fell ill, often turned to magical remedies. These women would not dream of taking their children to a pagan temple to be healed, but the magical and superstitious practices they employed also derived from demons, he warned. They were to be condemned just as harshly and avoided just as stringently as any more overtly pagan rites.

These examples highlight the complex difficulties inherent in attempting to separate fully Christian from pagan practice, as early Christian authorities sought to do. For centuries, as Christianity spread across the Roman Empire, the new faith existed side by side with the vibrant paganism of the classical world. Christians and pagans married, and clearly Christian mothers whose children had fallen ill sought all available means to cure them, doubtless using prayer and the sign of the cross, but also turning to other ritual remedies and herbal medicine without hesitation. Some Christians, indeed perhaps most average Christians, saw no inherent conflict between devotion to their faith and continued use of at least some of the many magical rites offered in the ancient world. Julius Africanus (ca. 160–240), a Christian layman who wrote as much for Roman society in general as for a specifically Christian audience, saw nothing wrong with the use of magical rites for healing, love spells, or the use of magic to defeat enemies in battle. Among Christian authorities, however, this opinion was decidedly a minority view, and the practice of magic in almost all forms was condemned as inherently super-stitious, pagan, and incommensurate with the Christian faith.

In a general sense, Christianity's sweeping condemnation of magic and the assertion that almost all forms of magical practice were inherently un-Christian were based on what has been called the "demonization of magic" that occurred early in the Christian era.[1] Many magical rites in antiquity were premised on human magicians' invocation and control of supernatural spiritual forces or entities called *daimones* in Greek and *daemones* in Latin. In the classical view, these spirits were not necessarily evil or antagonistic to humanity. While some were often conceived as malevolent, others might be ambivalent or even benevolent in nature. Classical Greek philosophy, in par-ticular, seems to have moved far toward a rejection of any malevolent *daimo-nes*, although this view never became widely accepted among nonelite classes, and in late antiquity certain philosophical systems, notably Neopla-tonism, reintegrated the notion of potentially harmful and evil *daimones* into their thought. The ancient Hebrew tradition also knew of such spirits, described more fully in apocryphal literature than in the canonical books of scripture. In Hebrew thought, also, these spirits were more uniformly evil and were often associated with illicit magical arts. The apocryphal Book of Enoch, for example, described how the spirits Semjâzâ and Armârôs taught enchantments and herb-lore to human beings, while Barâquîjâl, Kôkabêl, and Sariêl taught astrology and how to discern signs in the movements of heavenly bodies. Christianity took over these Jewish ideas, shaping demons into purely evil creatures and, critically, expanding their active role in the world.

Demons were present in Christian thought from the earliest days of Chris-tianity: witness the statement of Paul to the Corinthians mentioned above. Origen, writing in Egypt in the early third century, did much to define the role of demons in the Christian cosmos, especially in terms of their relation to magicians and the magical arts. Also in the deserts of Egypt in the third and fourth centuries ascetic practices developed that would eventually blos-som into the earliest forms of Christian monasticism. These early ascetics, withdrawing from the world into lives of severe religious contemplation in the desert, perceived demons as terrifyingly present and active forces bent on the temptation and corruption of Christian souls. Such ideas fit easily with, and reinforced, the broader Christian conception that all pagan rites were simply masks for demonic forces, and especially that most magical activities were inherently demonic and thus evil and directly opposed to Christianity.

Although Christianity's moral condemnation of magic was, from the start, powerful and virtually all-encompassing, formal prohibition of magical activities for Christians nevertheless came more slowly. In 306, in what is now Spain, the Synod of Elvira proclaimed that Christians known to have practiced *maleficium* should not receive last rites. This ruling was based on the notion that magic was demonic and thus that the involvement of any Christian with these arts was a serious offense against the faith. Still, although one must bear in mind that the term *maleficium* was increasingly used at this time in a general sense to denote any kind of condemned magical activity, the employment of the term here may indicate that some of the usual ancient concern to prohibit only those forms of magic designed to achieve harmful ends continued to inform Christian thought. In 314 the Council of Ancyra prescribed severe penances to Christians who practiced divination, while the first clear prohibition of magical rites more broadly defined for Christians was issued by the Council of Laodicaea in 375. This legislation pertained only to the clergy, however, not to the laity.

The fourth century marked a critical point in the history of Christianity, beginning with the conversion of the emperor Constantine (reigned 306–337) supposedly as a result of a miraculous vision he received before a crucial battle against an imperial rival in 312. The Christian writer Eusebius (ca. 263–340), in his *Vita Constantini* (Life of Constantine), claimed that he heard directly from the emperor how he had seen an image of the cross in the sky, along with the words "in this sign you will conquer." Constantine did conquer, and the next year he issued a decree of toleration, proclaiming Christianity to be an officially recognized and legitimate cult within the empire. He became a great patron of Christianity and Christian churches, and he presided over the first ecumenical council of Christian bishops at Nicea in 325. Christianity now had the weight of imperial power with which to enforce correct belief and practice, and imperial authorities were increasingly influenced by Christian doctrine. After Constantine, no non-Christian ever again ruled the empire, with the brief exception of Julian the Apostate (reigned 361–363), who, while he did try to restore some of the privileges of pagan cults, also issued a renewed edict of toleration for Christianity. Finally, during the reign of the emperor Theodosius I (379–395), Christianity became the official religion of the Roman state.

The advent of Christian emperors only gradually altered Roman legislation against magical practices, however. In 320, for example, Constantine issued laws against private divination; yet this was hardly a specifically Christian act on his part. Private divination had long been censured by pagan authorities, and Constantine was careful to permit the public rites of divination that were so essential to many Roman cults. Similarly, the emperor Valentinian (reigned 364–375) ordered death for anyone who ventured out at night to perform harmful magic. Yet his legislation was fully in accord with typical condemnations of secretive and harmful magic in the ancient world. He continued to distinguish beneficial from harmful magic and recognized legitimate forms of divination. Throughout the fourth century, Roman authorities clearly exploited the vague meanings of such terms as *magia*, *maleficium*, and above all, *superstitio*. Since "superstition" meant most basically illegitimate or improper forms of cultic rites, legislation condemning *superstitio* could be interpreted and enforced quite differently, depending on what sort of practices were actually viewed as improper in any given context. In 438, however, the emperor Theodosius II (reigned 408–450) issued a much stricter legal code. Christian ideology toward magic was far more thoroughly embodied in the law than ever before. All pagan rites were defined as superstitious, and all magical practices and forms of divination were uniformly prohibited. Not all ambiguities were eliminated, and certainly magical and other pagan practices were not eradicated from the empire; nevertheless, by the early fifth century, Christian understandings of magic and superstition dominated the Roman world and were ready to be passed on to the medieval West.

From Augustine to Isidore:
The Codification of Christian Magic

The early fifth century witnessed not only the dominance of Christian views of magic in Roman imperial law but also the most profound and influential formulation of Christian ideology regarding magic. Augustine of Hippo was the greatest of the Latin fathers of the church, and his writings became foundational sources for later Christian thought in medieval and early modern Europe. In several of his works, including *De civitate dei* (City of God), he dealt with the subjects of magic, superstition, and demonology, establishing their place in the natural and supernatural order of the Christian universe. In his writings on these topics, Augustine followed most of the basic ideas developed by earlier authorities, including those already discussed in this chapter. He argued, for example, that pagan gods were actually Christian demons in disguise, and that all pagan rites and practices were superstitions. His significance lies mainly in assembling these ideas into a fully coherent system and setting them within a comprehensive Christian worldview. He stressed the essential difference between Christian miracles, which drew on divine power, and magic, which drew on demonic forces. More than any earlier authority he developed the idea that a direct relationship or pact necessarily existed between human magicians and demons in order for magic to function.

Born in 354 in Tagaste in Roman North Africa (near modern Souk Ahras, Algeria), Augustine was educated primarily in Carthage, the principal city of the region. Although his mother was a Christian, he largely rejected her religion in his youth. Instead, he was drawn to classical philosophy, as well as to the heretical Christian sect of Manicheanism. Traveling first to Rome and then to Milan while seeking employment as a rhetorician and educator, he was drawn back to orthodox Christianity by another father of the church, Ambrose of Milan (ca. 340–397). After much consideration and a famous conversion experience recounted in his *Confessiones* (Confessions), he was baptized into the church in 387. Shortly thereafter, he returned to Tagaste. He intended to live a private and secluded life of contemplation and scholarship. While visiting Hippo Regius, however, a coastal city some sixty miles from his hometown, he was inducted into the priesthood, seemingly against his will, by the local congregation. He quickly rose to become bishop of the city, and he held that office for the rest of his life.

Augustine's earliest considerations of magic come from around 396. In question seventy-nine of a work entitled *De diversis quaestionibus LXXXIII* (On Eighty-Three Diverse Questions), he dealt with the biblical confrontation between Moses and Aaron and the priests of Pharaoh, whom Christian thinkers considered to be magicians. At around the same time, in his *De diversis quaestionibus ad Simplicianum* (Diverse Questions to Simplicianus), he discussed Saul's consultation of the sorceress of Endor in order to divine the outcome of a pending battle. Some of his most important discussions of magic and superstition, however, are found in his *De doctrina Christiana* (On Christian Teaching), begun in the mid to late 390s but completed only in 426. Here he established that all magical practices were superstitious, insofar as they relied on consultations with demons or contracts or other arrangements that magicians might enter into with them. He condemned spells and incantations along with many forms of divination, including astrology. He also attacked the widespread use of various amulets believed to have protective or curative powers as well as other forms of magical healing that he claimed Roman physicians also condemned. Here we can see that as much as Augustine was operating within, and indeed establishing, a Christian system for understanding, categorizing, and condemning magic, he was also an educated Roman and still drew on some criticisms of magic common to the classical pagan world.

In addition to active magical practices, spells, and curative rites, Augustine also criticized a host of common superstitions and the special observance of various signs. For example, if people tripped or stumbled upon leaving their houses in the morning, or if they sneezed while putting on their shoes, they might take this as an ill omen and stay at home for the day. Many people apparently believed that if child or a dog ran between two friends walking together on the street, or if those friends passed on opposite sides of a noticeable stone in the roadway, their friendship would dissolve. The solution was to strike the child or dog or tread upon the stone. Augustine had nothing but derision for such people. While stomping on a stone was harmless, if silly, he lamented for the poor children who suffered the blows of strangers. He wryly noted, however, that dogs struck for this reason sometimes bit back and caused these people to suffer real injuries on account of their superstitious fears. In his criticisms, of course, Augustine was not drawing on any particularly Christian notions. He asserted no demonic agency underlying these superstitions. Instead, he drew on the disdain common to Roman intellectuals for what they regarded as erroneous popular beliefs.

Augustine returned more directly to Christian themes in his *De divinatione daemonum* (On the Divination of Demons), written between 406 and 411. In 391 Christian authorities had destroyed the pagan temple of Serapis in Alexandria, and some people thereafter claimed that the priests of the temple had foreseen this event through their rituals. Since any special knowledge these priests possessed would, in the Christian view, have come from demons, Augustine wrote to demonstrate how such creatures might in fact appear to predict the future. Drawing not only on scriptural discussions of the nature of demons but also on classical conceptions regarding *daimones*, he maintained that demons were mainly spiritual creatures with airy bodies. They possessed preternatural senses, being able to perceive things indiscernible to humans, and they could move at tremendous speed across the world. Thus they were able to amass knowledge and information that often allowed them to predict future events with great accuracy, although without actually knowing the future. Only God possessed such actual foreknowledge, which he might reveal to legitimate prophets. The predictions of demons, although sometimes correct, were not infallible. Moreover, demons often sought deliberately to deceive the magicians who consulted them about future events; occasionally they would also "predict" events that they then caused in order to gain the trust and confidence of gullible humans. Ultimately demons could act only within the limits of divine permission, but God allowed them to engage in such activities in order to tempt and test human faith.

Augustine's fullest integration of magic and superstition into a comprehensive Christian worldview came in his *City of God*, written over the course of a decade from 413 to 426. In this sprawling work, he responded most basically to the pagan claim that the sack of Rome in 410 by Germanic Visigoths had resulted from the growth of Christian "superstition" in the empire and consequent weakening of Roman society. *City of God* addressed numerous historical, philosophical, and theological issues. Regarding the topics of concern here, Augustine forcefully reiterated the by then standard Christian claim that the real locus of superstition was in fact Roman and other pagan cults, not Christianity. He also dismissed pagan claims that their cultic rites accessed a higher or purer form of power than did the practices of common magicians. All such rites, he argued, drew on the power of demons; thus all were equally magical and superstitious. The only exceptions, of course, were Christian rites, which drew on divine power and resulted in miracles, not magic.

As *City of God* neatly illustrates, the definitive Christian statement against classical conceptions of magic and superstition came as the western Roman Empire, at least, was starting to dissolve as a unified political entity (the eastern Roman, or Byzantine, Empire would endure for another thousand years). Beginning in the fourth century and continuing into the fifth, Germanic peoples from northern Europe entered the empire in considerable numbers, sometimes by simple migration and sometimes in forceful waves that might accurately be called invasions. Although they eventually replaced Roman rulers with their own kings, these peoples hardly obliterated Roman society. Instead, a gradual process of cultural change consumed the western Roman world. Christian authorities continued to develop their understanding of magic and superstition while responding to new contexts created in this period, firmly grounded in the doctrines of Augustine and earlier authorities and always founded on the essential opposition of Christianity to paganism.

About a century after Augustine, Caesarius of Arles (ca. 470–543) incorporated the thinking of the bishop of Hippo, as well as other early Christian authorities, into his sermons, several of which dealt with superstitious practices supposedly common in his day and which in turn became important sources for later Christian authorities. Caesarius was a Gallo-Roman nobleman who, around 502, became bishop of Arles, a town on the Rhône River, near the Mediterranean coast. He was well trained in a classical Roman intellectual heritage that, while by no means yet eradicated, was by this time becoming increasingly rare. Although superstition was hardly an overriding theme in his sermons, he did decry superstitious and magical practices that he presented as prevalent in the region of Arles. These practices represented, for him, a persistent paganism that had to be eliminated. He warned, first and foremost, that pagan rites disguised the worship of demons and that all recourse to magicians, sorcerers, and seers of any kind was to be avoided. He condemned those whom he claimed perpetuated such blatantly pagan customs as worshiping trees or fountains, or performing elaborate rites while dressed as animals. He also warned against seemingly more benign practices, such as observing omens, signs in the heavens, or even interpreting sneezes as portents of good or ill fortune. He criticized those people who continued to regard certain days as portentous, finding some favorable for undertaking journeys, for example, and others not. All such practices, he maintained, were vestiges of paganism. Further, no one should consult with soothsayers about future events or turn to sorcerers to detect thieves or to heal injuries. Rather than use charms and amulets bearing "diabolical signs," sick people should go to church, be anointed with holy oil, confess, and pray.

The extent to which such practices actually existed, in the form in which Caesarius described, is difficult to determine. Certainly in many cases Caesarius shaped his rhetoric in accordance with accounts of magical and superstitious practice found in Augustine and other earlier authorities. On the other hand, there seems no reason to doubt that, despite strict Christian admonitions, many people continued to turn to magical remedies when they were ill, or sought to locate a lost or stolen item, just as they had done in Augustine's day. This problem of interpretation is evident, too, in Martin of Braga's (ca. 520–580) *De correctione rusticorum* (On the Correction of Rustics). This work, written in the wake of a church council held at Braga (in modern Portugal) in 572, was deeply influenced by Augustine's *De catechizandis rudibus* (On the Instruction of the Ignorant), and Martin was also certainly familiar with Caesarius's sermons. Martin followed Augustine in arguing strongly that all pagan gods were actually demons, and he echoed charges also made by Caesarius that many people continued to observe certain devotions in honor of pagan gods. Women, for example, still called upon Minerva when weaving, or observed the days of Venus when arranging a marriage. Again, how widespread such overtly pagan practices were at this time can be questioned. Doubtless, though, recourse to spells and other rites that church authorities would have perceived as masking devotion to demons was being used. Certainly, the perceived prevalence of superstition was a concern to those authorities meeting at the Council of Braga.

At the end of the sixth century, the Iberian peninsula produced the most learned Christian authority of that period. Isidore (ca. 560–636), bishop of Seville and advisor to the Visigothic kings of Spain, did not seek to address contemporary practices in his *Etymologiae* (Etymologies) so much as to summarize the totality of ancient knowledge, both classical and Christian. In doing so, he produced a veritable encyclopedia and perhaps the foremost general reference work for later medieval centuries. Following the Roman authority Cicero, he defined superstition as excessive or unwarranted religious rites or devotion, although of course as a Christian he saw all pagan rites and any practice that might entail demonic involvement as unwarranted. When he came to discuss magic in the eighth book of *Etymologiae*, he provided a complete history of the concept from ancient times. The first magician was the Persian king Zoroaster. Among the subsequent *magi* Isidore included the priests of Pharaoh who contended with Moses and Aaron, and the Greek sorceress Circe, who transformed Odysseus's men into swine. All such arts he linked to the instruction of "wicked angels," and he noted that *magi* were usually called *malefici* because of the inherently evil nature of their acts.

Isidore describes specific varieties of magical practice. Necromancy involved divination by summoning the spirits of the dead, while hydromancy involved conjuring visions to appear in clear water. Each of the other elements had a species of divination associated with it; hence geomancy, aeromancy, and pyromancy. Haruspices observed days and hours and pronounced what times were favorable or unfavorable for certain undertakings, augurs made predictions based on the flight of birds, and astrologers cast horoscopes based on the movements of the stars. Numerous other categories were listed, mostly concerning forms of divination, which was the principal intellectual magical activity in the ancient world, as opposed to the more practical spells and healing charms discussed by Martin of Braga and Caesarius of Arles. As with those authors, indeed even more so, one can ask to what extent Isidore's categories reflected actual magical practices common in his day. Yet this was not his real concern. Like Augustine two centuries before him, Isidore provided a comprehensive summary of Christian understandings of magic. Like Augustine, he separated all such activities sharply from proper Christian devotion, maintaining that all magical arts arose from a "pestilential association" between humans and demons. It matters less how much such categorizations reflected actual magical practice in early seventh-century Iberia as the degree to which they would shape all future understandings of magic and those beliefs and activities that authorities would label as superstitious in Christian Europe.

The Magic of Northern Paganism

Thus far we have explored the development of Christian categories of magic and superstition only in terms of Christianity's response to the pagan cults and ritual systems of the ancient Roman world, centered around the Mediterranean. This was, of course, the world in which Christianity first appeared and in which it grew to become the dominant cult. In the course of the fifth century, however, the influx of Germanic peoples from the north into Roman lands led to the gradual breakdown of imperial control and the eventual establishment of new Germanic kingdoms in Britain, Gaul, Italy, Iberia, and even North Africa. These peoples had their own religious and magical practices and beliefs, which had to be integrated into both classical and Christian systems. In the process, Christian ideas about magic were themselves changed, and they continued to develop as Christianity eventually expanded further into northern Europe, beyond the boundaries of the Roman Empire and into fully pagan territories in central Europe and Scandinavia.

What place magic held in the culture of northern Germanic peoples, or even whether a concept of magic comparable to that which had developed in the Greco-Roman world existed among them prior to their contact with Rome and Christianity, is very difficult to determine. The only written sources available to historians are those composed by Christian authorities typically hostile to Germanic paganism. Aside from the use of brief runic inscriptions, pre-Christian Germanic culture was entirely oral, and the earliest Germanic literature was written well after Christianization had taken place. To get some sense of pagan Germanic culture, historians usually turn to Norse literature, for Christianity came later to Scandinavia than to other regions of northern Europe, establishing itself as a real force in these lands only around 1000. Still, the majority of Nordic sagas and mythological accounts were only written down in the thirteenth century, although they typically reflected oral traditions that extended back at least to the period of Christianization itself. From these sources, from runic inscriptions, and from archeological evidence, some picture of the place of magic in pre-Christian Germanic culture can be developed.

As in the classical world, so in early Germanic culture there seems to have been no significant distinction between magic and religion. Thus an account of magic and magicians in the Germanic world can begin with the gods, who often seem to have employed spells, enchanted items, or to have otherwise engaged in "magical" rituals. The main literary sources for Norse mythology are the *Eddas*, written in thirteenth-century Iceland, though based on earlier materials. Probably the most important and famous tale illustrating magical-seeming actions (to modern sensibilities and certainly to medieval Christian authorities) on the part of the gods was the account of how the chief god, Odin, hung himself on a tree for several days as part of a ritual to gain knowledge of the mystical runes. Obtaining hidden knowledge was a major goal of Norse rites. Odin also was thought to keep the severed head of the god Mimir, who had possessed prophetic powers, embalmed with various herbs and preserved by spells in order to continue using it to divine the future. Also, like many human wizards in Germanic tales, Odin was thought to be a talented shape-shifter. The principal disguise in which he wandered the world, an old man cloaked and hooded or wearing a great hat, helped to create an archetype for the appearance of wizards in much later European literature.

The rites and rituals that early Germanic peoples directed toward their gods were doubtless intended to produce certain protective, beneficial, or divinatory results, just as the cultic rites of the classical world. Much less information exists, however, about what these rites entailed or how they were performed than is extant for classical cults. Archeology can confirm that cultic sites existed, but it offers little solid information on their function. Literary sources seem to indicate that the performance of spells, charms, and other rites by human magicians was somewhat less associated with interactions with deities than in the ancient Mediterranean world, although of course no sweeping generalization should be made here. The process of ritual divination known as *seiðr*, for example, which was used not only to predict but also to some extent to control the future, certainly carried what might be seen in modern terms as religious overtones and was often employed by the Norse gods themselves.

To risk another generalization, the performance of magic in the Norse world, or at least in the Norse sagas, seems to have been more associated with the power of spoken or written words alone, absent other ritual actions, than in the classical world. One can, of course, wonder about the extent to which literary sources accurately reflected actual practices. Nevertheless, certainly the most famous and unique aspect of Norse magic, for which there is ample physical evidence, was the use of runic inscriptions. The earliest known examples of these date from the third century. Whether they were initially believed to possess or convey special power is unclear, but in any mostly non-literate culture, forms of writing are usually regarded as charged with power. The runes were never developed into a system for prosaic writing; they seem always to have been used for special, mostly magical purposes. Items inscribed with runes, which could include almost anything from swords to whale bones to pieces of bark, were imbued with uncanny powers, and runes could be used for divination. Aside from carved runes, Norse sagas also abound with spoken spells or incantations, often called *galdr*, an Old Icelandic word meaning a song or spell, from the verb *gala*, to speak or to say out loud.

The uses to which magic might be put were as varied in Germanic culture as in classical or Christian culture. Harmful and threatening magic abounded, and the spells of sorcerers could kill, injure, or bring disease. Magic could also be used to control the weather, to raise storms, and to conjure mists. Ranged against all this was an array of counter-spells and charms that could heal, ward off disease, or provide strength or protection from injury. Forms of divination were numerous, and the revelation of hidden fate or secret knowledge was a principal object of Germanic magical practices, as was also true for magical systems of other cultures. In one area Germanic conceptions of magic do seem to have been significantly different from those in more southern lands. Love magic always enjoyed a prominent place in classical and even in Christian thought. In the Norse sagas, however, while harmful magic could be employed to impede sexual relations, there are almost no examples of magic used to incite love or to arouse amorous desire.

Potential users of magic covered a broad spectrum of Germanic society. As in the classical world, virtually anyone might learn how to employ a magical rite, and some simple ritual practices, protective charms especially, were quite common. Warnings seem to have abounded, however, about the dangers of employing powerful magic without sufficient knowledge or skill. Examples can be found in the sagas of people who improperly inscribed runes, often with disastrous results. There were also, of course, specialists in the use of magic who claimed the necessary knowledge or experience to work powerful and dangerous spells. As in the classical world, at least in literary depictions, such specialists were often portrayed as women, although, again as with the classical world, questions could be raised as to how accurately such literary stereotypes reflected reality. In Norse as in classical literature, these magical specialists usually enjoyed a dark or evil reputation. Although anyone might employ certain common spells or charms, to be too deeply immersed in magical practices was clearly thought to be threatening and socially reprehensible.

The levels of condemnation that magical practices evoked in the Germanic world are, as with so much else, difficult to determine with any degree of accuracy. The Norse sagas and other literature more typically present accusations of magic and responses involving some form of counter-magic, rather than decribing legal proceedings or remedies. What legal sources do exist for the early Germanic kingdoms are extremely problematic, as all were composed in Latin in the wake of extensive contact with Roman and Christian culture. Not only were these codes, the earliest of which date from the fifth century, heavily influenced by Roman legislation, but they also largely adopted the categories of magic created by Latin terminology. The Burgundian Code, for example, included the practice of *maleficium* by a woman as grounds for divorce, provided a man could prove this charge against his wife. Condemnations of *maleficium* also appeared in other Germanic legal codes, and there seems little reason to think that harmful or destructive magic was not outlawed in earlier, preliterate Germanic culture, just as in other cultures that accepted the real efficacy of magical rites and practices. Also condemned, however, were various forms of divination, weather-magic, and magical healing and curing, as well as the use of protective amulets and talismans. Such prohibitions on positive or beneficial magic seem very akin to Christianity's more wholesale condemnation of all magical practices, and so may well not reflect earlier Germanic distinctions. Another aspect of the Germanic codes was that fines and other penalties were often leveled against anyone who unjustly accused another person of performing harmful magic or of being a witch. Again, however, the terms used were Latin—*malefica* or often *striga*—and there is no way to know what, if any, earlier Germanic concepts might have lain behind such legislation.

Germanic paganism was the principal but by no means the only form of pagan practice encountered by Christianity as it spread beyond the borders of the Roman Empire. Although the beliefs and practices of the Celtic peoples of Europe had, by the time of Christianity's rise, been significantly modified by centuries of Roman control and close contact with Roman belief, Celtic paganism was still strong on the fringes of Roman Britain and in Ireland. Many practices that could be labeled magical occupied a major place in Celtic culture, but the same problem with sources obtains in this case too. All written material describing Celtic beliefs or practices was composed by Christian authors. Celtic druids, like the priests of other cultures, must have performed a variety of protective and benevolent rituals, and they were believed to possess significant divinatory and astrological skills. Naturally, Christian sources presented them as magicians and claimed that all of their rites and knowledge stemmed ultimately from demons. In confronting Celtic druids, Christian missionaries, saints, and bishops often appeared to be magicians themselves, and many themes from Celtic legends were worked into Christian accounts. Irish saints' legends, for example, focus more than much other hagiographic literature on the wonderworking abilities of the saints, as they displayed the superiority of the power of Christ over the superstitious rites of pagan priests. In particular, Irish saints exhibited power over the elements of nature. Saint Colman mac Luachin was able to survive for an entire day beneath the water of a lake, for example, and the famous Saint Patrick survived unharmed in a hut that was set on fire, while a druid in a similar hut was consumed by flame. In another contest, Patrick caused a druid to rise into the air and then smashed him down on some rocks. The echoes of the apostle Peter's victory over Simon Magus are obvious in the story and show how Christianity's own mythology colored the confrontation with Celtic paganism.

There is no doubt that elements of Germanic and Celtic paganism, and of certain magical beliefs and practices derived from them, survived in Christian Europe, primarily in folklore and folk wisdom. Legends of fairies, belief in the special significance of certain locations, such as springs, trees, and groves, or traditions surrounding the special powers of certain plants, herbs, or stones, for example, had deep cultural roots. But such cultural beliefs were never absolutely fixed or unchanging, and to determine the exact nature of these beliefs in pagan times from the folk beliefs of later Christian centuries is impossible. The best historians can do is to be aware of the general ways in which earlier northern paganism may have influenced later Christian beliefs and practices.

Magic and Superstition in Early Medieval Europe

Turning to Christianity's expansion into the lands of northern Europe, its interaction with northern paganism, and the continued development of Christian ideas of magic and superstition, the sources become more plentiful, but they remain problematic. The story of Saint Patrick's confrontation with Irish druids recounted above gives a sense of the difficulties. Heroic descriptions of missionaries, saints, and early bishops engaging in contests of power with pagan priests were propaganda to valorize Christianity and to aid in further missionizing, not factual accounts. They often incorporate biblical models and draw heavily on the works of earlier Christian authorities. Above all Augustine but also writers like Caesarius of Arles and Martin of Braga, who as we have seen were not necessarily reliable reporters of their own circumstances and who drew heavily from one another, became standard sources that later authors followed when describing magical or suspected pagan practices. Neither in their accounts of initial confrontations with paganism nor in their condemnations of supposedly persistent pagan practices enduring well after Christianization can ecclesiastical sources—essentially the only written sources from this period—be fully trusted as accurate descriptions of contemporary context.

One typical response to this problem on the part of scholars has been to try to read through the sources, screening out patently Christian elements in order to recover the traces of "true" paganism. This is obviously a very difficult and inexact process, but more basically it may be profoundly misleading in that it creates a false impression of two wholly dichotomous systems—Christianity and the survivals of fully pagan practices and rituals—jockeying for position in early medieval Europe. Rather, what seems more likely in the long span from the sixth through tenth centuries is that Christian beliefs and pagan traditions developed together and integrated with one another; there is no point in attempting to sift out the diverse elements of the practices that emerged and label them either Christian or pagan. To speak of pagan survivals, as many critical Christian authors did in this period and as many scholars have done since is not really accurate, for, despite the tone readily apparent in strident attacks on magic and superstition, Christian authorities were not actually interested in fully eradicating all traditional practices rooted in earlier, non-Christian culture. Rather, they sought only to convert such practices into Christian ones. Pagan holy sites were made into Christian shrines and churches. Fairy wells were blessed by saints and their power Christianized in this way. Attributes of pagan heroes or gods were transferred to Christian saints or other figures, and traditional spells were made into Christian blessings.

The underlying meaning and overall significance of this process of adaptation has been much debated. Some scholars have argued that the adoption and toleration by church authorities of pagan elements overlaid with what seems only a thin veneer of Christianity represents a clear failure of Christianization—that the church was not strong enough simply to wipe away all vestiges of pagan culture or did not care deeply enough about the faith of the masses to bother trying. Others have argued, in a more nuanced fashion, that despite Christianity's rhetoric of complete rejection of all forms of magic and superstition, many in the church recognized that magical rites filled useful and necessary functions and sought to rehabilitate and preserve certain elements of magic. Such arguments, however, fail to take seriously what Christian elites defined as magical and what they did not.

Consider the case of a rite intended to heal the leg of a horse that had been injured or gone lame. An early Germanic spell is known to have existed that involved the invocation of Woden (Odin), who healed his horse after it had sprained its leg as the god rode through a forest. In Christianized versions of the spell, the figure of Woden was replaced by Christ riding a horse into Jerusalem, performing the same healing feat. This adaptation may appear to be a concession by Christian authorities to persistent pagan magical practices. These authorities, however, never had any doubt that horses' legs could be healed by supernatural powers, nor did they feel that such healing was, in and of itself, intolerable. They were concerned only that the act not involve the invocation of demonic power (for, of course, Woden was considered to be a demon, as were all pagan deities). To replace the figure of Woden with that of Christ as the object of the invocation changed the essential nature of the act. With divine instead of demonic power being employed, the healing was no longer magical; it was now miraculous. This is not to say that, on a practical level, such adaptations were not driven by a realistic recognition of the need to accommodate deeply entrenched cultural practices, but rather to stress that such accommodations were in no way incompatible with the basic theoretical structure that Christianity sought to impose on conceptions of magical acts.

What remain to be explained, if the general stance of Christian culture could be so fluid and accommodating of a variety of practices, are the strong, occasionally shrill condemnations of magic and superstition that continued to flow from the pens of Christian authorities during these centuries. Yet there is really no contradiction here. What we see is not evidence of Christianity decrying some magical practices while accommodating others. If a practice was magic, it was to be condemned; if it was not condemned then it need not be regarded as magic. This is not as preposterously circular a statement as it sounds. Christian authorities never wavered in their strong theoretical stance that magic was essentially demonic and therefore evil. Thus they stridently opposed any practice that had been definitively condemned as magical or superstitious. In the absence of authoritative condemnation, however, there was much room for debate about whether various practices were indeed demonic, as opposed to potentially drawing on divine power or simply being ineffective (drawing on no real power and therefore of no serious concern). One reason that later Christian authors followed the early church fathers so closely on matters of magic and superstition was not simple slavish devotion, or even the conviction that such evils were by nature perennial, but the fact that those early sources authoritatively labeled specific practices as demonic. So authorities could confidently condemn these practices, as well as the category of "magic" in general, just as stridently in the sixth, seventh, and eighth centuries as in the fifth (or later in the fifteenth). Meanwhile, given the cultural conditions of the time, they might also easily accommodate a number of contemporary practices that to modern minds can appear just as "magical" as those that were reviled.

An important source for early Christian interaction with magic in northern Europe is provided by the sixth-century bishop Gregory of Tours (ca. 540–594). In his *Historia Francorum* (History of the Franks) and other works, he described a world in which magic remained prevalent. At the lowest level of society, itinerant sorcerers traveled the countryside, claiming to carry holy relics but in fact only deceiving people with magical practices, for when examined, their "relics" consisted of nothing more than herbs, roots, and the bones of animals. Magic could also be found at the highest levels of society, and Gregory famously related how the sixth-century queen Fredegund was accused of using poisons and other harmful magic against her enemies. Gregory's basic message, when he dealt with magic, was the same as that found in other early Christian authorities—that pagan rites were demonic superstitions, that pagan deities were actually demons, and that all magic was to be avoided because it drew on demonic power. Gregory's world was also peopled by many holy men wielding tremendous divine power, which might appear magical to modern sensibilities. For example, when Saint Martin discovered a tree blown down across a road, he raised it up again by making the sign of the cross. Thereafter, the bark of this tree possessed healing powers. For Gregory, of course, the nature of this power was very different from that employed by common magicians.

Beginning in the sixth century, handbooks of penances, known as penitentials, produced by church synods and councils and circulating widely through Europe, provide another rich source of information about magical beliefs and practices. Remarkably, in light of the dire punishments handed down by Christian authorities in later centuries, these penitentials prescribed only relatively mild penalties for magic or superstition. People who engaged in magical or superstitious acts were required to repent and perform some type of penance, which might involve fasting for some period, visiting certain saints' shrines, or performing other devotional acts. No harsher punishments were issued, however, and the general tone of these works usually presented magical or superstitious practices as cases of foolish error rather than dangerous threats to the Christian faith. Also clear from these sources is the fact that, despite a rhetoric of absolute opposition to all magical practices based on their essential nature, church authorities still paid some attention to the supposed effects of magical acts. Penances were more severe for spells that involved killing or working harm. If an area of "compromise" is to be sought in Christian thought about magic, it may well be found not in the Christianization of pagan spells and rituals of power, but here, where Christian authorities seem tacitly to have adjusted to the common ancient practice of condemning harmful magic more severely than other kinds. This is an important consideration, given that Christian authorities would often reject such an approach to magic during the witch trials of later centuries.

Also during the sixth and seventh centuries, brief lists of superstitions, *indiculi superstitionum*, were produced, often in connection with ecclesiastical synods, and sometimes circulated with penitential literature. These lists were very cursory, usually simply naming practices that church officials were to guard against and condemn. They were also very formulaic, typically decrying the continued worship or special veneration of trees, stones, and springs, with special attention paid to supposed omens and other signs of future events, the use of any magical amulets or other figures, and consultation with soothsayers or sorcerers for any reason. As with all early Christian sources, one can question the degree to which these lists described actual practices. They certainly indicate the categories of concern that persisted in the minds of clerical authorities, however.

In the sixth century, the rulings of church councils and individual bishops against magic and superstition, as well as the authority of penitential literature, tended to be localized in extent. There was no centralized authority to regulate all of Western Christendom. The papacy began to expand its effective control over the bishops and other clergy of Europe somewhat in the seventh century. The most important unifying force, however, was the rising power of the Frankish kingdom in the eighth century, which would come to encompass much of western Europe. A Frankish dynasty emerged during the reign of Charles Martel (Charles the Hammer), who ruled not as king but as "mayor of the palace" from 714 to 741 (the Frankish kings of the Merovingian dynasty having by this time become mere figureheads). His son Pepin the Short ruled as mayor from 741 to 751, at which point he did away with the last of the Merovingian dynasty and assumed the title of king himself until his death in 768. His son Charles the Great, or Charlemagne, followed him as king until 800, when he assumed the even more exalted title of emperor, the Roman office that had been defunct in the West since the fifth century. Charlemagne certainly deserved this title, for by 800, and until his death in 814, he ruled a realm that encompassed all of modern France, the Low Countries, much of Germany and Austria, all northern Italy, and a slice of northern Spain—in short, almost the whole of what was at that time Western Christendom.

The power of the so-called Carolingian dynasty rested primarily on military might, but it also involved a close alliance with the Roman Church and the Roman papacy. As kings and emperors, the Carolingians sought to unify and regularize beliefs and practices within their vast realm. Already in 742, a reforming church synod issued a decree forbidding the casting of lots, augury, and other forms of divination, as well as the use of magical amulets and incantations. In 743 the list of superstitions appended to the official decrees or "canons" of the Council of Leptinnes (modern Estinnes) condemned the use of amulets, incantations, auguries, divination, and weather-magic. These decrees circulated widely throughout the Frankish realm and even beyond, into Britain and Ireland, for example, where they still benefited from the prestige of Frankish authority. At about the same time, a monk named Pirmin at a monastery at Reichenau (in modern Germany) wrote a treatise on moral guidance entitled *Scarapsus*. On the subjects of magic and superstition, he drew heavily on Caesarius of Arles, Martin of Braga, and Augustine of Hippo, ensuring that these early authorities continued to shape understandings of magic in medieval Europe.

Charlemagne issued a systematic and sweeping legal condemnation of magic in 789 in an *Admonitio generalis* (General Admonition) for his entire kingdom. Influenced perhaps by the stricter moral position of reform-minded clerics in his court, he took a harsh stance against magic reminiscent of late imperial Roman legal codes but based primarily on more literal readings of biblical condemnations of magic. The *Admonitio* outlawed all forms of divination and other magical practices and required all magicians or enchanters to repent their practices or be condemned to death. This legislation applied not only to the Franks but also to conquered peoples, including the still-pagan Saxons. Throughout his reign, Charlemagne continued to issue decrees against magical, superstitious, and supposedly pagan practices, and he instructed his emissaries to look for and root out such practices throughout his empire. In 800 a church synod at Freising issued instructions echoing Charlemagne's commands, ordering bishops to investigate thoroughly anyone suspected of performing divination, incantations, weather magic, or other forms of sorcery in their lands. This inquiry could involve the use of torture. Weather magic and the raising of storms was a much feared form of harmful magic, and this certainly seems to have been true during the Carolingian period. Around 820, Archbishop Agobard of Lyon (reigned 814–840) reported widespread popular panics arising from suspected magical destruction of crops by hailstorms and other means. Although Agobard himself argued that storms could only arise naturally or by divine causation, the fears that led to the apparently frequent lynching of suspected weather-working magicians (*tempestarii*) were certainly not limited to the common folk.

Efforts against magic and superstition continued after Charlemagne's death. In 829 a church council at Paris again issued a proclamation condemning all magical practices. The important intellectual authority Hrabanus Maurus, abbot of the monastery of Fulda from 822 to 842, composed a work *De magicis artibus* (On Magical Arts), which drew heavily on Isidore of Seville's categorizations and condemnations of magic and divination. Nevertheless, in 850, a synod at Pavia complained that magical and superstitious practices were still prevalent, especially magic used to arouse love or hatred and harmful sorcery used to injure or to kill. Such practices existed, or at least could be suspected, at all levels of society. In a famous case in 855, King Lothar II (reigned 846–879) divorced his wife Theutberga, who had proven to be barren, and married his mistress Waldrada. Archbishop Hincmar of Rheims (reigned 845–882) very much opposed this remarriage. In his *De divortio Lotharii regis et Teutbergae reginae* (On the Divorce of King Lothar and Queen Theutberga) he accused Waldrada of having used magic to prevent Theutberga from successfully conceiving a child. To support his argument, he assembled a long list of magical practices, all of which he naturally condemned.

By the end of the ninth century, Christian authorities in Europe were criticizing magic and superstition more uniformly and severely than at any time since the late Roman period. Drawing on sources from that period, especially the writings of Augustine, ninth-century authorities continued to link magical practices to paganism. Their concerns in this area were doubtless increased by Christendom's continuing expansion into pagan lands and the need to incorporate pagan peoples into Christian society at the borders of Europe. The heartland of western Europe, however, had been Christianized in the fifth and sixth centuries, and despite the continued production of formulaic literature decrying the persistence of pagan practices, there is no evidence that paganism survived in any real form into later centuries. Nevertheless, into the tenth and eleventh centuries, Christian authorities continued to think of magic primarily in terms of the remnants of pagan beliefs and practices (see figure 2.2).

A classic example of this connection, and one that would resonate with continuing importance through centuries of European thought about magic, was the so-called canon *Episcopi*. Named after its first word in Latin, *episcopi* ("bishops"), this canon first appeared in a collection of canon law, or official church decrees, compiled by Regino of Prüm just after 900. The canon was thought to date from the Council of Ancyra in 314, lending it tremendous age and authority. In fact, it probably originated no earlier than the mid-ninth century. In his collection, Regino gathered several texts condemning sorcerers and enchanters, as well as superstitious rites supposedly still performed before certain trees, stones, or springs as if they were altars. The canon *Episcopi* was by far the most important and influential of these texts. The canon actually consisted of two fairly distinct parts, which in the medieval understanding appear to have been largely conflated. The document began with a simple instruction: "Bishops and the officials and clergy of bishops must labor with all their strength so that the pernicious art of *sortilegium* and *maleficium*, which was invented by the devil, is eradicated from their districts, and if they find a man or woman follower of this wicked sect to eject them foully disgraced from their parishes."[2] The canon then described how "some wicked women, who have given themselves back to Satan and been seduced by the illusions and phantasms of demons, believe and profess that, in the hours of the night, they ride upon certain beasts with Diana, the goddess of the pagans, and an innumerable multitude of women, and in the silence of the night traverse great spaces of earth, and obey her commands as of their lady, and are summoned to her service on certain nights." No connection was drawn in the text between these women and the other people mentioned as performing harmful sorcery. Nevertheless, such a connection clearly existed in the minds of medieval authorities, and the canon *Episcopi* would become an important source for later images of witchcraft and especially nocturnal flight to witches' sabbaths.

In fact, the beliefs described in the canon *Episcopi* are an excellent example of the complex amalgam of classical, Christian, and Germanic thought that underlay medieval conceptions of magic and superstition. The ancient Greeks and Romans had believed in groups of spirits that traveled in the train of the frightful goddess Hecate, who had some associations with the goddess Diana even in classical times. More direct roots for the images in *Episcopi*, however, might be found in the Germanic notions of the Wild Hunt, a group of spirits or shades of the dead that would ride in the train of a goddess named

Figure 2.2   Anglo-Saxon depiction of the Egyptian magician Jambres speaking to his brother Jannes in Hades.

Hulda or Holle (or Berta, Perchta, or other variants). This goddess was associated in Germanic belief with fertility and the moon, and thus Christian writers steeped in the Latin tradition associated her with Diana, goddess of the moon and the hunt. The notion that the entire affair was thoroughly demonic was, of course, a purely Christian construction.

What actual beliefs or practices may have underlain the original composition of the canon *Episcopi* are, as is so often the case with magical traditions, impossible to determine with certainty. Studies have shown that as late as the sixteenth and seventeenth centuries in some corners of Europe popular beliefs existed that certain specially marked individuals would participate in nocturnal, visionary experiences that involved gatherings of spirits and travel in large groups, often to assemblies or to battles. In the sixteenth century, these beliefs were thoroughly Christian, although of course unorthodox and condemned by authorities; individuals claimed that they were summoned by and followed angels, and that they engaged in combat against witches and devils. Perhaps more pagan forms of these beliefs existed in the ninth century, or perhaps authorities simply paganized a set of popular beliefs that they deemed unorthodox and superstitious. The canon was quick to note that the women it described had been "seduced by the illusions and phantasms of demons," which caused them to "wander from the right faith and return to the error of the pagans."[3]

One final text can serve to complete this survey of early medieval Christian concerns with magic, superstition, and the supposed persistence of paganism. A century after Regino of Prüm, in the early 1000s, Burchard, bishop of Worms from 1000 to 1025, composed his *Decretum*, another important collection of canon law and earlier church rulings. He included the text of the canon *Episcopi* (as did all later collections of medieval canon law), and further condemned magical and superstitious practices in Book 19 of this work. His rhetoric will, by this point, be familiar. He forbade any Christian to consult with or otherwise solicit magicians or diviners, whose practices he labeled as pagan customs. He also condemned the "pagan traditions" of worshiping the sun and moon, or reading particular meaning into eclipses or other astral signs. He condemned various spells used for protecting animals from disease or death, controlling the weather, and arousing love or hatred. He also forbade any Christian to participate in rites or observances performed before various stones, trees, or crossroads in the manner of pagans.

As well as completing the survey of Christian thought on magic and superstition up to around 1000, and reinforcing yet again the conviction at least on the part of Christian authorities that such practices were connected to the remnants of paganism, Burchard also demonstrated what overall effect this conviction had on the church's reaction to magic. Although magic was utterly evil and demonic, Christian authorities were always necessarily confident in the superiority of divine over demonic power and the ultimate triumph of Christianity over paganism. Such attitudes are evident in Burchard's writings. Even when demonic, superstitious, and pagan magic might produce real effects and work real harm, Burchard consistently treated these practices as the foolish errors of misguided and uneducated people tricked or deluded by demons rather than as serious threats to Christian society. The penalties he prescribed were mostly penances, and much of his work was penitential in nature. Despite the numerous condemnations of supposedly persistent magical and superstitious practices over the centuries, as well as some relatively severe legislation, early medieval Christian society seems to have been generally confident regarding magic.

This general confidence may help to explain why, frequent and formulaic condemnations aside, so many apparently only lightly Christianized spells, charms, and ritual practices were readily tolerated in early medieval Europe. Again, however, the fact must be stressed that in Christian thought the change from a pagan invocation in a magical spell to a Christian invocation in a blessing was neither slight nor superficial but altered the essential nature of the act. Studies of spells, charms, and blessings in tenth- and eleventh-century Anglo-Saxon England have done much to illuminate how Christian beliefs and practices interwove themselves with older traditions in complex ways, producing not a crude amalgamation of two different systems but a coherent synthesis, fully Christian but easily accommodating a variety of practices. What appear to modern sensibilities to be magical formulae existed side by side with obviously Christian blessings in monastic medical literature, for example. To take one such case, if a horse had fallen ill because it had been "elf-shot," which at this point the church would have defined as a form of demonic or magical assault, the tenth-century *Bald's Leechbook* recommended making an ointment out of dock seed and Scottish wax that had been blessed by having twelve masses said over it and applying it along with holy water to the afflicted animal. Another manuscript described an enormously long and complex ritual for restoring fertility to fields ruined by harmful magic. The ceremony involved taking natural elements from the field—clumps of sod, bits of plants, and the milk of animals—blessing them with masses, fashioning symbolic crosses, and invoking divine power through Christ, Mary, the evangelists, and other saints, as well as saying prayers, but also invoking the powers of nature and performing specific ritual actions over the field.[4]

Although the authors of these Anglo-Saxon sources were still clerics, they may give a far better sense of the complex interminglings of ritual practices that occurred in early medieval Europe than do the numerous condemnations of magic and superstition from this era. Of course, the very fact that the rites described above were recorded with approval by monastic authors meant that, in contemporary terminology, they would not have been magical at all but were instead regarded as invocations of divine blessing. Or so, at least, authorities were convinced in these cases. Since we have only the record of what authorities approved or condemned, we have little way of knowing what most common people may have thought about the rites and practices in which they doubtless frequently engaged to protect themselves or their animals, to cure or to heal, to ensure fertility, and so forth. Studies of later centuries have indicated that, while most people willingly accepted ecclesiastical authority and the church's definitions of what was proper and improper, they gave less thought to the nature of the power by which these rites supposedly operated than to the practical effects they were thought capable of achieving. Such an attitude most likely characterized the majority of people in early medieval Europe as well.

This attitude can, in fact, be discerned even in many clerical condemnations of magic. Burchard of Worms and the other authorities whom he echoed were probably accurate in describing magical and superstitious rites mainly as the result of foolishness and error rather than any real malevolence. When they felt the need to condemn certain practices, authorities employed a strictly dichotomous rhetoric of pagan versus Christian, demonic versus divine. In practice, however, Christianity could accommodate many practices and rituals of power. This very ability to accommodate and tolerate, however, produced problems, as authorities were obviously and consistently concerned, over many centuries, that the common people, not sufficiently trained in the nuances between divine and demonic power, would fall into error, would go too far in their practices, and would become guilty of performing magic. These factors—the broad acceptance and toleration of practices designed to invoke or manipulate supernatural or occult powers, provided these could be seen as divine or in some cases natural and not demonic; the persistent fear of the possibility of error; and the tendency, when error was suspected, to fall back on extremely strict and dichotomous categories to understand and label the suspected practice—would continue to shape the history of magic in Europe for the remainder of the Middle Ages and beyond.

Notes

1. See Valerie Flint, "The Demonisation of Magic and Sorcery in Late Antiquity: Christian Redefinitions of Pagan Religions," in *Witchcraft and Magic in Europe: Ancient Greece and Rome*, ed. Bengt Ankarloo and Stuart Clark (Philadelphia: University of Pennsylvania Press, 1999), 277–348.

2. Translation in Alan Kors and Edward Peters, eds., *Witchcraft in Europe 400–1700: A Documentary History*, 2nd ed. (Philadelphia: University of Pennsylvania Press, 2001), 61–63.

3. Translation in Kors and Peters, *Witchcraft in Europe 400–1700*, 62.

4. Fully detailed in Karen Louise Jolly, *Popular Religion in Late Saxon England: Elf Charms in Context* (Chapel Hill: University of North Carolina Press, 1996), 6–8.

CHAPTER THREE

✦

Varieties of Magic in the High and Late Middle Ages, 1000–1500

Around the year 1000, medieval society underwent a number of profound changes, marking the end of the early medieval period and the beginning of the so-called high Middle Ages. Most basically, an agricultural revolution occurred in Europe in the course of the ninth and tenth centuries. New farming techniques and new technologies, as well as a climactic shift, combined to generate significant increases in agricultural production in many regions of Europe. This, in turn, spurred growth in other economic sectors; trade became more vigorous and basic manufacturing increased. As food became more plentiful and trade more regular and widespread, populations grew, and, for the first time since the Roman period, urban centers began to expand. These economic and social developments drove political and cultural ones. Society became more complex, and governments and legal systems became more structured. Intellectual life also developed, as cathedral schools and then early universities appeared, their growth driven largely by the need for more literate clerics to staff the burgeoning bureaucracies of both church and state in the twelfth and thirteenth centuries. All of these changes, but perhaps above all the new intellectual and legal developments of the period, greatly affected how magic was perceived, defined, and ultimately condemned.

The magnitude and scope of the changes during the high medieval period can create the impression that the early Middle Ages were something of a dark age in which economic activity shriveled to subsistence farming, roads fell into disrepair, cities became depopulated, and a slender thread of learning and culture was preserved only in a few monastic outposts. Such developments certainly did occur, but care should be taken to understand the real extent of both the post-Roman collapse and the tenth- and eleventh-century revival. The early medieval period was less of an economic, political, and cultural nadir than it sometimes appears, and for countless people in the high and the late Middle Ages, the dramatic developments of the tenth and eleventh centuries produced no significant changes. In regard to the subject of magic, the basic idea of an early medieval "dark age" followed by intellectual and cultural revival, as well as economic and social development, might contribute to the notion that sorcery and superstition were prevalent concerns in the early medieval world but became less central to the more developed and increasingly modern world of high and late medieval Europe. Nothing could be further from the truth. Basic understandings of magic and its place in European culture continued to be defined and determined by the Christian church, drawing on biblical and patristic foundations. The intellectual and legal developments of the high and late medieval period focused even greater attention on magical practices than had previously been the case and required that far more precise, systematic thought be applied to categories of magic.

Because of this increasingly rigorous intellectual effort, we know much more about magic from this period than from earlier ones. Clerical condemnations of magic and superstition continued, but philosophical and theological considerations of the workings of magic—the nature of the power of the stars, of demons, and of natural elements—became more intricate and thorough. Legal prohibitions continued and, particularly with the appearance of clerical inquisitors and the extensive records and theoretical literature that surrounded the practice of inquisitions, legal consideration of magical practices became far more advanced. Educated authorities began to regard at least some areas of magic as learned crafts rather than foolish superstitions: some directly magical literature survives from this period—treatises on alchemy, astrology, and astral magic, but also some necromantic texts, that is, writings that describe explicitly demonic magical invocations. By the end of this period, as the idea of demonic, indeed diabolical, witchcraft developed, a body of literature began to emerge on that subject, and the records from some early witch trials survive. Many of these now more plentiful sources continue to present the same basic problems we have already encountered in attempting to trace the history of magic in the earlier Christian era. Virtually all of the documents were written by clerics who, by virtue of their education and Latin literacy, were members of a small elite. Our only real access to common magical practices comes through the narrow window of their writings, supplemented by some archeological evidence. Moreover, most written sources were intended as condemnations of magical activity, and so they necessarily presented an extremely negative picture of magical practices. Nevertheless, the new wealth of recorded material allows for a much more accurate, though still far from perfect, picture of magic to be developed for the period from 1000 to 1500 than is possible for any earlier historical era.

This chapter presents an overview of the numerous forms that magical activities could take in the high and late Middle Ages, trying to read through the available sources to present a picture of actual practices. That picture will necessarily be a general one, especially in the first sections, which consider those forms of magic most commonly practiced in medieval Europe but least systematically described in the sources. More precision will be possible in the areas of learned astrology, alchemy, and demonic magic, or necromancy. The following chapter will consider the story that the medieval sources most directly relate—that of progressively escalating concerns over magic and developing legal condemnation, culminating in the emergence of the idea of diabolic witchcraft and the earliest European witch trials in the fifteenth century. The practices described in this chapter, as the forms of condemnation described in the next, were not at their root new to this period. Many varieties of common magic derived from early medieval or even ancient times. Likewise astrology, alchemy, and even demonic magic had ancient precedents. Yet all these varieties of magical practice were significant elements of European culture during this period, and especially the more specialized, learned forms of magic clearly underwent important developments during this era.

The Common Magical Tradition

Interest in magic extended across the entire range of European society in the Middle Ages. Popes and bishops, theologians, canon lawyers, inquisitors, kings, princes, and other ecclesiastical and secular officials were all concerned to understand how magical practices operated, and to identify people who they believed practiced magic. Because the basic Christian definition of magic as mainly drawing on evil demonic forces was theoretically absolute and broadly accepted, few people would have thought, in the medieval centuries, to have labeled themselves as magicians or claimed that they actually used magic. In fact, of course, just as in earlier periods, many people employed certain simple rituals or engaged in actions intended to invoke, coerce, or control natural or supernatural powers in ways that could appear magical to other contemporary observers (and certainly to modern ones). These practices varied widely, but taken in the most general sense their use extended across Western Christendom and cut across all social distinctions. Clerics as well as laypeople, nobles as well as peasants, intellectuals as well as the uneducated all engaged in some way in these activities. Any attempt rigorously to separate learned or elite from popular practices in this area can lead to the same kinds of essential, conceptual errors that can arise from attempts strictly to divide pagan and Christian practices when considering earlier centuries. Rather than drawing such divisions at the outset, it is better to begin by considering what Richard Kieckhefer has called the common tradition of magical practices employed to some degree by people from all levels of medieval society.[1] These general practices can then serve as a basis for understanding more limited, elite varieties of medieval magic as well as concerns about magic expressed by authorities during the Middle Ages.

Many of the practices discussed here will be familiar already from previous chapters. Likewise, although this discussion will focus on the high and late Middle Ages, the basic practices, purposes, and forms of common magic outlined could also largely be applied to later centuries. There is a danger, however, in assuming that common practices were entirely unchanging, providing an immutable bedrock upon which rested other elements of the historical understanding and treatment of magic in Europe. Such a view would follow too closely that presented by the majority of medieval sources, written by educated clerics who viewed many common magical practices as the perennial, foolish superstitions of the uneducated, even as they themselves made use of other such practices. This view would also rest too heavily on the assumption that ordinary laypeople in medieval Europe were essentially unaffected by the changing conceptions of magic developed mainly by religious elites but certainly diffused throughout much of medieval society. What does seem true, however, is that while intellectual and legal authorities were concerned largely with the means by which magic operated, most of those who engaged in common practices were concerned primarily with the ends that these rites could be used to achieve. Thus while particular methods of employing magic might develop or change, the purposes that the common tradition of magic served seem to have remained fairly constant over the course of centuries.

The most basic purpose for magical rites, items, and spells was to heal—unsurprising in a world fraught with injury and disease but lacking many effective means to treat these problems. A science of medicine based on theories of the body and the power of certain natural agents to affect health or disease existed in antiquity, and the study of medicine and emergence of a professional class of physicians advanced significantly in Europe during the high and late Middle Ages. Monasteries preserved much ancient medical theory as well as practical medical treatments, and already in the tenth century advanced medical training was available at schools in Palermo, drawing mostly on highly developed Muslim medical knowledge. By the thirteenth century, the development of universities in Europe, which usually contained specialized medical faculties, brought increasing organization. Still, the number of professionally trained physicians remained very limited, and of course by modern standards much of their knowledge and training was of questionable value. Most medical services were provided by barber-surgeons, midwives, and village healers. While such people often had considerable practical knowledge of the workings of the human body, they also employed a wide variety of charms, amulets, herbal potions, and unguents that blurred the line between medicine and magic.

In addition to healing, magical practices were also used to ward off disease and to provide protection from potential injuries. The health of animals too was a major concern, and healing and protective magic focused on domestic animals was very common. Likewise the health of crops was a critical factor in the heavily agricultural society of medieval Europe, and rites and practices intended to ensure the fertility of fields, to protect crops from disease or other harm, to elicit favorable weather, and to keep away harmful insects and other threats abounded. Ensuring fertility generally for crops, beasts, and humans was an important purpose of magical practices, so critical and so precarious was successful reproduction in all of these areas. Rarely, in fact, were common magical practices used to achieve great gains of wealth or power; rather, they were focused almost exclusively on the quotidian struggle simply to maintain and protect basic conditions of well-being and modest prosperity.

Of course, magic could injure as well as heal or protect from harm. While people in medieval Europe might readily admit to knowing and using beneficial or protective spells or charms, those accused of performing harmful magic more typically denied the act, the knowledge, or both. There is no way to be certain how widespread the actual use of supposedly harmful magic may have been in this period. Doubtless many accusations were false, but some people did openly threaten their neighbors with magical harm, and probably more than a few actually employed some spell or other magical practice to strike out at their perceived enemies. Certainly belief in the possibility of harmful magic was pervasive in medieval society. Magic was thought capable of causing injury, illness, or death; controlling the will or befuddling the mind; causing beasts to sicken or become infertile; preventing cows from giving milk or milk from turning to butter in the churns; causing crops to wither; and bringing storms and hail to destroy fields.

Against all of this potential magical harm were ranged magical protections and methods to counteract specific spells. Helpful and harmful magic were generally regarded as intimately related, and the same people who might proclaim their special knowledge or power to work beneficial spells were sometimes suspected by their neighbors of possessing more malevolent power as well. Likewise those who may have gained a reputation for working harmful magic might be sought out to undo some negative spell. The liminal position of all common magical practices is perhaps best exemplified by the various types of love magic that existed in medieval Europe. A number of spells, charms, philters, and potions existed that were believed to arouse love or amorous desire in one person for another, typically the individual who performed the spell or engaged someone to perform it. For the person who gained love, or at least a lover, such magic was beneficial and positive. Of course, these spells also had the effect of dominating another's will and forcibly arousing desire for someone who, assumedly, was not the object of any natural attraction—otherwise the spell would have been unnecessary in the first place. Like other forms of common magic, these spells also had their negative opposites. They might be used to arouse enmity, discord, or hatred between two parties who otherwise would have been amicable.

Another major purpose of common magic was divination. This general term could, in the medieval context, cover an enormous range of activities, active and passive, designed to discern the future in both a general and often a specific sense, as well as to gain knowledge of far off events or local secrets (the Latin *divinatio* was only one term used by authorities, and would certainly not have been applied by most people when they engaged in such activities). Such practices had this much in common with magical healing—they were typically protective or corrective in nature. That is, common forms of divination were rarely used to achieve great gains. Rather, they were used to perceive, and so avoid, potential misfortune or harm. People sought to determine fortuitous days to undertake major activities, such as long journeys, marriages, plantings, or harvests. Young people tried to discover whom they were destined to marry, and new parents sought to determine the general fate of their children. If children were particularly ill-omened, magical remedies might then be employed to improve their futures. Divination could also be used to redress crimes or common misfortunes. The location of lost items could be discovered, or the identity of thieves could be determined in the case of stolen items. Divination could also reveal the infidelity of spouses or the guilt of murderers.

Forms of Common Magical Practice

While the purposes of common magic, broadly defined, remained fairly constant throughout much of medieval European history, the means and the methods by which such magic was performed could vary enormously. Even if accurate information on all of the practices used across Europe in these centuries existed, a complete catalog would be impossibly long. Nevertheless, some general categories of practice can be identified that apply broadly throughout this period and extend into later periods as well. Perhaps the most immediately recognizable form of magical practice was that of a spell, charm, or incantation—a verbal formula designed to produce some more or less specific result. Ritualized, formulaic speech was always regarded as possessing power throughout the premodern world. The ancient Romans believed magicians often worked by means of *carmina*, that is, songs or spells, and Norse sagas recounted the use of *galdr*, meaning essentially the same thing. Belief in the power of ritualized speech permeated the Christian Middle Ages, and Richard Kieckhefer has usefully identified three varieties of verbal formula generally regarded as having special power—prayers, blessings, and adjurations.[2] Prayers implored the aid of some supernatural entity, most commonly God, the Virgin Mary, or a saint, although medieval authorities also believed that prayers could become corrupted and directed toward demons. Blessings, or their negative opposites, curses, were directed toward the person or thing to be affected, and usually specified the desired effect ("may you be healed") but did not necessarily indicate any specific entity or power being invoked to produce that effect. Adjurations were commands directed at natural or supernatural agents or entities, ordering them to perform certain actions, or to cease some action and depart.

All these forms of verbal formulas were closely connected to religious practices. Prayers and blessings were obviously so. Adjurations were closely related to the practice of exorcism, that is, commanding demons to depart. The basic notion behind exorcism, however, of invoking divine power to drive away a harmful entity, could also be applied against disease or indeed any negative agent. One adjuration, for example, commanded an irritation to depart an eye: "Thus I adjure you, o speck, by the living God and the holy God, to disappear from the eyes of the servant of God, N., whether you are black, red, or white. May Christ make you go away."[3] In medieval terms, none of these practices was magical, so long as they sought to invoke divine rather than demonic power. Clerical authorities, however, were highly suspicious of the widespread use of such formulas, for they feared that even apparently legitimate prayers, blessings, and adjurations might actually disguise some sort of demonic invocation. Moreover, even if these formulas were not demonic, they might still be superstitious in some other way; for example, they might invoke divine power improperly, or they might seek to achieve some effect that divine power could not be expected to perform, usually taken as an indication that they relied, in fact, on demonic power. Since God was good, benevolent blessings could more easily be accepted as employing divine power, while harmful curses would more readily be suspected of drawing on demonic force—although faithful Christians could, under certain circumstances, legitimately curse their enemies, and monks and other clerics sometimes engaged in such ritualized cursing. A formula might also be deemed superstitious if it seemed to command rather than to supplicate divine power. Yet here too, boundaries were blurred, because many standard prayers, elements of liturgical ritual, and so forth were held even by many authorities to produce virtually automatic effects.

Uncertainty also prevailed in the use of physical items, rather than verbal formulas, in ritualized ways to produce powerful results. Leaves, roots, herbs, stones, and gems were all believed to possess various properties and powers, often medicinal or protective in nature. Countless medieval remedies involved the use of such items by touch or by ingestion. While the bulk of such remedies can appear unscientific to modern minds, they may not appear especially magical. In medieval thought, too, such practices would not have been considered magical so long as they could be conceived as drawing on natural powers believed to be inherent in the items themselves. In addition to obvious natural properties, however, some items were believed to possess occult properties that could be accessed only in certain ritualized ways, or in combination with other magical elements. A root would need to be picked at a certain time of the day or night, for example (see figure 3.1), or a stone would need to be polished while reciting certain words. The leaves of a particular tree were deemed to provide effective relief from fevers, but only if one wrote an invocation of the Holy Trinity on them in Latin and said the Lord's Prayer over them on three consecutive mornings before administering them to the patient. Authorities judged many such practices to be superstitious, and they feared that knowledge of such secrets might have originated with demons.

In addition to being applied as medicinal potions or unguents, certain materials or items could be carried as amulets, usually for general protective

Figure 3.1   Illustration of a dog extracting a magical mandrake root from the ground.

purposes, although the functions amulets could perform were varied and some-times highly specific. Like the modern lucky rabbit's foot, a hare's foot was believed to offer generalized protection from harm. A sprig of rosemary placed at the door of a house would keep out snakes or, if carried on one's person, would keep away evil spirits. If one carried mistletoe, one could not be con-demned in court. If people gathered certain herbs under the astrological sign of Virgo, said three Lord's Prayers and three Hail Marys over them, and carried the herbs with them, they could be sure that no one would be able to speak ill of them. Here again we see various practices used in combination to produce a more powerful effect. Likewise blessings could be applied to certain items, imbuing them with power, and these items would then make effective amulets. Holy wax blessed on the feast of the Purification, for example, was sometimes believed to provide protection against lightning, and blessed wax from the tomb of Saint Martin of Tours would protect vineyards from hail.

In this last example, the wax amulet seems to approximate the power of a relic, that is, bones, body parts, or other items closely associated with a saint or tomb of a saint, and thus partaking in a degree of the saint's power. As long as the force providing protection to the vineyards was believed to be divine power invoked through the saint, with the wax being only an incidental element in that invocation, no magic was being performed (in the medieval sense). Yet, as always, authorities feared that people might succumb to superstition and would come to believe that the wax itself was somehow inherently powerful. They also feared that holy wax or other holy items would be used sacrilegiously for impious ends. Probably the most powerful such item in medieval Christendom was the wafer of the Eucharist, which, once consecrated by a priest, was believed to become the very body and blood of Christ. The importance of the Eucharist, always a central element of the Christian liturgy, increased steadily throughout the high and late Middle Ages. Devotions directed toward the consecrated host became extremely popular in the course of the twelfth and thirteenth centuries, culminating in the creation of the official feast of Corpus Christi (the body of Christ). In the course of this feast, a parish priest would usually carry a consecrated host from the church through the local village and fields to ensure fertility and to provide general protection from harm. This was an official ecclesiastical ceremony, but laypeople seem often to have appropriated consecrated hosts, either with or without the knowledge and complicity of a priest, for a variety of functions. Hosts were used in rites to protect fields, cure disease, and ensure fertility. Women might even hold the host in their mouths as they kissed a man in order to incite passionate love. As the Eucharist became the focus of greater popular devotion, legends also developed that Jews would steal the consecrated wafer, sometimes to use in magical rituals and sometimes simply to desecrate the host.

Beyond possessing some natural force or being imbued with power by prayer or blessings, items might be inscribed with certain formulaic words, or written formulas might themselves be carried as objects of power. Carrying the names of the three biblical magi on one's person was widely believed to ward off epileptic fits. There was also a specific series of various names of God that supposedly offered protection against fire, water, weapons, and poisons of all kinds. Gems and jewelry were among the favorite objects for magical inscription, at least among the upper levels of European society in the Middle Ages, continuing a tradition that extended into ancient times in both classical and Germanic cultures. Less wealthy people had to settle for magical inscriptions on more homely objects. For example, one source describes a seemingly nonsensical phrase that could be inscribed on a wand of hazel wood. If a man took this wand, hit a woman three times on the head with it, and then kissed her, she would supposedly fall in love with him.

In addition to simple objects, images could be fashioned for magical purposes. Human figures could be made from wax, wood, or other material, and then used as the focus of ritual actions. Most often the purpose here was not protective but harmful, as figures could be stuck with pins or otherwise mutilated to cause injury or suffering in the person with whom the doll was identified. The images used in such rites could also be fairly abstract, so long as they were ritually associated with particular people who were to be affected in some way. For example, two stones could be declared, in the course of a spell, to represent two people, or their names could be inscribed on the stones. Then the stones might be smashed together in order to incite enmity or discord between those individuals. Images thus empowered often gained further potency by being buried in or near the home of the person to be affected, or in other symbolically powerful locations such as crossroads, graveyards, or near gallows. The most common remedy against this sort of magical assault was to discover the location of the image, possibly by divination, and destroy it or perform counter-rites over it.

As with other areas of the common magical tradition, the forms that divination could take were manifold in medieval Europe. Yet divination differs somewhat from other areas of common magical practice in that many forms of divination could be largely passive, entailing only the observance and interpretation of certain signs rather than the active performance of some rite, spell, or charm, although there were certainly also active forms of divination. Simple awareness of signs and portents, however, was perhaps the more common form of prognostication, and such omens might appear in many ways. From ancient times, at least some dreams were widely believed to convey special significance. Within Christian culture, there was solid biblical support for the belief that dreams might reveal the future, if only they could be properly interpreted. While he was held captive in Egypt, for example, Joseph interpreted a dream of Pharaoh as portending famine and then advised what steps could be taken to ensure a steady supply of grain through the coming years of shortage (Genesis 41:1–36). Similarly, although on a far grander scale, the Hebrew prophet Daniel was able to interpret the dream of King Nebuchadnezzar of Babylon as laying out the entire history of the world down to the time of the apocalyptic coming of the kingdom of God (Daniel 2:1–45). Of course, in Christian thought such interpretations would not have been considered magical, or even forms of divination. Since they were presented in the Bible they would have been regarded by all medieval authorities as instances of divine revelation. Daniel, for example, explicitly contrasted his ability to interpret Nebuchadnezzar's dream to the useless efforts of Babylonian magicians and diviners. Still, the use of dreams as a means of divination was common throughout the Middle Ages, and at the higher levels of medieval society manuals circulated that outlined the procedures for the proper interpretation of dreams.

Aside from dreams, nature provided innumerable signs of the future, if only one knew where to look. Birds were often regarded as portents, depending on the direction of their flight, the time of day or time of the year in which they appeared, or the nature of their chirps and calls. The ancient Romans had developed complex systems of divination based on the flights and calls of birds, but most common medieval predictions were fairly basic. Merely to encounter a raven, for example, was considered unlucky in many parts of Europe. To hear swallows chattering on the roof of a house, however, was regarded by some as a good omen for those who dwelled inside. To encounter a black cat was widely believed to predict misfortune, but so was encountering a hare, at least at the outset of a journey. Rather understandably, the sight of hens gathering under a henhouse was taken as a prediction of coming rain. Less obviously, a cat lying on a windowsill in the sun licking its own posterior was believed to foretell the coming of rain sometime later that day, at least in certain regions of northern France and the Low Countries in the fifteenth century. Basic aerial or astral signs were also taken as profoundly portentous. Thunder, comets, and eclipses all might reveal the future, and were usually taken to signal coming misfortune, although methods of interpretation could vary greatly.

Throughout the Middle Ages the belief was also widespread that certain days were inherently ill-omened, especially the so-called Egyptian days, which derived from the ancient Roman belief that Egyptian magicians had determined certain days to be unlucky. Usually there were held to be two Egyptian days each month, although some sources gave other numbers, occasionally as many as thirty-two per year. As noted in the previous chapter, church authorities inveighed repeatedly against the special observance of certain days, whether they were considered to be lucky or unlucky, for they regarded this as pagan superstition. Nevertheless, belief in the Egyptian days, along with the observance of other special days and times, remained common down to the fifteenth century. So ingrained were these notions that for example many medieval calendars listed Egyptian days along with approved church feast days, despite the fact that no cleric would have (or should have) approved.

Of all common magical practices, divination was perhaps the most consistently opposed by church authorities. Suspicions of enduring pagan beliefs and fears about the possible involvement of demons were factors in this condemnation, of course, but most basically, clerical authorities regarded any attempt to predict the future, even in the most general terms, as a possible contradiction of the notion of human free will bestowed by God. They also feared that the common laity might believe such predictions actually curtailed the omnipotence and free action of God himself. All the more ironically, then, church figures sometimes became the basis for common divination. To encounter a priest or a monk at the outset of a journey, just like encountering a black cat, was widely believed to be an evil omen, although one could ward off the coming misfortune by making the sign of the cross. In certain regions, more specific versions of this general belief prevailed. For example, to encounter a white monk, that is, a member of the Cistercian order, known for their white garments, was unlucky, but to meet a black monk, that is, a member of the Benedictine order, portended good fortune.

Aside from the observance of signs and omens, more active methods of divination existed in the common magical tradition. Palm reading, or chiromancy, was widespread. Rolling dice or other means of casting lots was also a common way to discern the future. The so-called *sortes biblicae* involved randomly opening the Bible and interpreting whatever passage was first read as having prophetic meaning. The ancient Romans had used the text of Virgil's *Aeneid* similarly, and the practice of using the Bible in this way was widespread in medieval Europe. This was one of the few methods of common divination to enjoy a modicum of tolerance and indeed support from certain authorities, although many still decried it as superstitious. Slightly more elaborate rituals could also be used to discern the future or disclose hidden facts. To determine the sex of an unborn baby, salt could be placed on the head of a pregnant woman while she slept. Upon waking, if she first spoke a male name, she would have a son, but if she spoke a female name, she would have a daughter. To know whether a woman had been unfaithful in her marriage, a magnet might be placed behind her head while she slept. If unfaithful, she would fall out of the bed. If people were suspected of theft, they could be given a piece of bread on which a certain formula had been written. Thieves would be unable to swallow such bread, while the innocent would have no difficulty eating it. Another method of identifying a thief was to gather several suspects together in a room, draw the image of an eye on the wall, and drive a copper nail into it. The guilty person would cry out when this happened. Such methods were of course not uniformly accepted or practiced across Europe, but they give some sense of the manifold ways people sought to uncover secrets and reveal the future course of events.

When considering the sheer diversity of practices in the common magical tradition, the question naturally arises: was this a single tradition at all? Given that these rites and rituals, images, amulets, and devices were used by so many different types of people in so many different circumstances, can any essential unity be discerned behind all these various acts? Quite possibly, many contemporaries would have seen no significant similarity between a farmer performing a protective rite to shield his crops from inclement weather and a woman reciting a charm to help milk turn to butter in her churn. Belief in the power of word and ritual was so extensive that most people may not have automatically linked all of the ways in which this power could manifest. The farmer's rite would simply have been an aspect of agricultural practice; the woman's, an element of domestic craft. Yet there are also indications that some underlying unity was believed to exist between such practices. Farmers might know certain rituals to protect fields and aid cultivation, and midwives, for example, might be familiar with charms and amulets to fortify expectant mothers and newborn babies as one element of their occupation. Yet there were other people who claimed an expertise in all, or at least many, aspects of such practices.

Most aspects of the common magical tradition could be practiced by anyone, but some people, by virtue of long experience or sometimes because of some special mark, such as being born with the caul (the fetal membrane) still intact, came to be seen as experts. Such people were usually regarded has having special abilities in many areas—they could heal and harm through spells and curses, they had special knowledge of herb-lore, they could craft amulets and magical images, and they had extensive expertise in divination. These people might often be the wizened old women who later would be associated so powerfully in the popular imagination, as well as in authoritative thought, with witchcraft. Yet perhaps the most common such figure was neither female nor socially marginal; rather, he was the local village priest. There is ample evidence that priests were widely regarded as ritual experts whose special knowledge and power extended well beyond the official ceremonies their position required them to perform. There was almost no variety of common spell or charm that was not widely believed to be more effective if a priest performed it, no amulet that was not more potent if a priest blessed it, no means of divination that was not more reliable if a priest confirmed it.

The church also lent unity to the varied practices of the common tradition through its condemnations. Critical authorities would discuss healing, herb-lore, amulets, and divination in succession, lumping them all together under the categories of *magia*, *maleficium*, or *superstitio*. The unity they saw, of course, was the potential danger of demonic power and diabolical corruption lurking behind all these practices. As noted in the previous chapter, the degree to which most laypeople accepted these concerns and actively incorporated them into their own conceptions of such activities is difficult to determine. In general, medieval people were perfectly ready to accept the church's basic message about the power of demons and the pervasive menace they represented. In practice, however, people rarely seem to have been overly concerned that the devil or his minions might be lurking behind the specific practices with which they were familiar, and certainly not those which they themselves used. In Christianity's earlier days, clerical authorities mainly regarded such practices as foolish errors and holdovers from paganism. These required correction, but while they were certainly reprehensible and potentially corrupting, they were not perceived as deeply threatening. During the high and late Middle Ages, however, magic and superstition began to appear to authorities as increasingly dangerous. A chief reason for this was the rise, during this period, of varieties of magic that could not be dismissed as the foolish errors of simple people. Educated men, clerics themselves, began to study and develop elaborate systems of learned magic, firmly grounded in the best philosophy of the day, yet dangerously subversive of certain basic aspects of the Christian faith.

The Rise of Learned Magic

In the course of the eleventh, twelfth, and thirteenth centuries, intellectual activity in Europe became more vibrant than at any point, arguably, since the disintegration of the western Roman Empire and the slow dissolution of Roman culture that had taken place a half millennium before. Although formal education at any level, let alone the opportunity for advanced study, was never available to more than a small fraction of the overall population, the numbers of these men (for advanced education was available only to men) increased significantly. As inquiry expanded in many areas, magic became a field of serious study and experimentation. Some highly educated men began to dabble in magical practices, and some did much more than just dabble. Others examined magical practices as they believed they understood them, not necessarily to discredit such operations but to establish precisely how magical rites and rituals functioned and achieved their effects. Such considerations lent credence and indeed intellectual prestige to magic far beyond what the common tradition and centuries of persistent superstition had attracted.

Perhaps the most fundamental development of this period, in terms of intellectual activity both magical and otherwise, was the dramatic rise in schools. Throughout the early Middle Ages, many monasteries had operated schools and maintained libraries to preserve ancient texts, both Christian and classical. As the chief function of monks was to withdraw from the world, however, general access to these small centers of learning was limited. The eleventh century witnessed the rise of far more open schools, usually associated with great cathedrals and hence known as cathedral schools. By the later twelfth century, in Bologna, in Paris, and elsewhere, the first universities were developing from these schools. These were major intellectual centers training large numbers of students in all disciplines and supporting sizable faculties of scholars dedicated to the refinement and expansion of existing knowledge. These schools and universities had an insatiable hunger for the ancient, authoritative texts that provided the foundation for study in all areas—Aristotle for natural philosophy and physics, Galen for medicine, Augustine and the Bible for theology, and many others. Monasteries in the West had preserved much of the ancient intellectual tradition, but many texts, particularly those of the Greek rather than the Latin tradition, no longer existed in western Europe. They had been preserved in the Byzantine East, however, and had become the basis for the great intellectual achievements of the Muslim world in the eighth, ninth, and tenth centuries.

Thus a critical element of the revival of intellectual activity in medieval Europe was the reception of Arabic texts and learning. For obvious reasons, a ready exchange of knowledge between the advanced Muslim world and the Christian West was difficult. Opportunities for such exchange did exist, however, in Spain, Sicily, and southern Italy, where contact between the two religions was constant, where expanding Christian kingdoms often came to have sizable Muslim populations, and where Jewish communities, with considerable intellectual traditions of their own, could serve as mediators between the two dominant faiths. One of the earliest and most remarkable examples of such contact concerns Gerbert of Aurillac (ca. 940–1003), a Christian cleric and scholar who later became Pope Sylvester II (reigned 999–1003). Born in what is now southern France, he studied in Spain under Muslim teachers, learning mainly mathematics and astronomy. He then returned north and taught at the cathedral school at Rheims before continuing his rise through the ecclesiastical hierarchy. Already in the eleventh century, stories developed that he had studied magic in Spain, had used his occult knowledge to facilitate his rise to the papacy, and had established a school for magic in Rome.

Throughout the high and late Middle Ages, scholars who pressed too deeply into such advanced learning often were rumored to have become magicians. While the darker elements of such stories were usually pure fantasy, there were at least some grounds for the basic suspicion, because certain varieties of magic did have a place in Muslim learning, as well as in Jewish intellectual traditions. In particular, Muslim and Jewish scholars had taken over much astrological and alchemical knowledge from the Greeks and had expanded significantly upon it. This knowledge now made its way into the schools of the West. Among the earliest translations of Arabic texts into Latin, for example, those made by Adelard of Bath (ca. 1080–1155) included works on astrology and astral magic.

Astrology had always been known in medieval Europe, but in the twelfth century far more elaborate systems began to appear. The related subject of astronomy was one of the seven basic liberal arts (established around the fifth century as the *trivium* of grammar, rhetoric, and logic, and the *quadrivium* of arithmetic, geometry, music, and astronomy) studied in schools and universities. Some scholars distinguished sharply between astronomy, as the mathematical study of the heavenly bodies and their movements, and astrology, which dealt with the supposed effects those astral bodies could produce on earth. Many other scholars did not, however, and astrology was often defended as a legitimate science. Astrology was essentially a complex system for divination, and its most typical purpose was to develop horoscopes. By knowing the positions of the stars and planets at the time of a person's birth and other significant points in life, astrologers could make general predictions about that person's character, qualities, potential achievements, and so forth. Astrological predictions could also be made regarding events; the success of marriages, for example, or the outcome of battles might be revealed by the stars. More commonly than predicting an outcome, astrological knowledge could be used to determine when the most fortuitous time to undertake a certain action would be. Nuptials would be scheduled so that the influence of the planet Venus would be strong, and commanders might seek to engage in battle when the influence of Mars was dominant.

That astral bodies imparted energies that could influence terrestrial ones was hardly an outlandish idea—one had only to note how the moon influenced the tides or more basically how the rising sun warmed the air to be convinced of this fact. That the planet Mars could impart martial energies or that the power of Venus somehow facilitated amorous attraction or sexual

fertility was widely accepted in the Middle Ages, and much serious intellectual effort was spent working out exactly how these various forces operated.
Although learned astrologers sometimes made predictions about the future,
they would hardly have considered themselves diviners or magicians. Rather,
they would have presented themselves as wise men and philosophers exploring the forces of nature. Nevertheless, authorities opposed to astrology often
grouped it with other forms of divination. As noted above, critics condemned divination for seeming to impinge on the possibilities of human free
will. Similar charges were leveled against astrology, and here astrology's more
"scientific" aspects actually proved detrimental to its defense. A frequent
response to the free will criticism of divination was that signs and omens did
not cause certain actions, that is, they did not affect free will, but merely
revealed what those actions most likely would be. Theories of astral forces,
however, openly asserted that the position of astral bodies at certain times
directly caused certain actions on earth via the forces they exerted. So long
as these were actions in nature—temperature and tides, the force of winds
and storms—there was no serious problem. When, however, astrologers
seemed to imply that astral forces could influence or even compel a person
to undertake certain courses of action or to behave in certain ways, religious
authorities became much more concerned about the implications such theories could have. Thus while some aspects of astrology gained fairly uncontroversial acceptance, other aspects were frequently condemned as superstitious.

Astrological learning was also integrated into other more clearly magical
practices. Even common people, for example, made use of some basic astrological knowledge when they gathered herbs or performed other rites at specific times of the day or of the month, or under particular astral conditions.
Other areas of learned magic, as will be seen below, often incorporated far
more complex astrological elements into their procedures. Some astrologers
themselves, rather than being content to know what astral forces were dominant at any given time and what effects they could have, sought actively to
attract these forces and to direct them toward particular ends. Such activities
can be described as a form of astral magic. The practice of such magic often
involved inscribing rings, amulets, or other items with astrological symbols
that were intended to draw down the force of particular astral bodies. In
other situations, magicians might perform ceremonies involving spoken or
written invocations of astral forces. Theories of this more active sort of astral
magic were well developed in the Muslim world as well as in certain Jewish
traditions, and a substantial literature existed on the subject. The most well
known of these works, the Arabic *Ghayat al-Hakim* (The Aim of the Wise),

entered Europe during the reign of Alfonso the Wise, king of Castile (reigned 1252–1284), being translated first into the Castilian vernacular and eventually into Latin as *Picatrix*. This and similar works described elaborate rituals for creating astrological talismans and otherwise invoking and directing the power of astral bodies and astral spirits. Concerned Christian authorities were quick to detect the invocation of demonic powers in these ceremonies and to condemn them completely.

Aside from astrology, another major new area of occult, if not definitively magical, intellectual pursuit in the high and late Middle Ages was alchemy. Like astrology, this art developed in antiquity and survived in the Byzantine East, but only reentered the West via Arabic texts in the twelfth century. The first known translation into Latin of an Arabic alchemical treatise was that made by Robert of Chester in 1144. The basic purpose of alchemy was to transform one substance into another, most famously to change lead into gold. Like astrology, this practice rested on certain fundamental principles of ancient and medieval natural philosophy. In the case of alchemy, the principle involved was that all matter was composed of the same four basic elements—earth, air, water, and fire—merely in different proportions that gave particular substances their varied characteristics. If the proportions of these elements could be manipulated, alchemists reasoned, any substance might be transformed into any other. Such manipulation was no easy task, but might be accomplished through long and arduous series of meltings, boilings, evaporations, refinements, sublimations, distillations, separations, and combinations of various materials. To achieve their ends, alchemists employed some of the same basic equipment as modern chemical laboratories.

Alchemists, like astrologers, would certainly never have thought of themselves as magicians, but as natural philosophers exploring the hidden properties of nature, and in fact alchemy was only rarely condemned in the Middle Ages alongside other magical practices, far less often than astrology typically was. In its basic purpose of transforming materials, alchemy did potentially conflict with certain Christian notions that the nature of substances was divinely established and should not or could not be altered. In general, however, alchemy seems to have raised far fewer religious concerns than other magical practices. The most typical charge brought against alchemists was that they were simply quacks whose claims to be able to transform natural substances were ludicrous.

There were, however, considerable magical overtones to alchemy. For one, alchemy was often associated with other forms of magic. Links with astrology and astral magic were highly pronounced. Many basic metals were believed to be connected to particular heavenly bodies—gold with the sun, for example, silver with the moon, quicksilver with Mercury, iron with Mars, and lead with Saturn. Alchemists needed to take the astral forces of these bodies into account when they performed their experiments, and astral magicians might use these metals in their rituals to attract and focus the power of these bodies. Since alchemists claimed to be able not only to transform substances but also to unlock occult properties within them, alchemical practices could be used to distill very potent healing potions, or poisons, or to purify other materials for use in magical rituals. Purity was an obsession in alchemy, extending not only to the materials used but also to the alchemists themselves, who often believed that they had to observe numerous taboos—remain chaste, for example, or wear only white garments—in order to avoid contaminating their experiments with their own impurities. These concerns point to a basic fact linking alchemy to other forms of magic. Alchemists regarded the precise actions required by their experiments essentially as rituals that needed to be performed correctly and that could be affected by improper actions that, to modern minds, would be entirely unconnected to the physical processes the alchemists were trying to generate. In this regard, alchemy was very much a part of the world of ritual power that defined so much of medieval magic.

Magicians at Court, Magic at the Universities

Since learned magic of all sorts required training and education, not just in the immediate art but also in underlying principles of mathematics, physics, or astronomy, these varieties of magical activity tended to center around schools and universities. Because these arts often required significant economic resources to equip astronomical observatories or alchemical laboratories, and to allow the uninterrupted work demanded by complex alchemical experiments or detailed astrological observations, they just as often centered on political courts. Throughout the high and late Middle Ages, many political leaders maintained astrologers at their courts to offer prognostications and advice. This fact is telling, but less certain is the degree to which kings and princes took the services of their court astrologers seriously. Studies of late medieval England, for example, indicate that English kings regularly disregarded the predictions and advice of their astrologers. On the other hand, the chronicler Matthew Paris related that the German emperor Frederick II (reigned 1215–1250) would undertake no major action without first consulting his astrologers and giving careful consideration to their advice. Alchemists were also frequently employed by kings and other nobles, for obvious reasons. Yet literature existed warning nobles not to invest much faith, or many resources, in the work of alchemists, for most of them were described as fools and frauds. Interestingly, there was also alchemical literature that advised alchemists to avoid entering the service of princes, warning that their constant demands would disrupt the slow and delicate work required for successful transmutations.

Of course, astrologers and alchemists were perfectly ready to admit that their complex labors often ended in failure. Astrologers frequently made incorrect predictions and alchemists regularly failed to produce gold from their furnaces. Errors at any point in the process would result in invalid or unsuccessful results. Thus a king might firmly believe in the principles of astrology and yet still ignore the advice of his astrologers. Moreover, there is ample evidence to show that astrologers and even alchemists might have been maintained at courts for less serious purposes, to provide entertainment or diversion. Other types of magicians also filled such roles, performing simple tricks or illusions very similar to modern stage magic. How exactly medieval audiences would have viewed such entertainments, when most of them probably also believed that these magicians possessed serious knowledge and commanded real power, is very difficult to determine. What is clear is that the world of learned magic had multiple aspects—serious and frivolous, respected and condemned.

Beyond the involvement of educated men in magical practices, the reaction of intellectuals to these forms of magic was also complex. In general, the basic principles of alchemy and astrology, grounded as they were in ancient traditions and established in ancient, authoritative texts, were widely accepted. Nevertheless, many alchemists (perhaps most) seem to have been regarded as fools incapable of producing the transmutations to which they aspired. Perhaps for this reason, or perhaps because, as noted above, alchemy did not seriously conflict with major Christian principles, intellectual authorities, all of them clerics, rarely condemned alchemy to any great extent. Astrology, on the other hand, aroused extensive debates and much conflicting opinion at the very centers of learning in Europe. The practice, so widespread in ancient Roman society, had been widely condemned in early Christian literature as superstitious and essentially pagan. The seventh-century authority Isidore of Seville had included astrology in his catalog of condemned magical practices, and this list became more or less definitive for the remainder of the Middle Ages. Yet with the recovery of so much ancient knowledge concerning astrological systems in the eleventh and twelfth centuries, many European intellectuals were no longer willing to dismiss astrology as entirely superstitious. The difficulty lay in rescuing some acceptable systems of astrology from the condemnations of earlier authorities, and from the dilemma that the determinative power of astrological forces seemed to conflict with the important Christian notion of human free will.

Ultimately a middle way was found that solved both problems, perhaps best exemplified in *Speculum astronomiae* (The Mirror of Astronomy) usually attributed to the theologian Albertus Magnus (ca. 1200–1280). This work advanced the relatively uncontroversial position that astral bodies did indeed exert influence on terrestrial ones. This influence extended to human bodies as well. Weak human wills might often succumb to the influences generated by their physical bodies, and so astrologically based predictions about the nature and quality of individuals, and their behavior in certain situations, might often prove true. Nevertheless, a sufficiently disciplined human will could always overcome the base influences of its body, and thus the divine promise of free will was not impinged. If this compromise was accepted, then the condemnations of earlier church authorities could be read as referring only to the notion that astral forces were entirely dominant over human will, which could still be declared to be superstitious. Thomas Aquinas (1225–1274), a student of Albertus and probably the most important intellectual figure of the high Middle Ages, accepted this line of argument, as did many other medieval authorities. Yet for various reasons this solution was not entirely successful. Doubts remained about the exact nature and extent of astral influence, and some authorities denied such influence altogether. The very skeptical theologian and natural philosopher Nicholas Oresme (ca. 1325–1382), for example, maintained that astral bodies projected no forces toward the earth aside from light and heat.

If the nature and status of astrology aroused much debate in the schools and universities of medieval Europe, astral magic aroused far more definitive condemnation from most intellectual authorities. In his important *Summa contra gentiles* (Summa against the Gentiles), for example, Thomas Aquinas argued extensively against the notion that the ceremonies, incantations, signs, and inscribed symbols of astral magicians could do anything to attract, focus, or control the forces that astral bodies naturally emitted toward the earth. He fully accepted that these forces existed, but he contended that they were not and could not be the source of power upon which these magicians drew. Most basically he noted that the ceremonies of astral magic entailed invocations, supplications, and adjurations, either spoken or set out in written characters. Such invocations could have no effect on inanimate natural objects or forces, he argued, but had to be addressed to some intelligence, which then responded to them. The nature of this intelligence was, for Aquinas and other medieval clerical authorities, a foregone conclusion. They saw the power of demons at work behind this magic.

Much intellectual discussion of magic in fact centered not on magical practices themselves but on demonology, that is, considerations of the nature and power of demons. For centuries, Christian authorities had been deeply concerned about the possibility of demonic power operating behind most forms of magic. In late antiquity, church fathers such as Origen in the third century and Augustine in the early fifth had devoted considerable attention to the subject of demons, but early medieval Europe had seen few developments in demonological thought. Beginning in the twelfth century, the scholastic theologians of the high and late Middle Ages returned to this topic and developed far more rigorous systems for understanding demonic operations. They drew on early Christian authorities, of course, but also incorporated the Aristotelian philosophy now dominating the schools and universities of Europe into their theories of how demons manifested and exercised power in the material world. Thomas Aquinas, for example, in sections of his *Summa theologiae* (Summa of Theology), dealt extensively with the various ways in which demons tempted humans and the abilities through which they achieved their ends. He and other theologians worked out intricate arguments about how demons could manipulate physical substances, including the airy bodies in which they cloaked themselves and human bodies as well. Such arguments ranged from how demons, lacking vocal chords, imitated human speech when they appeared to sorcerers, to how, lacking generative organs, they could impregnate women (in what became the standard explanation, demons first assumed female forms to seduce men, then gathered the seed from these encounters and assuming male forms, used it when copulating with women).

In general, scholastic authorities concluded that demons were able to control most aspects of the natural world and that they possessed a great deal of occult knowledge, such that they could produce many wondrous effects. Some powers were forbidden to them. They could not, for example, control human will, although they could generate bodily impulses and appetites to which weak-willed people might respond. They could not alter essential substances, although they could manipulate the air around objects or simply manipulate human organs of perception so that changes would appear to occur. Everything they did was subject to the ultimate authority of God. Yet authorities were convinced that by calling on demons, magicians could achieve a multitude of effects, and they now offered detailed explanations for how specific magical results were attained. At times they disagreed with one another in the details of their arguments, and some took issue with earlier authorities—even so great a figure as Augustine—on particular points of demonic nature. But by demonstrating in intellectually rigorous ways the terrible range of demonic powers, their work added significantly to the growing seriousness with which all varieties of magical practice were regarded in this period.

The prince of demons, Satan, also became a more solidly defined figure at this time. Christianity derived its concept of the devil from the ancient Hebrews. The Greek *diabolos*, used frequently in the New Testament, was a translation of the Hebrew name Satan, meaning "adversary." In early Judaism, however, Satan was an ambiguous figure, appearing in the Book of Job, for example, as a servitor in the heavenly court. The concept of Satan as "the devil"—the single great opponent of God and enemy of humankind—emerged more fully in later, apocalyptic strains of Judaism and then completely in Christianity. The New Testament clearly describes Satan as a rebellious angel cast out of heaven. For example, in Luke 10:18, Christ tells his disciples that "I watched Satan fall from heaven like a flash of lightening" (this, in turn, led to Satan being identified as Lucifer, the "light-bearer," originally a name applied to a fallen king of Babylon in the Book of Isaiah). The image of the devil as chief of all demons and the militant foe of God was most fully developed, however, in the Book of Revelation, Christianity's own apocalyptic text. As with so much Christian doctrine, the early church fathers solidified the authoritative understanding of Satan in the fourth and fifth centuries.

Despite such roots, while the devil did appear as a tempter and a deceiver, especially in monastic literature of the early Middle Ages, he was not always a truly awesome opponent. Particularly in common understanding, the image of the devil became infused with aspects of pagan spirits and deities (just as the original Hebrew idea of Satan had been informed by other ancient Near Eastern deities and demonic entities). While often still terrifying, at times the early medieval devil could be merely a malicious trickster, one who could often be tricked in turn by clever monks or even wily peasants. This image of the devil endured into later centuries. Late medieval and early modern magicians were sometimes depicted bartering with and even trying to dupe the demons they summoned. Yet in general, beginning in the twelfth and thirteenth centuries, scholastic theologians restored much of the terrible majesty of the apocalyptic Satan, the great dragon of Revelation. This in turn significantly affected authoritative perceptions of magical operations and magicians. As we will see in the remainder of this chapter and in the next, medieval conceptions of magic and the medieval condemnation of magic increasingly focused not just on the involvement of magicians with demons but also on their subservience to demons and ultimately to a single diabolical master.

The Rise of Demonic Magic

Anselm of Besate, a cleric living in the eleventh century, related how his cousin Rotiland had once taken a young boy to a hidden location outside of town, buried him to his waist, burned substances that emitted acrid fumes around him, and called upon demons with an incantation that involved the use of Hebrew or some other foreign language. He commanded the demons to bind women to him in love, or at least sensual lust, just as the boy was bound in the earth. In the mid-twelfth century, in his *Policraticus*, John of Salisbury (ca. 1110–1180) recounted a similar tale. He told how, as a youth, he had studied Latin under a certain priest who on one occasion called John and another boy to him, anointed their fingernails with holy oil, and delivered a strange incantation that John was sure included the names of demons. The purpose of this ceremony was to divine the future by conjuring images in the boys' fingernails. The other boy claimed that he actually saw certain misty figures appearing, but John saw nothing and was never used in such a ritual again. In the early thirteenth century, in his *Dialogus miraculorum* (Dialogue on Miracles), Caesarius of Heisterbach (ca. 1180–1240) related the story of a certain knight who did not believe in the power of demons. One night, a monk took him to a deserted crossroads, traced a circle in the dirt, and placed the knight inside it. The monk then summoned numerous demons, which came at his command and circled around the knight in horrifying forms. Finally, the devil himself appeared as a huge, dark figure towering over the nearby trees. He indicated that the monk was a good friend of his and proceeded to make many requests of the knight, all of which the terrified man refused. Finally, the devil tried to snatch him out of the circle, but at this point the monk stepped forward and all the figures vanished. The knight, although unharmed, was profoundly shaken and never again doubted the reality of demonic power.

These stories, spanning nearly two centuries, all tell of demonic magic being worked by educated men through relatively complex rituals. While Christian thinkers had associated magical activity with the secret invocation of demons since before the time of Augustine, early authorities had made this connection by conflating pagan rites, or the perceived remnants of pagan practices, with demonic rituals. Those guilty of performing such rites were typically regarded as simple folk, foolish or misinformed, who may well have been duped by demons and had no idea of the true nature of their actions. In the eleventh, twelfth, and thirteenth centuries, however, concern over a different sort of demonic magic seized the minds of clerical authorities. The demonic elements of this magic did not arise from any error or lack of proper understanding; rather, these practices entailed the explicit invocation of demons, often by name. Moreover, these rites were performed by educated men, usually clerics, who deliberately engaged in what they knew to be dark and forbidden practices.

This magic was most often termed *necromantia* (necromancy) in the texts that described and condemned it. The term necromancy technically referred to divination by means of summoning the spirits of the dead (derived from the Greek *nekros* and *manteia*). This practice was well known in ancient times, both to the Greeks and Romans and to the ancient Hebrews. The classic biblical example of necromancy was the occasion on which the Hebrew king Saul sought out a diviner in Endor who summoned the shade of the dead prophet Samuel to predict the outcome of an impending battle (1 Samuel 28). This sort of divination was condemned, along with other varieties, by all major early Christian authorities, and necromancy made its way into the authoritative list of magical categories compiled by Isidore of Seville in the early seventh century. Christian authorities had difficulty, however, accepting the notion of necromancy in a strict sense. Isidore, for example, was careful to define necromancers as those who, by their incantations, *appeared* to summon the spirits of the dead. In Christian conceptions of the afterlife, souls of the dead were believed to rest securely in either heaven or hell or, by the later medieval period, in purgatory, from which they could not be released or recalled by any human means. Authorities posited, therefore, that the supposed shades of the deceased that appeared to necromancers were in fact demons, and *necromantia*, along with its near cognate *nigromantia*—the black arts—was used as a general term for demonic invocation.

Necromancy was not so broad a term as to cover all varieties of magic that were suspected by authorities of involving demonic power, however. Rather, it was a decidedly learned art involving complex rituals and ceremonies, often patterned on the church's own liturgical rites, and knowledge of this art was typically conceived as being contained in books or manuals. Anselm of Besate, for example, noted that his wicked cousin had a book of spells from which he conjured demons. William of Auvergne, a scholar at the University of Paris, and bishop of Paris from 1228 until his death in 1249, claimed that he had seen several books of necromancy years earlier as a student in Paris. In 1277 another bishop of Paris, Etienne Tempier, formally condemned such books as dangerous to proper faith, good morality, and the well-being of Christian souls. A century later, the inquisitor Nicolau Eymeric (ca. 1320–1399) reported in his great inquisitorial manual *Directorium inquisitorum* (Directory of Inquisitors) that he had confiscated and burned many such texts from magicians whom he had tried, including such famous magical tomes as *Clavis Salomonis* (The Key of Solomon) and *Liber iuratus Honorii* (Sworn Book of Honorius the Magician), whose names were known across Europe. In the early fifteenth century, the theologian and religious reformer Johannes Nider (ca. 1380–1438) reported that he knew a certain monk in Vienna who, before entering the religious life, had been a necromancer and had possessed several demonic books. Some of these texts survived inquisitorial flames and now allow remarkably direct access into one area of the world of medieval magic. For example, a fifteenth-century necromantic manual from southern Germany, probably not dissimilar to the demonic books that Nider's monk once possessed, has been discovered and studied in great detail.[4]

Since necromancy was essentially a bookish art, its practitioners necessarily belonged to the small, educated elite who possessed the Latin literacy necessary to use such manuals. This meant that necromancers were virtually always clerics. The ranks of the clergy in the Middle Ages extended down from priests through a variety of more minor orders, and it was these lower orders that most likely supplied the majority of necromancers. Medieval schools and universities were religious organizations, so most students were formally required to become clergy. Thus virtually all educated people were by definition clerics. After receiving their degrees, however, these men might have few or no official ecclesiastical functions. Beyond their education, necromancers' clerical status could affect their magical activities in other ways. Although authorities would condemn them as being in league with demons and entering into pacts with them—as Caesarius of Heisterbach and many other authorities would put it, of being a "friend" to demons—necromancers sometimes defended themselves by claiming that they in fact commanded demons to perform their bidding. Much Muslim and Jewish magical literature discussed invoking and controlling demons or spirits in the name of God, and, as with other areas of learned magic, these traditions informed much Christian practice, but clerical necromancers could also trace this authority to command and compel demons back to the biblical accounts of Christ granting the power of exorcism to his disciples and to all the faithful. Among the lowest clerical offices into which these men would have entered was, in fact, that of exorcist.

The heart of any necromantic magical act usually involved a verbal formula, sometimes of supplication but typically of compulsion, addressed to one or more demons. Necromantic texts are replete with phrases containing the words *conjuro*, *adjuro*, or *exorcizo*—meaning I conjure, I adjure, or I exorcise, but in fact all used interchangeably to mean I command. These relatively simple and direct formulations were then surrounded by elaborate rituals, some lasting for hours or even days and requiring extensive preparations. Magic circles formed a major element of necromantic ritual, although not usually in the way described by Caesarius of Heisterbach, or indeed as is probably most common in the modern imagination, as protective circles in which the magician or some other person could remain unharmed by the powerful forces the ritual was to unleash. Rather, magic circles were typically forms traced in the earth or simply drawn on a piece of paper or parchment. The circles were filled with symbols and writing designed to focus the power of the spell (see figure 3.2). Rituals also frequently involved offerings of some kind to the demon being summoned (lending credence to authorities' concerns that necromancers were supplicating, rather than commanding, demons). Animals such as bats or birds, especially hoopoes, might be sacrificed, or other kinds of offerings could be made, such as milk or honey, cheese, or almost any other type of material or item. In some rituals incense was burned, or candles were lighted, or songs were sung to honor demons and attract them into the magician's presence. Various other forms of magical practice often bled into necromancy; for example, astrology often figured in necromantic rituals. Either the invocations themselves had to be made under certain astral signs, or the materials to be used in the ceremonies needed to be collected or prepared under specific astral conditions. The range of ritual practices that could be incorporated into necromancy was enormous.

The purposes to which necromancy might be put were also broad and very diverse. Since in the Christian worldview almost any type of magical practice could be suspected of being demonic, naturally demonic invocation could be seen as capable of achieving almost any type of magical end. Necromancy might be used for divination, since demons possessed a great deal of secret knowledge that they could reveal. A frequent purpose of necromantic rituals was to create "illusions" that involved conjuring materials, items, or animals to appear. For example, a magician might conjure a horse or a boat to bear him on a journey, or food-laden tables for a banquet. Authorities believed that the effects of these conjurations could be quite real. That is, a person might in fact be transported over considerable distances by a conjured horse. What made this act an illusion, however, was that according to authorities the horse in this case would actually have been a demon taking on the appearance of an animal, not a real horse that the magician had caused to

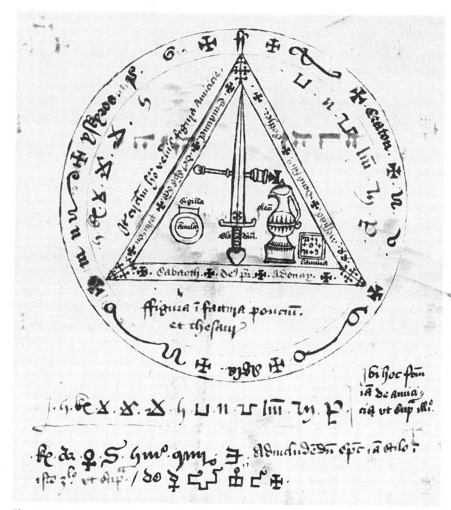

Figure 3.2 Necromantic magic circle from the fifteenth century.

appear. Demons could either alter their own forms or they could affect human perception so that people thought they saw a horse, a boat, a banquet, or anything else the magician might desire. Aside from deceiving the senses, demons could also affect the human heart and mind, and so necromancy could be used to arouse love or hatred, to bring calm or incite agitation, and so forth. Just as in divination, here too there were debates about

the extent to which human will might be directly affected by magical practices. Many authorities reasoned that demons only had power over human
bodies, but that by affecting the body in certain ways (manipulating bodily
humors, for example), they could induce various mental states, or at least
cause people to succumb to such states more readily. Demonic power over
bodies of course allowed them to inflict physical harm on people and to cause
disease. They could also heal, however, and so through them necromancers
also commanded all these powers.

Even if necromancy was only used to heal, however, or to entertain by
creating inoffensive illusions, authorities were certain to condemn it in all
its forms. The belief that interaction with demonic forces was inherently evil
and corrupting had been an essential aspect of church doctrine since the
earliest days of Christianity. From the time of Augustine, Christian authorities had condemned magic primarily because of the potential involvement of
demons in the rituals and practices that they deemed to be magical. They
could hardly now fail to condemn ritual that was explicitly demonic in
nature. That some necromancers claimed, by virtue of their position as clerics and more basically by the power of Christ, that they could interact safely
with demons and command them toward positive ends was hardly an effective defense; in fact it constituted a significant challenge to the longstanding
position of the church. Augustine had noted that most magic was based on
evil associations between humans and demons, and Aquinas had argued that
even when a magical ritual did not contain any explicit submission to
demons, nevertheless a tacit pact might be supposed to exist between the
magician and the entities he summoned. Necromancy, a type of magic contained in Latin manuals and performed by clerics, was probably the form of
magic most familiar to Christian authorities in the high and late Middle
Ages. As concern on the part of authorities over magic grew in this period
and condemnations of magical practices increased, they were shaped largely
by conceptions of elite necromancy, but applied ultimately to all varieties of
magic and superstition.

Notes

1. Richard Kieckhefer, *Magic in the Middle Ages* (Cambridge: Cambridge University
Press, 1989), 56–57.

2. Kieckhefer, *Magic in the Middle Ages*, 69–70.

3. Kieckhefer, *Magic in the Middle Ages*, 3.

4. Richard Kieckhefer, *Forbidden Rites: A Necromancer's Manual of the Fifteenth Century*
(University Park: Pennsylvania State University Press, 1998).

CHAPTER FOUR

The Medieval Condemnation of Magic, 1000–1500

With the rise of specifically learned varieties of magic in the high and late Middle Ages, authorities came to regard magic more seriously, and as a more serious threat, so that this era was also marked by the increasingly rigorous and intellectually specific condemnation of many forms of magical practice, as systematic demonology and awareness of explicitly demonic necromancy fed longstanding Christian concerns about the potentially demonic nature of all magic and the demonic threat behind superstition. Legal advances also took place in this period, above all the use of inquisitorial methods in court proceedings. These methods allowed more readily for prosecutions and convictions in cases involving charges of magical practices. In addition, specially designated inquisitors began to appear who (eventually) brought cases of heretical demonic magic under their jurisdiction. To support these new procedures and personnel, advanced legal literature and theory developed, which defined the illicit qualities of magic more precisely than ever before. Legal condemnations of magic thus became as profound and encompassing as earlier moral condemnations had been.

Throughout its history, magic had always faced two essential kinds of condemnation—moral and legal. Since ancient times, social and cultural authorities of various types—philosophers, poets, and priests—had often castigated magic quite broadly as foreign, antisocial, and generally disreputable. Legal authorities, however, usually refrained from sweeping condemnations of entire categories of action and focused instead only on those cases in which magical practices were believed to produce specific harmful or otherwise criminal effects. In the early Christian era, this general distinction continued to pertain, despite Christianity's stringent rejection of almost all magical practices. Clerical authorities linked magic categorically to pagan rites and demonic powers, and thus they condemned all magical activity as inherently immoral and illicit for Christians. When Christians were found to have engaged in such activity, however, the responses ecclesiastical officials prescribed were relatively mild, typically involving correction and penance rather than more severe forms of punishment, as befitted an essentially moral failing. Kings, princes, and other lay leaders, who sometimes did bring harsh penalties to bear against alleged magicians, continued to focus largely on the supposed use of magic to kill, steal, or otherwise work harm.

Of course, these distinctions were never clear-cut or absolute in practice, as moral judgments were always deeply intertwined with legal rulings. Even in the ancient world, legal condemnations could become quite general in tone, and any type of illicit magical practice could be regarded as a threat to the community's harmonious relationship with divine or spiritual forces. In Christian Europe, kings and princes relied heavily on clerics and on the church to buttress their authority. Thus the church's condemnation of magic had legal effects, and law codes were always based on Christian morality. In the high and late Middle Ages, however, the church itself became a much more legalistic entity. Canon law, based on church rulings or "canons," developed into a science at the new schools and universities that appeared in this period, and increasingly the church came to define itself and its authority in terms of these legal codes. Ecclesiastical courts developed to enforce this law, which applied to all Christians. Ultimately, specialized officials appeared—inquisitors whose purpose was to root out the worst offenders against church law, those Christians who denied or rejected essential elements of their faith or aspects of church authority and so became heretics. Because of their perceived involvement with demons, people who engaged in many types of magical practices were eventually included in this category.

The history of the condemnation of magic in this period culminated in the emergence of the essentially new category of diabolical, conspiratorial witchcraft. Although people had been suspected, accused, and prosecuted for performing harmful or malevolent sorcery—*maleficium*—throughout the Christian era, as in antiquity, only in the fifteenth century did the idea develop that people might engage in *maleficium* as members of heretical, demon-worshiping cults, offering themselves to Satan in exchange for power and acting at his direction to corrupt and subvert all of Christian society. Defined in this way, witchcraft was essentially a double crime, entailing the terrible moral and religious violations of idolatry and apostasy from the faith, as well as the more secular crimes of causing death, illness, and destruction by magical means. The perceived threat represented by witches was therefore of concern to both secular and religious authorities, and suspected witches could be tried in either lay or ecclesiastical courts. This dual character helped give witchcraft its unique status in both legal and moral thought and continued to define it throughout the period of Europe's major witch hunts in the sixteenth and seventeenth centuries.

Ending around 1500, this chapter adheres fairly closely to what is more or less the traditional divide between the medieval and early modern periods in European history. Recently much scholarship has begun to point out the artificiality of this division, and the subjects of magic and especially witchcraft can figure prominently in such arguments. The story of the "medieval" condemnation of magic could easily be continued unbroken to include the witch hunts of the sixteenth and seventeenth centuries. Nevertheless, within the history of witchcraft, certain divisions can be discerned between earlier and later periods. Initially, rising concern over magic, superstition, and ultimately witchcraft developed among clerical authorities, and most of the earliest witch trials in the fifteenth century were conducted by clerical inquisitors. Witch hunting subsided in the early sixteenth century, however, as the religious energies of Europe focused on the tumults of the Reformation. Only in the later sixteenth century did witch hunting begin to rise again, now directed mainly by secular rather than ecclesiastical officials. More generally, although the Reformation had little direct effect on ideas of witchcraft—Catholics and Protestants proved equally willing to prosecute suspected witches and conducted these trials in roughly the same way—the religious divisions created in the sixteenth and seventeenth centuries dramatically affected how Europeans thought about heresy and superstition. The witch hunts of the sixteenth and seventeenth centuries, as well as other aspects of the history of magic in that period, will therefore be treated separately in subsequent chapters. Yet their essential connection to earlier developments must also be borne in mind. I have deliberately included the fifteenth-century origins of witchcraft in this chapter, not so much to reinforce the traditional break between the medieval and the early modern in European history as to highlight the fact that the idea of diabolical witchcraft underlying the major early modern witch hunts grew directly out of medieval developments. Thus I want to stress continuity of traditions, or at least the continuing trajectory of certain traditions, throughout the entire period from 1000 to the end of the seventeenth century.

Canon Law, Heresy, and Inquisition

Christian bishops and church synods had issued rulings on magic and superstition for centuries before the process of collecting and systematizing these decrees into codes of canon law began, and the earliest collections made in medieval Europe included material on these subjects, such as the canon *Episcopi* in the tenth-century collection of Regino of Prüm, and the material in Book 19 of Burchard of Worms's *Decretum* in the eleventh century (as discussed in chapter 2). These early attempts to codify church law were impressive and influential but ultimately limited in scope. With the rise of schools and universities in the twelfth century, much more thorough compilations were possible. Moreover, a network of legal faculties and professional canon lawyers developed that demanded a single, coherent system of law. The fashioning of such a system out of centuries of diffuse rulings was largely achieved by Gratian, a monk in Bologna, site of one of the first universities in Europe. Around 1140 he produced his *Concordia discordantium canonum* (Concordance of Discordant Canons), more commonly known as the *Decretum*, which became a standard legal text across Europe and served as the basis for the church's *Corpus iuris canonici*, or Code of Canon Law. The work was divided into various "cases," and *Causa* 26 dealt with the issues of sorcery and divination. Here Gratian set side by side many earlier decrees, concluding with the canon *Episcopi*, which of course directed bishops to forbid the practice of sorcery and harmful magic (*sortilegium et maleficium*) in their diocese. He also introduced the subject of magic in *Causa* 33, dealing with marriage, when he considered the possibility that magic could impede sexual union or conception. Here he drew especially on Hincmar of Rheims's treatise discussing the divorce of the Frankish king Lothar.

Gratian's purpose, as the full title of his work indicates, was to compare earlier rulings and derive from them coherent legal principles. Unsurprisingly, then, he largely reiterated early medieval attitudes toward magic and superstition. He presented superstitious beliefs mainly as foolish error. Demons were able to trick simple people by means of illusions and deceptions, just as the canon *Episcopi* related concerning those women who supposedly believed that they traveled at night with the goddess Diana. Likewise, magical practices generally warranted only a moderate response. Religious officials should forbid sorcery and divination, and anyone who persisted in such acts was to be excommunicated and removed from the community. This was by no means a negligible penalty, especially in the tightly knit social world of medieval Europe, but it was only a shadow of the later religious and legal reactions such practices would incur. Even the apparently stringent passage in Exodus 22:18, which instructed, "You shall not permit a sorceress to live," was in this period interpreted with at least some moderation. Since Christianity and the Roman Church were considered to represent the community of the (spiritually) living, authorities read this passage as requiring only that sorcerers be excommunicated and exiled, not that they necessarily be executed.

This (somewhat) moderate attitude toward magic and suspected magicians began to change in the course of the twelfth and thirteenth centuries, however, at least partially in connection to growing concerns over heresy and heretics within Western Christendom. As already recounted, as late as the year 1000 Christian authorities still associated magic and superstition mainly with paganism or the remnants of paganism. They regarded these illicit beliefs and practices as errors that would eventually fade when confronted with proper instruction in the Christian faith. After 1000, concern over the survival of pagan practices declined while concern over heresy, that is deliberate error emerging from within Christianity, grew. Heresy had been an important issue in the early days of Christianity, as various groups espousing somewhat different doctrines vied for supremacy within the Christian community. After the fifth century, however, heresy had receded as a major concern of religious authorities in Western Christendom, although of course it never disappeared altogether. Reports of heretical groups began to circulate again in the late tenth and eleventh centuries, and 1022 saw the first execution of heretics in the West since late antiquity: the burning of a group of clerics in the city of Orléans. The severity of this judgment aside (this group of clerics was connected to the French royal court and political factors figured heavily throughout the case), authorities typically reacted to heresy in the eleventh and into the twelfth century by calling for more effective instruction, correction of errors, and usually banishment as the harshest penalty directed against stubborn heretics. Over the course of subsequent centuries, however, reaction became more severe, as many authorities came to see heresy as deliberate, pertinacious, and a very dangerous threat.

This danger was by no means simply imagined. Heretical movements of considerable size and impressive tenaciousness (in the face of concerted and often violent church opposition) existed from the twelfth through the fifteenth centuries. Catharism was deemed to be rampant in northern Italy and southern France until virtually eradicated by a crusade in the early 1200s and by sustained inquisitorial activity for most of the rest of that century. Waldensianism grew from the teachings of Valdes of Lyon, a merchant who in the mid 1170s heeded Christ's call to poverty, abandoned his wealth, and, ignoring episcopal and ultimately papal commands that as an uneducated layman he should not preach, began to evangelize. His followers, sharing his rejection of ecclesiastical authority and increasingly moving into some doctrinal error as well, persisted in regions of France, Italy, and the German Empire for the rest of the Middle Ages. The unorthodox Oxford theologian John Wyclif (ca. 1328–1384) inspired Lollards in England and also to some extent Hussites in Bohemia. Named after the Prague preacher Jan Hus (ca. 1373–1415), Hussitism was more a movement of religious reform and nascent nationalism than a doctrinal heresy. Hussite forces seized effective control of Bohemia in the early 1400s and beat back several military campaigns directed against them by the church and the German emperor. Yet however real or imagined the actual religious deviance of various heretical groups was, their existence deeply agitated many clerical authorities and seemed to provide direct evidence of demonic activity in the world.

Growing concern and increasingly harsh ecclesiastical (and secular) reaction to heresy affected concerns over magic, because authorities increasingly linked magic with heresy in this period, and eventually those specialized ecclesiastical authorities who prosecuted heretics also took responsibility for handling cases involving magical practices. Heresy could be seen as involving superstitious errors, and like so many forms of superstition it was often regarded as being demonically inspired. An account of the heresy at Orléans in 1022, for example, included a description of heretics participating in a secret, nocturnal gathering where a demon would appear in bestial form to receive worship. The heretics also supposedly engaged in wild sexual orgies on these occasions and murdered young children. The influence of this description on accounts of witches' sabbaths centuries later is obvious. In the late twelfth century, the Cistercian monk Ralph of Coggeshall (died 1227) reported a case of heretics who were also sorcerers in league with demons. Heretics known as Publicans (supposedly related to the Cathars) were discovered in the French city of Rheims, he related, and one old woman was brought for questioning before the archbishop and his assembled clergy. Although they debated with her on many points, they could not convince her to acknowledge the error of any of her positions, and so she was sentenced to death. Even as the fires were being lighted, standing before the whole assembly she produced a ball of thread from her garments and threw it out a window while crying "catch." Immediately, she was lifted from the ground and carried away, obviously (to the assembled clergy, at any rate) by demonic spirits.

The similarity of Ralph's story to the apocryphal account of Simon Magus carried into the air by demons while engaged in a contest of power with Christ's disciple Peter is clear, and his report of these supposed events need not be taken as a factual account of either heresy or sorcery. Yet it points to the connections that clerical minds were drawing at this time. Equally fanciful, perhaps, were the reports extracted from suspected heretics in the Rhineland only a few years later, in the 1230s, by the inquisitorial official Conrad of Marburg (ca. 1180–1233). A true fanatic, Conrad was obsessed with the perceived threat of heresy, and he coerced lurid confessions of demon worship and demonic gatherings from suspects. These accounts took on great significance when they were related to Pope Gregory IX (reigned 1227–1241), who accepted them wholeheartedly and, in response, issued the decree *Vox in Rama* (A Voice in Rama) in 1233, in which he described a gathering of heretics who summoned a demon. This creature appeared in various guises—as a giant toad, a pallid man, or an enormous cat—and received homage and worship from the assembled heretics, who also engaged in depraved orgies in its presence.

Ralph's and especially Conrad's accounts evince a strong sexual motif associated with demonic heresy, and this may have affected clerical authorities' conceptions of demonic magical practices as well. Of course, as indicated in previous chapters, certain sexual undertones and gendered connotations had always existed at least in literary depictions of magic, but association with heresy could certainly have added to these. Clerical officials were obsessed with the idea of highly sexualized heretics engaging in orgies with one another and with demons. Ironically, many of the heretical movements in the Middle Ages, founded on religious idealism, advocated at least as strict a control over sexual behavior as did orthodox Christianity. But in the development of a stereotype, authoritative imaginings were far more powerful than reality. Perceptions of deviant behavior, rather than its reality, were equally important when stereotypes of Jews were imported into conceptions of magical practice.

As concern over heresy rose in the eleventh, twelfth, and thirteenth centuries, Christian reaction to the other major religiously "dissident" group in Europe, the Jews, also became more severe. Jews were never regarded as heretics, since by definition a heretic was a Christian who had fallen into error. Nevertheless, Jews were often depicted as sharing many of the same characteristics as heretics. Officially, the medieval church tolerated Jews and preached that the continued existence of Judaism was necessary and divinely ordained, if only to allow for the prophesied conversion of the Jews at the end of time. In practice, the Jewish communities of Europe suffered from a marginal and precarious status, and Jews were often suspected of being sorcerers. Of course Jews engaged in common magical practices of all sorts, just as Christians did. In addition, as noted in the previous chapter, elements of learned Jewish magical traditions had powerfully influenced the development of astrology, astral magic, and even demonic magic in the medieval West. Jews were seen as possessing ancient knowledge, and spells or invocations employing Hebrew, believed by many authorities to be the original language spoken by Adam, were often regarded as especially efficacious.

Of course, because of their rejection of Christianity, Jews were easily depicted as being in league with demons. One legend related how the early sixth-century Christian saint Theophilus had been tempted by a Jewish sorcerer into signing a pact with the devil in order to gain magical powers. This story became an archetype for later notions of diabolical pacts associated with magic and witchcraft (see figure 4.1). In the twelfth century, accusations of ritual murder began to be leveled against Jews. In 1144 Jews were accused of murdering a young Christian boy near Norwich, England, and from this point the belief that Jews killed and often cannibalized Christian children as part of demonic rites designed to denigrate Christianity developed and spread across Europe. In the thirteenth century, as Christian devotion came to focus more on the Eucharist, Jews were accused of stealing consecrated hosts in order to desecrate them. Charges of ritualized infanticide, cannibalism, and host desecration were also made against heretics and were later closely associated with sorcerers and especially witches.

By the thirteenth century, the repression of heresy in certain regions had become the full-time occupation of specially deputed men—inquisitors. Although the term "inquisition" is often bandied about, there was no such thing as "The Inquisition" in the Middle Ages. An inquisition, *inquisitio* in Latin, did not imply an ominous institution, but simply meant a process of legal inquiry. Bishops and their officials were expected, as a matter of course, to inquire into any potential errors of faith within their jurisdictions. By the twelfth century, as heresy became a greater concern, inquisitorial procedures became more intense and systematized (since *inquisitio*, by itself, could refer to any type of inquiry, the more exact phrase *inquisitio heretice pravitatis*, or inquiry into heretical depravity, was used to designate a heresy inquisition). In 1184 Pope Lucius III issued the decree *Ad abolendam* (In Order to Abolish), formally condemning all forms of heresy and ordering all bishops to conduct a thorough inquiry at least once or twice every year into suspected heresy in their diocese. In regions where heresy was, or was perceived to be,

Figure 4.1 Theophilus making a pact with the Devil, then repenting before the Virgin.
Source: Réunion des Musées Nationaux / Art Resource, NY.

intense, such inquiries proved too taxing for bishops and their officials, who of course also had to perform numerous other duties, and specialized inquisitors began to be appointed. In 1231 Gregory IX authorized the first papally appointed inquisitors, that is, officials who received their authority directly from the pope, although they still were supposed to operate in close conjunction with bishops and other local authorities.

The emergence of inquisitions and inquisitors can be seen as part of a more general shift in the nature of the church's application of its authority in medieval Europe. Ecclesiastical officials, who in the earlier Middle Ages tended to be concerned mainly with enforcing correct religious observance and outward practice, in the later medieval period increasingly tried to guarantee that proper belief would underlie practice. The Fourth Lateran Council, convened in 1215 by Pope Innocent III (reigned 1198–1216), marked a key point in this shift. This ecumenical council issued many rulings, including some touching on heresy. More revealing than any of these, however, may be the fact that Lateran IV mandated regular yearly confession for all Christians. Seemingly distant from the process of inquisition, confession was actually closely related, for it involved, or was supposed to involve, a personal inquiry by an individual, although directed by a priest, into his or her own beliefs and moral state, leading to acknowledgment and repentance of any errors. This was also the underlying moral goal of an inquisition, and authorities' growing preoccupation with uncovering and uprooting potentially improper beliefs was a critical factor in the developing condemnation of heresy, as well as the condemnation of magic and superstition.

Aside from indicating general moral imperatives, growing reliance on inquisitions marked the emergence of a new type of legal procedure in Europe, one far better suited than earlier methods to trying cases involving charges of magic. In the earlier Middle Ages, courts typically followed what has since been labeled "accusatorial procedure," based largely on Germanic practices. In this procedure, an accuser would initiate a case by bringing a charge before the court. This person then had the obligation to prove the charge, essentially acting in the role of prosecutor. Accusations of magic, however, were extremely difficult to prove, since magical activities were usually conceived as being inherently secretive and covert. In such situations, courts often turned to the use of judicial ordeals. For example, suspected sorcerers might be required to grasp hot irons, and in several days their wounds would be examined to determine whether they were healing properly (little or no healing was a sign of guilt), or suspects might be bound and dunked in water to see how quickly they rose to the surface (floating too quickly was a sign of guilt). Such methods were not quite as "irrational" as they might initially seem to modern sensibilities. These rituals were performed publicly, and the ultimate determination of guilt or innocence often relied on the general acclamation of the gathered witnesses, who determined whether a burn was sufficiently scabbed over or a suspect had remained submerged for an adequate amount of time. Judgments in these cases would have been informed by the deep knowledge people living in tightly knit communities usually had of their neighbors' general character.

When suspects were acquitted under accusatorial procedure, following the principles of *lex talionis* (literally, the law of retaliation) their accusers faced legal retribution for bringing false charges. Thus in the absence of clear physical evidence or eyewitnesses, rare in cases of magic, there was a strong disincentive to make any accusation unless the accusers were absolutely sure that they stood in higher regard within their communities than did the accused. Certainly if an entire community regarded an individual with suspicion, punishment could occur, and it was often severe. In 1075 for example, citizens of Cologne threw a woman from the town wall because they believed she was practicing magical arts. In 1128 the people of Ghent eviscerated an "enchantress" and paraded her stomach around the town. These were extralegal events, however, and generally under accusatorial procedure suspicions of sorcery led to formal accusation and prosecution far less often than under the later system adopted in Europe.

Between the twelfth and fifteenth centuries, accusatorial procedure fell out of use across much of Europe. This is not to say that accusatorial practices disappeared entirely. In later centuries, for example, witches might still be "swum," that is, dunked in water to determine their guilt. But such practices were rare and usually were held in disrepute by authorities. Instead, legal professionals came to rely on inquisitorial procedure, based on ancient Roman judicial practices rediscovered and revived as part of the general intellectual recovery of the twelfth and thirteenth centuries. The church dealt a major blow to the old accusatorial methods when, in 1215, the Fourth Lateran Council forbade clergy to take part in judicial ordeals. Inquisitorial procedures were developed first in ecclesiastical courts, but by the fourteenth and fifteenth centuries they had become common in many secular courts in Europe as well.

Under inquisitorial procedure, guilt or innocence was proved by the active investigation, or inquiry, of a judge or magistrate into the details of a case. An investigation could still be initiated by an accuser bringing a specific charge before the court. In other cases, however, a magistrate could undertake an investigation on his own initiative, based only on general reports of an individual's "ill fame" (*infamia*), exactly the sort of vague disrepute that often hovered around those suspected of performing sorcery. Papally appointed inquisitors developed a relatively standard procedure for launching their investigations. An inquisitor, along with a small staff, would arrive in a town or village, and enlisting the support of local clerics and secular officials, he would preach a public sermon, usually a fairly pointed one focused on the evils of heresy. He would then call for people to come to him with confessions, accusations, or merely with suspicions. Having assembled a list of suspects, he would proceed with his investigation, questioning the accused and calling other people to testify. Under this procedure, accusers were not responsible for the veracity of their accusations, and of course inquisitors would not suffer any legal reprisals for proceeding with questionable investigations that ultimately resulted in acquittals.

Also under inquisitorial procedure and of particular advantage when dealing with cases of heresy or magic, inquisitors and other magistrates could use torture if no clear evidence of guilt or innocence was available. The use of torture was also an ancient Roman legal practice revived in Europe in the thirteenth century. The first evidence of the legal use of torture comes from statutes of the Italian city of Verona in 1228, regarding the use of torture by secular courts. In 1252 Pope Innocent IV (reigned 1245–1254) permitted papal inquisitors to use torture to extract information from suspects. To obtain a conviction for a potentially capital offence, standard legal procedure came to require either the testimony of two eyewitnesses or the confession of the accused. Given the clandestine nature of most magical practices, eyewitnesses were usually out of the question. Authorities certainly recognized the potential of torture to extract false confessions, and they devised methods and imposed limitations intended to reduce this risk. Nevertheless, especially in cases involving accusations of demonic sorcery, authorities often set these restraints aside. The unrestrained use of torture would become a hallmark of most of the major witch hunts of subsequent centuries.

Given the importance of inquisitorial procedure in the escalating condemnation of magic in medieval Europe, it is interesting to note that papally appointed inquisitors were initially precluded from investigating cases of sorcery per se. In 1258, only a few years after papal inquisitors appeared in Europe, Pope Alexander IV (reigned 1254–1261) ordered that they should not involve themselves in cases of divination or sorcery unless the magical practices involved appeared to be manifestly heretical. This decree entered canon law in 1298 when it was included in the *Liber sextus* (The Sixth Book [of canon law]) issued under Pope Boniface VIII (reigned 1292–1303). Boniface also added his own injunction to Alexander's prohibition. The ultimate effect of these decrees should not be exaggerated, however. The standard gloss on the *Liber sextus* by the legal scholar Johannes Andreae (died 1348) indicated that magical practices were to be deemed heretical if they entailed the invocation and worship of demons, which many authorities suspected of most forms of magic, or if they involved the misuse of sacraments, particularly the Eucharist, which entailed grave superstition. Already in the thirteenth century, theological authorities such as Thomas Aquinas had been considering the demonic nature of magic in detailed and systematic ways. In the fourteenth century, legal and inquisitorial authorities would have reason to look just as closely at magical practices and superstitions.

Growing Concerns in the Fourteenth Century

Beginning around 1300, the level of authorities' concern over magical practices, especially harmful and supposedly demonic sorcery, seems to have risen significantly. In addition, accusations and trials for sorcery rose throughout the century. This may reflect more widespread concerns, or simply the greater ease with which such trials could be conducted under new legal systems. To determine the root causes for this growing anxiety, we must consider several possible candidates, for the fourteenth century was a period of profound crisis in Europe. Early in the century, from 1315 through 1317, a series of major famines devastated much of Europe. Then, beginning in 1348, the terrible plague known as the Black Death swept across the continent, carrying off perhaps as much as a third of the European population by 1350, with plague outbreaks recurring sporadically for the rest of the century. Many people chose to see the Black Death as a sign of God's wrath, but the church was in a poor position to offer comfort in the face of these natural disasters. From 1309 until 1378, popes resided not in Rome but in the small papal territory of Avignon in southern France. This long exile, later known as the Babylonian Captivity, damaged the spiritual authority of the papacy, yet the attempted resolution proved an even greater catastrophe. The return of the papacy to Rome in 1378 quickly produced a schism in which some cardinals elected a second pontiff, who promptly returned to Avignon. The church, and Western Christendom itself, split over which pope was legitimate. This confused situation persisted and grew worse with the appearance of a third pope in 1409. Unity was finally restored only in 1417. The religious uncertainty created by this schism, and the blatantly political maneuverings of the various popes, seriously damaged the prestige of the church and the clergy in the eyes of many Europeans.

These natural and manmade disasters helped to shape the general temperament of Europe in this century, producing a climate of terrible uncertainty and consternation. This atmosphere may also have contributed to the greater level of concern about magic and the threat of demonic power evident in this period, as well as increasing paranoia regarding heretics and Jews. Direct connections, however, are difficult to find. In several important areas, anxieties about magic were rising well before most of these events occurred, and these concerns culminated in the concept of diabolical witchcraft and the earliest witch trials only in the generally more stable fifteenth century. Rather than look to these broad crises as direct causal explanations for any of the developing ideas, concerns, or reactions regarding magic in this period, a better course is to examine such developments in their immediate contexts. The condemnation of magic had already gathered considerable energy prior to 1300. This history, along with a range of particular factors, now drove that condemnation forward.

Numerous accusations of magic and involvement with demonic forces appeared within the very highest circles of secular and ecclesiastical power in the early fourteenth century. These cases may reveal little about more general levels of concern regarding magical practices in this period, but by virtue of their high profile they were unusually influential. The earliest case, and among the most cynically employed for purely political purposes, involved charges brought against Pope Boniface VIII by the French king Philip IV (reigned 1285–1314). Boniface and Philip were locked in a bitter struggle over effective control of the clergy in France. The struggle ended in 1303 when Philip convened a council of French nobles and bishops, which then accused Boniface of heresy as well as possession of a familiar demon from whom he regularly took counsel. Philip dispatched troops into Italy to bring the pope to France to stand trial. The French soldiers actually seized the aged pontiff at his residence at Anagni, but a local crowd forced them to release him. Boniface was spared a trial, but not his ultimate fate; the experience of his capture had so shaken him that he died soon thereafter. Philip refused to let the case die with the man, however. In order to justify his actions against Boniface, in 1310 he began pressuring the new pope, Clement V (who had just taken up residence in Avignon at the borders of French territory), to hold a posthumous trial. The charges against Boniface were now expanded, so that he was accused of having possessed three demonic familiars as well as an additional spirit that he kept bound in a magical ring.

The trial never took place, because Philip and Clement reached a settlement beneficial to the French king.

Even as this case was unfolding, Philip launched another venture in which he employed charges of heresy and diabolism for political gain, directing them in this instance against an entire religious order, the Knights of the Temple of Solomon, or Knights Templar. French knights had founded the Templars as a crusading order in the Holy Land in the early twelfth century. The order became famous and extremely popular, attracting tremendous support and substantial donations of land and other forms of wealth across Europe in order to support its activities in the Crusader States. The last Christian outpost in the Holy Land, the port of Acre, fell in 1291, however, and the Templars' opponents now began to argue that they served no ostensible purpose. By 1307 Philip had devised a plan to dissolve the order and appropriate its extensive property for the French crown. He instructed Guillaume de Nogaret (ca. 1265–1313), the same man who had directed the accusations against Boniface, to bring charges against the Templars. Various accusations were made, ranging from charges of heresy and sodomy to the worship of demons, particularly a demonic head supposedly known as Baphomet. Royal agents arrested the Templars across France. Torture was applied, and many knights confessed to even the most outlandish charges, although many also later recanted. Once again, an agreement was reached with Clement V, who disbanded the order in 1312 without officially acknowledging any of the charges brought against the knights. For having recanted their earlier testimony, a few Templar leaders, including the grand master of the order, Jacques de Molay, were burned in 1314. Although charges of magical practices per se did not figure in the trial of the Templars, the episode grimly foreshadowed many of the excesses of sorcery and witch trials to come, particularly in the use of torture to extract false confessions.

In the actions taken against Boniface and the Knights Templar, supposed concern over magical practices, divination, and involvement with demons clearly served only to mask ulterior political motives on the part of the French king. Not all such concern was cynical or false, however, and the fear of magic was very real in this period, especially at the French court. When Philip's queen, Joan of Navarre, died in 1305 at the age of 32, suspicion of murder by poison or other magical means began to circulate, and charges were brought against Bishop Guichard of Troyes. Political factors drove these charges to some extent, but they also reflected real fears, almost paranoia, about magic that existed in Paris at this time. Similar rumors of magical assassination surrounded the deaths of Philip himself in 1314, and the deaths of his sons Louis X in 1316 and Philip V in 1322.

Perhaps the clearest example of the coexistence of cynical political maneuvering with real concerns about demonic magic can be found in the papal court at Avignon, especially during the pontificate of John XXII (reigned 1316–1334). Almost immediately upon ascending to the papal throne, John began to charge his political opponents with performing magical acts. In 1317 he had Hugues Géraud, bishop of Cahors, arrested on suspicion of trying to murder him through sorcery. The bishop was tortured, convicted, and burned. In 1318 Robert Mauvoisin, archbishop of Aix, was charged with performing illicit magic, although he ultimately escaped conviction. In 1319 the Franciscan Bernard Délicieux was tried in Toulouse for possession of books of sorcery. In 1320 Matteo Visconti, the ruler of Milan, was accused along with his son Galeazzo of plotting against the pope by means of sorcery. And from 1320 until 1325, a whole series of accusations were leveled against John's political opponents in the Mark of Ancona. Some of these charges were better grounded than others. Both John and his opponents would have believed in the efficacy of many magical rites, and surely some of his enemies were not above using such means to attempt to strike out at the pope.

Whatever the level of actual magical threat against John personally during the course of his reign, the pope was clearly deeply concerned about the danger demonic magic posed to all Christians. In 1320 he directed William, Cardinal of Santa Sabine, to issue a letter to inquisitors in Toulouse and Carcassonne, both relatively near to the papal seat at Avignon, ordering these men to take action against all sorcerers (maleficos), whom John regarded as infecting the community of the Christian faithful by sacrificing to, worshiping, doing homage to, and entering into pacts with demons. Several years later, in 1326, the pope issued the important decree Super illius specula (Upon His Watchtower), in which he pronounced a sentence of automatic excommunication against anyone who invoked demons in order to perform magic or divination. Tellingly, John referred to such magic as a "pestilential disease" infecting all of Christendom. Super illius specula provided a basic foundation for the condemnation of sorcerers and later witches for the remainder of the Middle Ages. In fact, John's concerns clearly focused not on the sort of common sorcery that characterized witchcraft, but on the elaborate, ritualized necromancy with which he, as an educated cleric, would have been more familiar. In the document, he described magicians who offered sacrifices to demons or fashioned images or objects such as rings or mirrors with which to summon them. As discussed in the previous chapter, such magic certainly existed in the fourteenth century. In 1323, for example, an ecclesiastical court near Paris heard a particularly gruesome case involving both clerics and laypeople who attempted to invoke the demon Berech using a magical circle fashioned out of strips of cat flesh.

Even as Pope John was worrying over magical assassination and the corruptive threat of necromancy in the papal palace at Avignon, in distant Ireland, a strangely precocious case was unfolding that brought together elements of political and upper-class intrigue, concerns over demonic magic, and inquisitorial technique. Alice Kyteler of Kilkenny had aroused a good deal of local resentment by outliving several husbands, from whom she had gained considerable wealth. Among her principal opponents were some of these men's children by other marriages, who felt that Alice had worked to deny them their appropriate inheritances. They suspected, moreover, that Alice had somehow enchanted their fathers with love magic, and perhaps done away with them by magical means as well. When Alice's fourth husband began to sicken in 1324, charges were brought before Richard Ledrede, bishop of Ossory, who had been educated on the continent and had spent some time at John XXII's court in Avignon.

The charges developed in the course of the investigation, and ultimately Alice and a group of accomplices were accused of having renounced the Christian faith, of worshiping demons, and of gathering at night at crossroads to offer sacrifices to them. Alice also supposedly had a demonic familiar who was her lover. Most of these charges rested on the confession of one of Alice's servants, Petronilla of Meath, who was tortured to extract a confession and then burned for her involvement in these supposed crimes. Alice escaped, probably to England, and was never heard from again. Many of the elements here—the performance of harmful magic, accusations directed against a group of supposed sorcerers who gathered to worship demons, and sexual intercourse with demons—would become standard fare in later witch trials. Such trials would not begin in earnest for another century on the continent, however, and in Ireland this sort of case would not occur again until the seventeenth century, and then only rarely. The Kyteler affair, therefore, may be seen as a telling aberration, illustrative of some aspects of the course that the condemnation of magic would take in coming years, but having no real influence on those future developments.

Another notable event with far more direct consequences for the developing condemnation of magic in Europe took place in 1324, when the prominent inquisitor Bernard Gui (1261–1331) completed his *Practica inquisitionis heretice pravitatis* (The Practice of Inquisition into Heretical Depravity), a comprehensive manual of inquisitorial procedures. Gui was a papally appointed inquisitor in Toulouse from 1307 until 1324, and so he would have been one of the officials to receive John XXII's directive of 1320 to take action against sorcerers and diviners who engaged with demons. Records indicate that Gui never actually sentenced anyone for sorcery during his tenure in office, but other inquisitors in the region were conducting such trials, and the *Practica* reveals that Gui clearly felt such matters fell within inquisitorial jurisdiction. He categorized sorcery and divination as one of six standard varieties of heresy that inquisitors might expect to encounter. The procedures he outlined for use against sorcerers reveal an awareness of many elements of common magic. Gui instructed his fellow inquisitors to ask suspects about magical healing, common divination, and love charms, for example. His most extensive accounts of magical practices, however, dealt with complex necromantic rituals, describing sacrifices and other forms of overt homage shown to demons, along with the misuse of sacraments, especially the Eucharist, in magical rites. These sorts of practices, Gui noted, were typically performed by educated clerics, not common sorcerers. Nevertheless, he considered all the magical practices he described to be demonic in nature. His manual was widely copied and was influential on all later inquisitorial thought and practice.

Inquisitorial concern about demonic magic continued to develop over the course of the fourteenth century, and theories regarding the essentially demonic nature of most forms of magic became increasingly elaborate and definitive. In 1376 the Catalan inquisitor Nicolau Eymeric (ca. 1320–1399) wrote his important and influential manual *Directorium inquisitorum* (Directory of Inquisitors). He too dealt with sorcery and divination as part of his comprehensive treatment of all matters of concern to inquisitors. Whereas Gui had mainly presented practical instructions for how inquisitors should proceed against various heresies, Eymeric was more concerned to develop legal and theological theories to support inquisitorial authority. With magic, he set out to demonstrate that most forms of sorcery and divination were demonic, and beyond this that all demonic magic was inherently heretical. He was familiar with books of necromancy, and clearly intended to counter the main defense that necromancers sometimes offered, namely that they piously commanded demons in the name of Christ rather than subserviently worshiping them. Eymeric responded that even to invoke demonic power was illicit for Christians, since the very act of invocation demonstrated forms of worship or veneration due only to God or the saints. Thus most magic could be equated to idolatry. Drawing on Thomas Aquinas, he argued that even if magicians displayed no overt signs of worship, and even if they did not intend to do so, they entered into tacit pacts with demons whenever they performed magical rites. Although Eymeric, as all medieval authorities, set aside certain forms of magic as potentially drawing on natural rather than demonic powers—occult properties of herbs, the force of astral bodies, and so forth—his was the most comprehensive condemnation of magical practice yet produced, and his arguments proved influential beyond inquisitorial courts.

As the fourteenth century progressed, condemnations of magic came from outside inquisitorial circles as well. At the very end of the century, fear of assassinations by poison or other forms of magical assault again flared at the French royal court. In 1398 two Augustinian monks were executed in Paris after they had failed in their attempts to relieve the intermittent madness of the French king Charles VI (reigned 1380–1422) and then accused his brother Louis of Orléans of having used magic against him. Louis' wife was also accused of practicing sorcery. After Louis' death in 1407, charges of magic again circulated against him. Most importantly, in close connection to this web of concern at the royal court, the theological faculty of the University of Paris, the preeminent intellectual institution in medieval Europe, issued a broad condemnation of sorcery, divination, and superstition in 1398. The twenty-eight articles of the Paris condemnation tended to dwell mostly on the sort of elaborate, ritual magic that clerical necromancers would perform. Yet they were general enough to apply to almost any form of magical practice. They echoed Eymeric in asserting strongly that all magic that relied on the power of demons was inherently idolatrous.

The rising concern over magic in the fourteenth century and the increasingly severe condemnation of magical practices were most evident within elite groups—nobles, members of royal or papal courts, theologians, or highly placed inquisitorial officials. Yet, mainly through the offices of inquisitors, these concerns could make themselves felt at any level of society. As early as Bernard Gui's manual, a conflation of common magical practices and more complex, learned forms of overtly demonic necromancy was evident, as well as a conviction that the same demonic menace lay behind all such sorcery. The Kyteler case, isolated as it was, predicted the end to which these concerns could lead. In the coming century, concern over common superstitions would escalate, and the condemnation of magic would blossom into witch trials and the concept of diabolical witchcraft.

Fears of Superstition and the Rise of Witchcraft
in the Early Fifteenth Century

In the early years of the fifteenth century, clerical authorities revived concern over superstition in Europe. Throughout the high and late Middle Ages, Christian thinkers had continued to regard many magical practices as forms of superstition, but as they came to associate magic less and less with the remnants of paganism, they generally reduced the emphasis on superstitious error in their condemnations of magic in the period after 1000. Foolish superstition, as opposed to deliberate heretical deviance, seemed to have little place, for example, in the world of educated, clerical necromancers. Nevertheless, even learned magicians, insofar as they sometimes claimed that their magic did not function in the ways that the church determined it did, might be guilty of superstition. And as the concerns of clerical authorities began to swing back toward common magical practices, superstition again became an important category in their considerations.

In the early years of the fifteenth century, the influential theologian and chancellor of the University of Paris Jean Gerson (1363–1429) wrote several tracts on magic and superstition. He dealt with all manner of beliefs and practices, for example, condemning the common belief in unlucky days, especially the so-called Egyptian days, and disavowing the notion that a crow croaking on the rooftop of a house foretold misfortune for those who dwelled inside. He also denounced more elite forms of magic such as the improper use of astrology or astral magic, and in one tract he argued particularly against the use of astral talismans by members of the medical faculty of the university at Montpellier. Many of Gerson's sentiments were echoed by Nicholas Magni of Jauer (ca. 1355–1435), a theologian at the University of Heidelberg, who in 1405 wrote an influential treatise entitled simply *De superstitionibus* (On Superstitions). Nicholas seems to have been inspired, or at least had his concerns piqued, by the case of an Augustinian friar, Werner of Friedberg, whom the theological faculty at Heidelberg had questioned earlier that year regarding various superstitious beliefs that he held.

One of the charges against Werner focused on a common charm that he knew in the German vernacular, and of which he approved: "Christ was born, Christ was lost, Christ was found again; may he bless these wounds, in the name of the father, son, and holy spirit." A woman had asked him whether she might use this charm to heal her son's injured hand, and he responded that she could. He maintained this position before the assembled theologians of Heidelberg, arguing that the blessing invoked divine power and was in no way illicit. Werner maintained that he had used this spell successfully to heal several injuries, although at one point during his questioning he curiously professed that he did not believe it could cure wounds. The basic effectiveness of his spell, however, was not really the center of debate. Authorities' concern focused on the potentially hidden means by which this spell might have operated. In his treatise, Nicholas of Jauer argued at great length that words could have no effective power other than to invoke and command (or supplicate) conscious intelligences, an argument ultimately derived from Thomas Aquinas. The suspicion of the Heidelberg faculty, of course, was that this spell did not draw on divine power, as Werner maintained, but on demons. If Werner could be proved to be in error about the nature of the power his spell invoked, he would be guilty of superstition.

The decision of the Heidelberg faculty in this case does not survive, and Werner may well have been set free. The concerns his case engendered did not abate, however, and in his treatise on superstition, Nicholas of Jauer devoted much space to discussing the potential extent of demonic powers in order to demonstrate the great range of magical effects they could be employed to cause. He also discussed the range of natural powers on which magical practices might draw and outlined the limits of the natural properties of herbs, stones, and astral forces. Similar themes were explored in subsequent literature on superstition. In 1412 another Heidelberg theologian, Johannes of Frankfurt, produced a disputation on the ability to coerce and control demons, concluding, akin to Nicolau Eymeric, that demons could not be invoked without at least inadvertently offering them some form of worship. In 1415 an anonymous author, probably a Cologne theologian, wrote a treatise *De daemonibus* (On Demons) to similar effect, and in 1425 the Cologne theologian Heinrich of Gorkum wrote a treatise simply titled *De superstitiosis* (On the Superstitious).

All of these works demonstrated a willingness on the part of their authors to apply demonological theories developed in the preceding centuries not only to elaborate, necromantic rituals or other varieties of learned magic but also to the more simple and mundane spells, charms, and other common magical acts that proliferated in late medieval Europe. This newly rigorous focus on common beliefs and practices was due in part, perhaps in large part, to a new variety of theology emerging in this period. Rather than continuing to focus on grand questions about the nature of divinity or the essence of morality, as had the earlier, all-encompassing systems of Aquinas and others, many theologians now sought to apply these systems to practical and pastoral ends. At Paris, Gerson championed this move to apply theology to specific issues and problems within Christian society, and he clearly identified super-stition as an area in which correction was needed. His ideas proved very influential, especially in the lands of the German Empire, where several uni-versities had recently been founded (at Prague in 1348, at Vienna in 1365, at Heidelberg in 1385, and at Cologne in 1388). Each of these schools, and each of their new theological faculties, was eager to find a purpose, and the extirpation of superstition was one cause to which they applied themselves.

Another factor underlying rising concern over superstition in the fifteenth century was the intense desire for reform within the church, and within Christendom generally, that developed in reaction to the prolonged papal schism that began in 1378 and finally ended only in 1417. Both Jean Gerson and Nicholas of Jauer, for example, attended the great church council held at Constance from 1414 to 1418, where the schism was resolved and a single pope elected, and Gerson played a leading role there. Aside from settling the schism, the Council of Constance sought to reform church governance and ecclesiastical institutions, and even more generally many council members sought to revitalize religious life and the practice of the faith across Europe and to bring about moral and spiritual regeneration throughout Western Christendom. Reformers of this bent, both at Constance and elsewhere, as the reforming impulse spread, refused to tolerate any kind of demonic and therefore corruptive magical practices or superstitions, or indeed any kind of moral turpitude whatsoever. The fiery Italian preacher and reformer Bernar-dino of Siena (1380–1444), for example, strongly opposed not just sorcery, but also usury, which he associated with Jews, and homosexuality (sodomy in his vocabulary), all of which he felt were sapping the moral and spiritual strength of the communities in Italy through which he traveled. Through his popular sermons, he incited a series of sorcery trials in 1426 in Rome by warning the citizens that if they did not reveal all suspected sorcerers to the authorities, they would be just as guilty in the eyes of God as those sorcerers themselves, and divine wrath would descend upon their city. A year later, he tried to incite more trials in his hometown of Siena but met with less success (see figure 4.2).

Although Bernardino of course focused on the demonic threat that he saw lurking behind most magical practices, the descriptions of sorcerers he offered in his sermons make clear that most of the people accused in these trials were not practicing overtly demonic magic, nor were they typically even performing harmful magic. Rather, they were healing, using herbal rem-edies, and often performing love magic via spells or potions. That Bernardino was able to persuade people to inform on individuals who filled a basically

Figure 4.2   Bernardino of Siena preaching against witchcraft in the Piazza del Campo in Siena.

Source: Scala / Art Resource, NY

useful role in their communities gives some sense of the seriousness with which the common laity took authoritative warnings about demonic power and the threat of demonic operations. In the course of the trials, many of the accused, more often women than men, were also charged with killing children, not in the manner usually ascribed to heretics in clerical authorities' descriptions of demonic, cultic gatherings, but by stealing in upon them at night and sucking their blood. This charge seems to have been based on popular folklore stretching back to the ancient belief in the vampiric creature known as the *strix*—an indication, perhaps, of how most laypeople envisioned demonic threats. One trial for which excellent records survive confirms this basic pattern. In 1428 in the town of Todi, a woman named Matteuccia Francisci was initially accused of casting curative spells and performing various types of love magic, including brewing potions both to incite desire and to serve as contraceptives. In the course of her trial, she was also charged with murdering children as a *strix* and of traveling to a diabolical gathering at distant Benevento in order to worship demons.

Because of this last element, the trial of Matteuccia can be seen as representing a new step in the condemnation of magic in Europe. Medieval authorities had always recognized harmful magic, generally termed *maleficium* in Latin sources, as a criminal act, just as authorities had since ancient times. Yet they did not usually regard it as a collective or conspiratorial act. Individuals who performed such magic might be accused of consorting with demons, but they typically were not thought to act in concert with other men or women. This changed early in the fifteenth century. In 1409 Pope Alexander V (reigned 1409–1410) wrote to the inquisitor Pontius Fougeyron about reports he had heard concerning "new sects" of both Christians and Jews that were beginning to appear in Europe, and he warned of the new threat posed by sorcerers, diviners, and other superstitious people. A later pope, Eugenius IV (reigned 1431–1447), wrote again to Fougeyron in 1434 about the danger posed by demonic sorcerers, both Christian and Jewish, and in 1437 he pronounced that Christian sorcerers forsook their religion by worshiping demons and becoming members of diabolical sects. Members of these sects were still generally called *malefici* (men) or *maleficae* (women), but the meaning of *maleficium* itself took on an added connotation. The term no longer meant just harmful magic, or even demonic magic, but now also implied participation in a diabolical cult. This conspiratorial stereotype would characterize witchcraft, at least in the minds of most authorities, for the next several centuries.

Already by the time Eugenius was issuing his pronouncements on magical sects, several other sources had taken up this idea. All of these accounts were composed in lands clustered around the western Alps, and all were written within about a decade of one another, such that this time and place may be viewed as the birthplace of the idea of witchcraft in the form in which it largely persisted through the era of the major early modern witch hunts. Even as Matteuccia Francisci was sent to the flames in Todi in 1428, trials were taking place in the Alpine region of Valais that claimed perhaps as many as 100 victims. These trials served as the basis for an account written by Hans Fründ, a lay official and chronicler in nearby Lucerne. He described people performing harmful magic—killing, causing disease, and raising storms with lightning and hail to destroy crops—but he also described these sorcerers as members of a large cult, meeting at secret, nocturnal gatherings where they would foreswear their Christian faith, worship demons, engage in sexual orgies, and feast on the flesh of babies. Similar reports came from Claude Tholosan, a secular judge and chief magistrate of Briançon in French Dauphiné from 1426 to 1449. Around 1436 he produced a treatise *Ut magorum et maleficiorum errores manifesti ignorantibus fiant* (That the Errors of Magicians and Witches May Be Made Manifest to the Ignorant), based on trials he had conducted. He too described not only basic *maleficium* but also participation in diabolical, cultic activities. In these accounts, the horrific idea of the witches' sabbath can be seen taking shape—an imagined gathering where witches gave full vent to their supposedly debased and immoral natures and at which they symbolically acted out their subservience to demons and affirmed their membership in a diabolical cult bent on destroying Christian society.

In addition to laymen like Fründ and Tholosan, clerical authorities also advanced this idea. Sometime in the mid-1430s, an inquisitor in Savoy, most likely in the valley of Aosta, composed a tract known as *Errores Gazariorum* (Errors of the Gazarii—a somewhat generic term for heretics or malefactors). This short document included graphic descriptions of diabolical cults gathering at what was here, as in other early sources, termed not a sabbath but a synagogue. This document included a detailed report of how new members of the witches' cult were required to renounce Christianity and swear homage to a presiding demon in exchange for magical powers. It is also the earliest known description of witchcraft to mention a pact between witches and demons written in blood. In 1437 and 1438 the Dominican theologian Johannes Nider (ca. 1380–1438) wrote a long moral treatise titled *Formicarius* (The Anthill—ants being a symbol for well ordered, productive society), the fifth book of which dealt with "Witches and their Deceptions." He claimed that he took many of his accounts of witchcraft from conversations with a secular judge, Peter of Bern, who had conducted trials in the mountainous Simme valley in Bernese territory years earlier. Interestingly, Nider actually depicted two different forms of magical activity. In general, he described witches operating in organized sects, gathering secretly to renounce Christianity, worship demons, devour babies, and so forth. He also discussed a single witch several times, a man named Staedelin. This person also performed harmful and demonic magic (at one point, according to Nider's account, explicitly offering a sacrifice to demons in exchange for their causing a thunderstorm), but Nider never described him as a member of a diabolical cult or group of any kind. Thus in one source we can see both the newer idea that "witchcraft" was coming to entail and the older notion of individual practitioners of harmful demonic sorcery.

Staedelin, the principal witch Nider described, was male, as were two other witches associated with him, a man named Hoppo and an individual called Scavius (literally, "the scabby man"). Nevertheless, the image of witchcraft emerging at this time was becoming even more strongly gendered than earlier conceptions of common *maleficium*, and most witches were female. Nider appears to have been the first author to address this point directly, devoting one (small) section of his *Formicarius* to explaining why witches were more often women than men. The reasoning he offered was not remarkable for a medieval cleric. He maintained, based on sound biblical and Aristotelian knowledge, that women were inferior to men physically, mentally, and spiritually. Thus they were more prone to demonic temptations. In particular, they were more vain than men and more carnal, so demons could easily seduce them with blandishments and the promise of sexual pleasure. They were also quicker to anger and so sought power to strike out at their perceived enemies. Moreover, they were prone to gossip, so that once one woman attained access to demonic power, she would soon spread this knowledge to others.

The explanations Nider gave for women's proclivity for witchcraft drew on standard strains of medieval misogyny familiar to other clerical authorities. In particular, fear that women were especially susceptible to demonic influence seems to have been growing in the early fifteenth century, evident also, for example, in clerical concerns over cases of female mysticism and suspected demonic possession. Such developments were an aspect of authorities' generally escalating concerns about demonic activity founded on the increasingly rigorous demonology coming out of the schools since at least the thirteenth century. Yet we should not suppose that scholastic demonology or clerical animus against women was the sole cause of the strongly gendered image of witchcraft. Magic had a long history of sexualized and gendered associations in the Christian West as well as in antiquity, and such associations were widely accepted throughout society. Late medieval trial records are spotty at best, but already in the latter half of the fourteenth century, women comprised a clear majority, just under 60 percent, of those accused in sorcery trials, and in the first half of the fifteenth century they comprised roughly 60 to 70 percent of those accused of witchcraft. The reasons for these percentages, which rose still higher in subsequent centuries, were enormously complex and will be addressed more fully in the following chapter. While numbers of accusations cannot serve as an exact gauge of popular opinion, they do seem to indicate that the propensity to associate harmful magic or witchcraft with women was broadly diffused through late medieval (and early modern) society.

The interplay between authoritative tracts and treatises describing diabolical sects of witches and ideas about the practice and practitioners of harmful magic developing in contemporary trials was intricate and difficult to determine. Both Fründ and Tholosan supposedly based their accounts on trials, while Nider claimed to take much of his information from a lay judge, and the author of the *Errores Gazariorum* was most likely himself an inquisitor. The overall number of trials for *maleficium* seems clearly to have been rising in the early decades of the fifteenth century, especially in the lands from which these sources emerged. Yet the earliest trial records known to survive from this region are later, pertaining to cases heard in an inquisitorial court in the diocese of Lausanne in 1448. These records, and those of still later trials, indicate that most initial accusations brought before courts at this time focused only on harmful magic, and that ideas of sects of witches and other demonic elements such as described in authoritative literature typically emerged only in the course of the trials, usually introduced by inquisitors or other magistrates. This is not to say that most people rejected, or even resisted, authorities' notions of diabolical cults of witches. The laity of the late Middle Ages was well schooled through sermons and other means about the dangers of demonic power and the sort of person who might be expected to interact with demons. Still, in the common imagination, concern over magic seems almost always to have focused on the direct harm that magical practices were believed to cause, not the diabolical fantasies that filled the minds of authorities.

The Development of Witchcraft to the
End of the Fifteenth Century

The immediate influence of the new conception of witchcraft being developed in trials and treatises in the early 1400s should not be overestimated. These ideas were initially fairly localized to Savoy, Dauphiné, and what would become western Switzerland. They spread slowly to the eastern Alps, and in northern Italy, where there were many sorcery trials at this time, these ideas did not take immediate hold. There, accused witches, usually women who claimed some expertise in healing or love magic, were often still prosecuted as individuals, and, significantly, charges of infanticide and cannibalism, while present, continued to owe more to longstanding concepts of vampiric *striges* than to the idea of depraved witches' sabbaths emerging to the north. Nevertheless, ideas developed in the western Alps gradually spread, in no small part thanks to the major church council that took place in the city of Basel just to the north of the lands that cradled the earliest conception of fully diabolical witchcraft. Like the earlier council at Constance, the Council of Basel (1431–1449) was a major ecclesiastical assembly drawing clerics from across Europe, and like Constance, Basel also had a strong reformist bent. Among the authors discussed above, Johannes Nider was an important member of the council for several years, and the *Errores Gazariorum* probably circulated in the city. From the council, a network radiated out, and many other figures associated with the spreading idea of diabolical, conspiratorial witchcraft were either present at Basel or were influenced by men who had attended the council.

One figure who spent several years in Basel was Martin le Franc (1410–1461), one of the most important French poets of the fifteenth century. While at the council, as secretary for Duke Amadeus VIII of Savoy (reigned 1391–1439, when he abdicated to accept the council's appointment as anti-Pope Felix V, reigned 1439–1451), Martin composed his long poem *Le champion des dames* (The Defender of Ladies) between 1440 and 1442. In this poem he included an extended section on witchcraft and the particular association of women with this crime. Through the voice of his "Champion," Martin defended women from such charges as much as he could. He especially questioned the supposed flight of witches. As the idea of the witches' sabbath developed, so did the notion that witches typically flew to these gatherings. This concept probably owed much to beliefs common in Alpine regions that sorcerers would fly to distant mountain peaks, often to raise storms and hail. Such a depiction of flight appeared explicitly in the *Errores*

Gazariorum, for example. Among educated authorities, the *locus classicus* of the idea of flight in the service of demons was the tenth-century canon *Episcopi*, which also associated this practice exclusively with women. Yet the canon presented such flight as a demonic illusion, and if flight to a sabbath was only an illusion, then the horrific activities that supposedly transpired there, and much of the image of diabolical witchcraft, must be illusory as well.

Although the newly elaborate stereotype of conspiratorial witchcraft focused heavily on witches' supposed participation in depraved diabolical rites at sabbaths, arguments intended to undermine the reality of these supposed gatherings ultimately did little to deter the condemnation of witches, because zealous authorities maintained that even an imagined association with demons was idolatrous. Nevertheless, the issue of the reality of flight continued to plague theorists of witchcraft, and often provided a point of attack for skeptics. In 1458 Nicolas Jacquier (died 1472), an inquisitor in northern France who earlier had attended the Council of Basel, wrote his *Flagellum haereticorum fascinariorum* (Scourge of Heretical Witches), arguing that witches represented a new and dangerous heretical sect unknown to earlier authorities. Among other conclusions he drew from this general proposition was that while the canon *Episcopi*'s dismissal of the reality of flight may have applied to heretics and demon worshipers of that era, it did not necessarily apply to contemporary witches. Jacquier also appears to have been the first authority to designate witches' gatherings "sabbaths" rather than "synagogues."

New terms and new arguments did not end debate about flight or other aspects of witchcraft. By mid-century, this new stereotype of harmful, demonic magic performed by members of conspiratorial, diabolical cults was well established in the European imagination. Around 1450 Jean Vineti (died ca. 1475), an inquisitor in southern France, wrote a treatise *Contra demonum invocatores* (Against Invokers of Demons), in which he maintained, like Jacquier, that witchcraft was an essentially new form of heresy. Also like Jacquier, he fully accepted the reality of flight and of the sabbath. Secular authorities also accepted these ideas. In 1456 Johann Hartlieb (ca. 1410–1468), court physician to Duke Albrecht II of Bavaria, wrote a *Buch aller verbotenen Künste* (Book of All Forbidden Arts) in the German vernacular, focusing mostly on learned and courtly magic such as necromancy and astrology, but also including accounts of witchcraft. In 1459 and 1460 several witch trials took place in the French town of Arras, leading to the arrest of thirty-four people and the execution of twelve. Based on these trials, Johannes Tinctoris (ca. 1400–1469) wrote *De secta Vaudensium* (On the Sect of Witches) in 1460.

Of course these works, learned and mainly composed in Latin, were not intended for widespread consumption. But the ideas they advanced did affect common conceptions of magic and witchcraft. They served as a source for preachers searching for material to include in sermons. Also at this time visual depictions of witches began to appear, at first closely associated with written descriptions of witchcraft. One of the earliest known depictions of witches flying on brooms is a marginal drawing in a manuscript copy of Martin le Franc's *Champion des dames* (see figure 4.3), and an illuminated manuscript of Johannes Tinctoris's treatise contains an elaborate illustration of witches worshiping the devil in the form of a goat. In the later fifteenth century, the development of printing allowed for the much wider dispersion of written materials, but also of visual images in the form of woodcuts. Many early printed treatises on witchcraft contained illustrations, and other works dealing with moral virtues and vices often included images of witches. Woodcuts also appeared in widely distributed pamphlets and on their own. By the end of the century, visual images of witchcraft in various forms circulated throughout European society.

Also toward the end of the fifteenth century appeared arguably the most famous treatise on witchcraft ever written, *Malleus maleficarum* (The Hammer of Witches), composed in 1486. This work is commonly attributed to two German inquisitors, Heinrich Kramer and Jakob Sprenger, although Kramer was by far the principal, most likely the sole, author. Kramer (ca. 1430–1505), also known by the Latin version of his name, Institoris, was a Dominican friar appointed in 1474 as an inquisitor in southern German lands. In this capacity, he came to work with his fellow Dominican Sprenger (ca. 1436–1495), a professor of theology at Cologne and also a papally appointed inquisitor. Kramer, at least, was clearly a very abrasive figure who often aroused antagonism, and the two men seem to have encountered significant resistance from various local authorities as they attempted to pursue their investigations into witchcraft. They complained of this in 1484 to Pope Innocent VIII (reigned 1484–1492), who responded by issuing the bull *Summis desiderantes affectibus* (Desiring with Greatest Ardor), in which he stated his alarm at reports of widespread witchcraft in German lands and explicitly authorized Kramer and Sprenger to take action against suspected witches. Innocent also ordered all officials, ecclesiastic and secular, to cooperate fully with the inquisitors in their investigations. The effectiveness of this bull can be questioned, for when Kramer undertook another witch trial in Innsbruck

Figure 4.3 Marginalia from Martin le Franc's *Le champion des dames* (1440–1442) of witches in flight.

in 1485, he again encountered stiff opposition from local officials, including Georg Golser, the bishop of Brixen, and ultimately he had to abandon his efforts. These men opposed Kramer not because they disbelieved in demonic witchcraft, but because they felt Kramer was overly zealous and too extreme in his methods. Golser went so far as to accuse Kramer of being senile.

Following this setback, Kramer began to write *Malleus maleficarum*. When the work was printed, the bull *Summis desiderantes* was included, lending an air of papal approval and authority to the treatise, although the bull was actually in no way related to the work. In addition, Kramer seems to have contrived to get a falsified approbation for his treatise from the theological faculty of Cologne. The inclusion of Sprenger as nominal coauthor, even though he appears to have contributed little to the work, may have been part of a similar strategy. As a theologian, Sprenger was a more respected figure within the Dominican order and the church as a whole than was Kramer. Moreover, *Summis desiderantes* mentioned Kramer and Sprenger in conjunction. In fact, there is substantial evidence to show that Sprenger, far from an ally and coauthor, actually became an opponent of Kramer, ultimately forcing him to leave the Dominican province of Teutonia, which Sprenger came to head.

The first argument Kramer advanced in the *Malleus* was that all those who maintained witchcraft was not a heresy were themselves guilty of heresy. Thus the function of the treatise as a retort to anyone who attempted to stifle Kramer's inquisitorial activities against suspected witches is clear. From this point, Kramer produced the longest and most detailed work on witchcraft yet written. He drew heavily on his own experiences as an inquisitor, as well as culling material from earlier literature, for example, from his fellow Dominican Johannes Nider's *Formicarius*. In addition to describing the nature of witchcraft as a diabolical heresy and presenting extensive accounts of the supposed activities of witches, the *Malleus* also served as a practical handbook, laying out precisely how inquisitors or other authorities should proceed in cases of witchcraft.

Most famously, the *Malleus* dwelled on the gendered nature of witchcraft, more so than any earlier account, and more than many later ones as well. Indeed, the almost exclusive association of witchcraft with women was perhaps the work's most original point. Other authorities writing on witchcraft at this time often included examples of female witches in their accounts, and Johannes Nider had offered the first sustained explanations for women's particular disposition to witchcraft in his *Formicarius*. Kramer relied heavily on Nider's basic arguments, but he elaborated on them and greatly expanded his own treatment of witches' gender to become a central point of his entire discussion of witchcraft. He also focused far more extensively on the supposed carnality of women, maintaining that their uncontrolled sexual lust was the primary factor leading them into the snares of demons. In fact, at one point he even addressed the perplexing problem of why large cults of witches seemed to have appeared only recently in Europe. Although Kramer maintained that there had always been witches, he also argued that witch cults were becoming more numerous because growing female lust now allowed demons to seduce more women in the current depraved era.

Gender would remain one of the defining characteristics of witchcraft throughout the period of the major witch hunts in the sixteenth and seventeenth centuries. While most later authorities accepted that witches were primarily women, however, many accorded relatively little direct attention to the issue of gender in witchcraft, and none ever made gender or sexuality so central a point as did Kramer in the *Malleus*. Although often viewed as some kind of definitive statement on witchcraft, exercising an absolute influence on all later thought on the subject, the *Malleus* was, in fact, nothing of the kind. Kramer made far more of certain aspects of the witch stereotype than did other authorities (for example, gender), and he made much less of others. He devoted relatively little attention to descriptions of witches' sabbaths, for example, although he did draw on such lurid earlier sources as the *Errores Gazariorum*. He also largely ignored the question of the reality of the flight of witches, which other authorities found to be of such central concern, although he did at certain points argue for the possibility of nonillusory flight.

Certainly the *Malleus* was influential. Between 1486 and 1520 it was printed in fourteen separate editions. From 1576 to 1669 it was reprinted an additional sixteen times, although by that period numerous other comprehensive manuals on witchcraft were available. Undoubtedly many authorities found the *Malleus* useful. Nowhere, however, were its positions regarded as definitive. Just as there was no single, institutional "Inquisition" in the Middle Ages, so there was no single, absolute statement about witchcraft. In 1489, only a few years after the *Malleus* appeared, the jurist Ulrich Molitor (ca. 1442–1507/8) composed a treatise *De lamiis et phitonicis mulieribus* (On Witches and Women Who Prophesy). Written at the behest of Archduke Sigismund of Austria (reigned 1446–1490), this work took the form of a conversation between Conrad Schatz, a magistrate of Constance who accepted all of the ideas of diabolical witchcraft that had developed in the fifteenth century, Molitor himself, who was more skeptical, and Sigismund, who served as arbiter between them. Molitor denied outright the reality of the sabbath and the flight of witches, as well as their ability to change shape. Moreover, he concluded that witches could not control the weather, nor could they impede human sexual fertility, unless God should allow this through his power. Yet Molitor did not deny the existence of witches, that is, people who had entered into pacts with the devil and believed that they had gained such powers, for the devil often deluded witches into thinking that they had caused events, such as storms, that had in fact occurred entirely naturally. For Molitor, these witches were still guilty of terrible crimes. Even if the sabbath was only an illusion, the fact that witches had in their imaginings been willing to worship demons and desecrate holy objects meant that they were idolaters and apostates, just as if their actions had been real.

The stereotype of witchcraft that emerged in the course of the fifteenth century was not an absolutely stable idea that once constructed, remained constant and unchallenged in all its aspects. Most people accepted the potential reality of harmful magic and feared its power, and basic notions of demonic threat hiding behind common magical practices and superstitions were widely accepted, certainly among authorities. Even when authorities disagreed about the extent of demonic power in the world, they acknowledged the existence of the devil and his desire to corrupt Christian souls. These concerns had always been an essential part of the condemnation of magic in Europe, however, and were not unique to the late medieval conception of witchcraft. The idea of diabolical, conspiratorial witchcraft was simply one stage in the long historical development of concern about magic and conceptions of how it functioned and what sorts of associations it entailed. This notion proved a critical development, of course, in terms of the major witch hunts that would erupt in following centuries. Even those hunts, however, did not hold Europe nearly so universally and uniformly in their grasp as is often believed.

CHAPTER FIVE

Witchcraft and Witch Hunting in the Early Modern Period, 1500–1800

In the mid to late 1620s, the central German city of Bamberg found itself in the midst of a major panic over witchcraft. Between 1626 and 1630, civic officials executed around six hundred people for this crime. Among them was the mayor of the city, Johannes Junius. He was brought into court in the summer of 1628, when other accused witches confessed to having seen him attending various witches' sabbaths, including at least one gathering in the town's own electoral council chamber. Junius maintained his innocence, and so the court turned to its usual method for obtaining truth. Thumb and leg screws were applied, crushing his hands and leaving him lame for weeks. His torturers stripped and searched him, and when they found a bluish mark on the left side of his body, they pricked it three times. He felt no pain, and no blood issued forth, so the presiding officials deemed this to be a devil's mark, a brand given to Junius by his demonic masters. Finally, they turned to one of the most commonly employed methods of torture used in this period, the strappado. Binding Junius's arms behind him and attaching them to a rope, they raised him off the ground. Eight times he was raised up and then let drop before the rope was jerked tight just before he hit the ground, wrenching the arms backward, an excruciatingly painful procedure that usually dislocated the shoulders. Through all of this, Junius grimly maintained his innocence. The court returned him to confinement to meditate on his crimes and his terrible pain, and a week later, on July 5, recalled him for more questioning. No further torture was needed, however. Under "urgent persuasion," Junius began to confess.[1]

One can only imagine the terrible week that Johannes Junius spent suffering in his prison cell after being tortured, but we do not need to surmise what his thoughts were as he determined, finally, to confess to being a witch. Junius was able to write a letter from prison, probably with the collusion of some of his jailers, to his daughter Veronica. Authorities intercepted this letter, however, and added it to his trial dossier, where it has been preserved. In it Junius explained why, although innocent, he was ready to admit to a crime that would mean his certain execution. Even as he was being taken away from his initial torture session, he wrote, the executioner (the official who performed the torture under the direction of higher magistrates) implored him to admit to being a witch. "Confess something," the man urged, "whether it be true or not. Invent something, for you cannot endure the torture which you'll be put to; and, even if you bear it all, yet you'll not escape." And so, after much thought, Junius confessed. He asserted that he had been seduced into a diabolical cult by a demon appearing to him in the form of a beautiful woman. He had engaged in carnal relations with this woman and had traveled to many witches' sabbaths, usually riding on a large black dog that would appear to him whenever he was summoned to attend. When pressed, he also identified other witches living in Bamberg, whom he claimed to know from these gatherings. All that he confessed was false, he assured his daughter, and yet he had to, "for they never leave off with the torture till one confesses something; be he never so good, he must be a witch." In early August, the court convicted Junius of witchcraft, and he was burned at the stake.

This case, unusual because of the high rank of its victim and the remarkable documentation that has survived, nevertheless exemplifies many of the horrors commonly associated with the term "witch hunt"—the highly questionable accusations, usually coming from other suspects, the presumption of guilt, the near impossibility of maintaining innocence under torture or the threat of torture, and the necessity to implicate others as well as admitting one's own crimes. In fact, Junius's trial represents the most severe form of witch hunting in Europe. It occurred in the midst of a major hunt, when authorities had become convinced that Bamberg and its surrounding territory were rife with witches, when accusations multiplied due to extreme applications of torture by the courts and the spread of panic through the community, and when each new accusation seemed ultimately justified by a confession wrung from the accused. The trial also took place in the region of Europe most prone to major hunts, the fragmented territories of the German (Holy Roman) Empire, particularly those states ruled by ecclesiastical princes, and it occurred in the period when these hunts were most intense, the fifty years from around 1580 to 1630. Thus the trial stands at the very high water mark of European witch hunting.

Yet how common were such trials? The early modern period, especially the sixteenth and seventeenth centuries, is sometimes described as the "age of witch trials" or the period of the "great European witch hunts." Such phrases can easily conjure an image of ruthless authorities persecuting countless innocent women and men (far more women than men) virtually continuously, of an entire continent gripped by fear and fanaticism for hundreds of years. The numbers sometimes associated with witch hunting reinforce this sweeping image. One still encounters claims of hundreds of thousands, occasionally even millions of dead. In fact, the sixteenth and seventeenth centuries did witness the elevation of witchcraft to a severe and specifically defined crime across Europe and saw far more extensive legal prosecution for this crime than at any other point in history. Nevertheless, witch trials were always sporadic occurrences, and truly major hunts claiming hundreds of victims, while certainly devastating, were actually very rare. Moreover, patterns of prosecution varied widely in different regions of Europe, the period of truly intense hunting was far more limited than is often assumed, and the overall number of victims was far lower than is sometimes claimed. Emerging out of late medieval concepts and concerns, witchcraft formed an important element of early modern culture. Yet witch trials and the few intense witch hunts that did occur must ultimately be set in their proper place within the much larger context of the history of magic and magical beliefs in Europe.

The Meaning of Witchcraft

Like magic itself, witchcraft is a term that carries manifold connotations. Very broadly construed, it can simply denote wicked or harmful magic. Witchcraft also typically entails common or low magic worked via simple spells, charms, and curses, as opposed to the complex ritual systems of high or learned magic. Those who perform these spells and charms are often regarded as being in league with dark and demonic forces. In this fairly general sense, witchcraft may be said to have a long history. As seen in chapter 1, the ancient Greeks castigated *goētes* for their association with spirits of the underworld, and the Romans outlawed *veneficium*, a term that meant poisoning but could also encompass more generalized magical harming. The most common Latin term for harmful magic, however, was *maleficium*, and this continued to be the designation favored by Christian authorities throughout the Middle Ages. A person who performed such acts was *maleficus*, or more typically the feminine *malefica*. The English "witch" derived from the Anglo-Saxon *wicca* (feminine, *wicce*), a general term denoting a spell caster. By the fourteenth and fifteenth centuries, *wicche* clearly meant *malefica*, or at least the one could be given as a translation for the other, although additional terms remained in use, both in Latin and in the vernacular. At the same time, other European languages developed their own terminology, for example, the French *sorcière* (derived from the late-Latin *sortiarius*, or diviner) and German *Hexe*.

To many who used them, these various terms may still often have meant only a person who used harmful magic, casting simple spells against her neighbors. As seen in the previous chapter, however, beginning in the early fifteenth century certain authorities, both clerical and secular, firmly linked a number of other elements to the practice of *maleficium*, notably apostasy, or the formal renunciation of the Christian faith, explicit worship of demons, and membership in diabolical cults. This more specific concept of conspiratorial, diabolical witchcraft would largely define what was meant by the designation "witch," at least for authorities, throughout the early modern period and across most of Europe. To be a witch was as much about a person's essential identity as it was a description of certain practices, for unlike other perceived practitioners of magic, witches were not just individual agents of harm or malevolence in the world. Instead, they became members of a vast, diabolical army bent on corrupting and subverting everything that was good and decent in society. To their opponents they were the most profoundly wicked enemies humanity had ever faced.

The full horror of the particular late medieval and early modern European conception of diabolical witchcraft was most fully captured in the notion of the witches' sabbath. The first major theorists of witchcraft, writing in the early fifteenth century, described groups of witches gathering to worship demons, engage in orgiastic sex, desecrate crosses, befoul consecrated hosts, and murder and devour babies at cannibalistic feasts. For all the fantastic and monstrous acts authorities envisioned taking place at sabbaths, however, they still could place them in fairly mundane and realistic settings. Small groups of witches would gather in cellars, caves, or other isolated but entirely worldly locations. Such images clearly derived from medieval notions of supposed diabolical gatherings of heretics or from the blood rites that clerical authorities often convinced themselves that Jews performed. Yet the imagined gatherings of witches at sabbaths could become far larger, more elaborate, and more fantastical than any of these earlier notions, owing mainly to the connection drawn between witches' assemblies and the concept of night flight.

Perhaps the most familiar element of the stereotypical image of the witches' sabbath was the nocturnal flight of witches to these gatherings, sometimes on animals but most often on staves, brooms, or other common household implements (see figures 4.3 and 5.1). Indeed, a witch flying on a

Figure 5.1 Dürer's *Witch Riding Backwards on a Goat* (ca. 1500–1501) illustrates the inversion and perversion of witchcraft.

Source: Bildarchiv Preussischer Kulturbesitz / Art Resource, NY

broomstick is surely the most iconic of all images of witchcraft. Yet the idea of such flight is arguably the strangest element of the European witch stereotype, always contested and often denied outright by certain authorities from the fifteenth century onward. Notions of flight have no basis in medieval antiheretical or anti-Jewish writings. Instead they seem to have been rooted in elements of ancient folklore dealing with the nighttime journeys of spirits in the train of various goddesses. The medieval church encapsulated such beliefs and condemned them as demonic superstition in the canon *Episcopi*. Yet despite centuries of clerical opposition, folk beliefs in the nocturnal travels of spirits, or groups of women, led by a female figure known as Holda, Diana, Dame Abundia, or other names, were common across much of Europe well into the early modern period.

These beliefs appear to have had tremendously deep cultural roots, into which authoritative constructions of witchcraft inadvertently tapped. In many premodern societies, including early European ones, certain people were believed to possess the ability to interact with the spirit world while in a trancelike state. These individuals, whom scholars now typically refer to as shamans, confronted evil spirits and sought to protect human communities, working to guarantee fertility, abundant crops, and successful harvests. The superficial although inverted similarity of such figures to witches, who were typically accused of impeding fertility and destroying crops, is clear, and in the 1960s, the Italian historian Carlo Ginzburg discovered a remarkable historical convergence of these beliefs.[2] Delving into inquisitorial records from the sixteenth and seventeenth centuries pertaining to the remote northern Italian region of Friuli, he encountered a group of people known as *benandanti* (literally "those who go well"). They were identified within their communities at birth by being born with the caul, the inner membrane covering the fetus, intact. They and their neighbors all believed that, upon reaching adulthood, they would undertake periodic journeys into the spirit world. The outcome of the battles they engaged in there with other spiritual foes would determine the abundance of crops for the coming season.

Clearly representing the remnants of deeply rooted shamanistic beliefs, the *benandanti* nevertheless situated their activities within an entirely Christian worldview. They boasted that they were called to battle by the angel Gabriel and that the opponents they encountered in the spirit realm were in fact witches seeking to destroy crops and bring disease and hardship to their communities. Many *benandanti* also claimed to possess magical powers, to be able to heal, for example, in the physical world. Inquisitorial authorities did not immediately condemn these beliefs, but eventually they decided that the *benandanti* must themselves be witches. Over time, they convinced most native Friulians and even many *benandanti* of this. Since Ginzburg's discovery, other scholars have identified similar remnants of shamanistic practices surviving in folklore and folk custom in many regions of Europe. Precisely how these affected the developing stereotype of witchcraft is uncertain. In Friuli, for example, inquisitors already had a fully developed notion of witchcraft and the witches' sabbath into which they ultimately fit the beliefs of the *benandanti*. Nevertheless, such widespread beliefs and practices clearly contributed to the complex notion of witchcraft that developed in the early modern period.

That the idea of the witches' sabbath could encompass and incorporate such diverse elements gives a sense of how flexible (although also in many ways increasingly precise) the stereotype of witchcraft was in the sixteenth and seventeenth centuries. Of course, that stereotype was never uniform across Europe, but certain basic elements of witchcraft, including many of those encompassed in the idea of the sabbath, were widely accepted, particularly by authorities. Surely the most critical of these in terms of the terrible fear that witchcraft inspired and the severe forms of prosecution it engendered was that witches were organized servants of Satan and members of diabolical cults. The presence of one witch in a region therefore indicated the existence of more, and a captured witch could reasonably be expected (and frequently forced) to identify others. This notion that witches were not merely individual malefactors but members of a satanic conspiracy bent on subverting Christian society led not only religious but also secular authorities to treat witchcraft very harshly. The threat posed by witchcraft was seen to be so great that authorities in many jurisdictions declared it to be a *crimen exceptum*, an exceptional crime. This meant that normal legal procedures could be suspended. Rules restricting certain types of questionable evidence were abandoned, the threshold for proof of guilt might be lowered, and perhaps most importantly, limitations on the use of torture could be ignored.

Equally defining of witchcraft was the belief, again never absolutely uniform but certainly very broadly held, that witches were typically women. The roots of this notion were extraordinarily diverse, but it too can be seen to be at least implied in the idea of the sabbath, insofar as sabbaths emphasized the sexual congress of witches with demons and more basically their submission and subservience to demonic masters and ultimately to the devil, who was of course conceived as being male. As noted in the previous chapter, medieval authorities never held a particularly favorable view of women. In the early modern period, this general animus became, if anything, even more severe as both clerical and secular authorities laid increasing stress on notions of patriarchy in politics, society, and even within households. Biblical commandments and classical Aristotelian philosophy both were marshaled to prove that women were inferior to men spiritually, mentally, and physically. They suffered weaknesses and corruptions in their bodies, which in Aristotelian thought were imperfectly formed versions of male bodies, and they were spiritually and intellectually more vulnerable to the deceptions and seductions of demons. Yet throughout the early modern era, many authorities largely avoided much specifically gendered theorizing about witchcraft. If "witch" often meant "woman" in this period, this seems to have been due less to abstract philosophy or theology than practical reality. That is, far more women than men were being accused of witchcraft in the courts. Across Europe an average of 75 percent of witchcraft accusations focused on women, and in some regions the percentages rose into the nineties. In Siena, for example, of more than two hundred witches tried from the late sixteenth to the early eighteenth century, over 99 percent were women.

Certainly one powerful reason for these percentages was the simple fact that women were, on the whole, far more legally vulnerable than men in this period, often having no legal status apart from their fathers and husbands. The fate of an accused witch might often depend on whether any man was willing to rise to her defense. Spinsters or widows were especially vulnerable. A widow, of course, might have male children, but as she aged, they might come to regard her more as an impediment standing between them and their father's inheritance than anything else. Across Europe, statistics varied considerably depending on location, but in general not only were far more women than men accused of witchcraft, but of those accused a higher percentage of women were convicted, and of those convicted a higher percentage of women were executed. These figures reflect legal biases but also an underlying reality that most people in early modern Europe seem to have linked women to the practice of *maleficium* more readily than they did men. Women themselves shared this belief, and numerous accusations were made by women (often acting through a male relative) and arose from animosities between female neighbors. Many cultures have associated various forms of magic more with women than with men. In early modern Europe, much common magical activity, and especially much of the harmful magic that characterized witchcraft, encompassed issues of fertility—love potions and charms for potency, but also withered crops, withered male members, and murdered children. Thus concerns over witchcraft naturally focused on the female domains of reproduction, childbirth, and nurturing.

For all that the predominance of women among those executed for witch-craft is a clear and grisly fact, still witchcraft was never exclusively a female crime. Although authorities believed they had strong intellectual grounds for considering women to be more susceptible than men to demonic temptation, they never argued that men were unlikely to be seduced into witchcraft. And although social and legal biases combined to facilitate accusations against women, on average 25 percent of the accused in witchcraft cases were men. Moreover, there were large regions of Scandinavia, eastern Europe, and vari-ous smaller pockets throughout western Europe where gender ratios were far more equal or even tipped to a majority of men. Three-fourths of accused witches in Normandy were male, for example, and in Iceland, over 90 per-cent of all accused witches, and twenty-two out of twenty-three executed, were men.

The meanings and implications of witchcraft were constructed in many different ways and at various levels of early modern society. Legal authorities produced legislation and learned theorists wrote treatises. Ordinary laypeople heard sermons, witnessed executions, and told stories among themselves. They were also called to testify in courts, where they did not just passively confirm authorities' pronouncements but introduced and sometimes insisted upon their own ideas about witchcraft, which thereby entered into elite dis-course. Yet we should not think of two distinct cultures, the popular and the elite, holding fully separate notions of what witchcraft entailed and only occasionally interacting. Rather, ideas and images of witchcraft permeated many areas of early modern culture and society. Witches figured in plays and popular ballads, as well as in the visual arts. As mentioned in the previous chapter, woodcuts depicting witches were used to illustrate broadsheets or pamphlets or even full treatises, and beginning around the year 1500 artists such as Albrecht Dürer (1471–1528), Lucas Cranach (1472–1553), and Hans Baldung Grien (ca. 1484–1545) began producing notable paintings and engravings on the theme of witchcraft. These artists drew from common cultural perceptions but also added their own emphases.

Prior to 1500 most visual images of witchcraft were very directly modeled on written descriptions and frequently focused on witches engaged in harm-ful magic. From the early sixteenth century on, artists became more indepen-dent in their use of witchcraft, developing their own themes and points of emphasis. In particular, visual depictions tended to focus much more intensely than written treatises on witches' gender and on the fantastic events of the witches' sabbath, at least partially because of specific artistic concerns that could be addressed through these topics. Images of (typically nude) female witches allowed artists to explore issues of sexuality and depictions of the human body that were certainly part of the general cultural conception of witchcraft at this time but were also of particular interest to those engaged in the visual arts. Dürer and Baldung, for example, both produced several important works focusing in complex ways on the nude bodies of female witches (see figures 5.1 and 5.2). Extravagant images of sabbaths, at which many early modern artists excelled, allowed them to explore themes of imagination and fantasy.

For all the elements that came together to create the stereotype of European witchcraft, and for all the factors that made it such a culturally potent concept, actual cases of witchcraft were still almost always at their root about harmful magic. While courts could and did initiate hunts on their own, the vast majority of witch trials throughout the early modern period responded to charges of simple *maleficium* brought by ordinary people when, for example, a cow died or a child sickened unexpectedly. Such occurrences did not automatically raise suspicions of witchcraft; unexplained misfortune was common in premodern Europe. Yet if some particular animosity existed between the victim or the victim's family and another person, and if that person had a reputation for wielding malevolent magical powers, or if there had been some direct sign of magical attack, however slight—a muttered curse, a threatening gesture, or even a baleful stare—then a public accusation might be made. Authorities, when the accusation was brought to their attention, could add charges of diabolism, apostasy, and attendance at sabbaths, and wring out confessions through torture.

Whatever specific conceptions of witchcraft they held, most early modern Europeans imagined witches as the absolute antithesis of proper moral and social order, completely destructive to their communities. Not surprisingly, then, those accused of witchcraft were typically the persons most marginal, or most easily marginalized, in a community. Variations were wide across Europe, but witches were more often old than in the prime of life. They were more often poor than rich. And in a society so completely imbued with notions of patriarchal power, where fathers headed households, kings were the fathers of nations, and God was the father of all, witches were more often women than men. Each segment of society made its own contributions to the idea of witchcraft, and each made its own use of that idea. Small rural communities expressed deep anxieties over agricultural failures, infertility, and unexpected death or disease through suspicions and accusations of witchcraft, even as they also revealed very particular local animosities and tensions between close neighbors. Many men, no doubt, expressed their con-

Figure 5.2 Hans Baldung Grien's *Witches Preparing for the Sabbath* (1510) depicts a sexualized gathering of witches.

Source: Réunion des musées nationaux / Art Resource, NY

cerns about dangerous female sexuality, just as many women expressed concerns about bad motherhood and the improper nurture of children. Religious authorities and secular officials alike expressed concerns about religious deviance, moral corruption, and demonic threats to proper Christian social structures. Witchcraft was so terrible not because it was a weapon of one particular segment of society against others, but because it was thought to be so broad, because so many concerns fed into it, and because all of European society contributed to it.

The Rise of the Witch Hunts

As shown in previous chapters, evil and harmful magic was legally condemned in antiquity and in medieval Europe. Judicial prosecutions for magical crimes were always possible, and in certain instances, particularly during the Roman period, major waves of legal repression could occur. Yet the number of trials conducted in the sixteenth and seventeenth centuries, while more limited than is sometimes imagined, was significantly greater than at any other point in European history. A rise in trials is already visible in the fifteenth century, occurring in close conjunction with the development of the notion of diabolical, conspiratorial witchcraft. These early trials were initially limited to a relatively small area in and around the western Alps and northern Italy, and in fact rather different notions of witchcraft seem to have been operating in Italy as opposed to French- and German-speaking regions in this area. Later in the century, however, the idea of witchcraft spread more widely across Europe, as did witch trials. Numbers increased steadily throughout the 1400s and into the early 1500s. Then, for a generation, from about 1520 to 1560, there was a lull. Trials tapered off, although they certainly did not cease, and the general level of fear over supposed cults of demon-worshiping witches seems to have diminished somewhat. For example, the criminal code issued in 1532 for the entire German Empire by the holy Roman emperor Charles V (reigned 1519–1556) ignored the concept of diabolical witchcraft entirely and dealt only briefly with harmful magic, *maleficium* in the old sense. Also tellingly, the *Malleus maleficarum*, which had been printed in fourteen separate editions between 1486 and 1520, was not issued again until 1576.

Also in the early sixteenth century, important skeptical voices began to be raised against witchcraft and especially against the abuses and excesses of many witch trials, which were already becoming apparent. In his famous *Encomium moriae* (Praise of Folly) of 1509, the Dutch humanist Erasmus

(1466–1536) did not mention witchcraft directly but was sharply critical of fanatical church inquisitors, whom he labeled as bloodthirsty and themselves superstitious. In 1515 the young legal scholar Andrea Alciati (1492–1550) condemned witch hunts that had taken place in the Italian Alps in his report *De lamiis seu strigibus* (On Witches), labeling these trials a "new holocaust" (*nova holocausta*). In 1519, in the city of Metz, in Alsace, the humanist scholar Heinrich Cornelius Agrippa von Nettesheim (1486–1535) came to the defense of an old woman accused of witchcraft by the Dominican inquisitor Nicolas Savini, arguing that the woman was senile and deluded, not a servant of Satan. Agrippa was himself a student and practitioner of learned magic. He wrote a major study, *De occulta philosophia* (On Occult Philosophy), when he was only twenty-four, although he did not allow it to be published for many years. Throughout his life he defended himself against charges that his own magical activities involved the supplication and worship of demons.

These and other skeptics of witchcraft from this period were all scholars influenced by the intellectual movement of humanism emanating from Renaissance Italy. Humanism had developed in the fourteenth and fifteenth centuries in direct opposition to the leading medieval intellectual system of scholasticism, and so humanists were often inclined toward a general skepticism of scholastic thought. Most of the major fifteenth century treatises on witchcraft, such as *Malleus maleficarum*, were essentially scholastic, and this may have contributed to some humanists' opposition to witchcraft. Like medieval scholasticism, however, Renaissance humanism fully accepted the intellectual basis on which the notion of witchcraft rested—the real power of demons and the devil in the world, and thus the real possibility of harmful, demonic magic. Many humanists readily believed in the possibility of witchcraft and the existence of some witches. As the examples given above show, these men objected most directly not to the underlying notion of witchcraft but to excesses in legal prosecutions and the overzealousness of prosecutors, which they feared were leading to numerous innocent victims being found guilty of this terrible crime. Although trials did abate somewhat in the first half of the sixteenth century, perhaps in part because authorities' zeal for prosecuting witchcraft had been called into question, they never ceased. For example, trials occurred steadily in the Low Countries throughout this period, a cluster of trials affected the Basque lands in the 1520s and 1530s, and a panic afflicted Catalonia in 1549. No less a figure than Martin Luther (1483–1546) could write already in 1516 in his commentary on Paul's letter to the Galatians that, while witches had been common in his youth, they were now no longer so frequently found. Nevertheless, Luther was no skeptic in regard to either witchcraft or witch hunting. He later wrote that he had no compassion for witches: he would burn them all.

The Protestant Reformation was, of course, the great event of the early sixteenth century in Europe. It began in 1517, when Luther circulated his ninety-five theses challenging basic doctrines of the Catholic Church at the University of Wittenberg. Within a few years he had moved into an open break with Rome, and winning broad support across much of the German Empire, he permanently shattered the religious unity of Western Christendom. The profound political, social, and religious forces unleashed by the Reformation dominated European history until well into the next century. That the major period of witch hunting in Europe corresponded almost exactly to the Reformation era has often been noted. Yet the relationship between witch hunting and the forces of reform, both Protestant and Catholic, was complex. On the one hand, Protestant authorities had even more cause than Renaissance humanists to devalue all medieval theology, upon which notions of witchcraft and the rationale for witch hunting rested. On the other hand, Christian notions of the essentially wicked, demonic nature of most magic derived from the earliest church fathers, to whose authority Protestant leaders saw themselves returning. Ultimately Protestantism, in all its forms, developed its own systems of demonology and theories of witchcraft that differed very little from Catholic ones.

Much ink has been spilled over whether Catholic or Protestant authorities executed more witches, but in the end the numbers tell no clear story. Some Protestant authorities conducted numerous witch trials; others conducted very few. Many of the most severe hunts occurred in Catholic regions, but other Catholic lands executed very few witches. Notably, the kingdom of Portugal, with over one million people, executed fewer than a dozen. Moreover, the religious confession to which any particular government or group of judicial officials adhered seems to have had little direct relation to their propensity to conduct witch hunts. Most of the largest hunts occurred in the territories of Catholic prince-bishops in the German Empire, for example, yet this owed not to the Catholic character of these lands or their governments. Rather, it was due to their lack of any well-developed, centralized governmental restraint over courts. The accusation and prosecution of witches were above all local events, typically fed by local concerns and conducted by local authorities. Across Europe, trials and especially major hunts occurred most frequently in regions where local jurisdictions had greater autonomy from typically more cautious central governments.

While the overall period of religious reform in Europe corresponds to the period of the most severe witch hunts, the early Reformation corresponds to a decades-long lull in the trials, and its onset may well have contributed to that lull. Accusations of witchcraft arose when people perceived that their particular misfortunes might be due to *maleficium*, and trials required that authorities officially abet these concerns. Somewhat ironically, but also understandably, in times of clear crisis and social strain deriving from an obvious source, such as war or plague, concern over witchcraft tended to recede, and authorities, occupied with other matters, gave less attention to any accusations that continued to arise. Official concern would return, often with a vengeance, however, in the period following the crisis, when social strains persisted but the immediate cause was no longer evident. This basic pattern, clear in many particular situations across Europe, also holds for the general onset and development of the Reformation.

When trials began to rise after 1560, they did so in both Protestant and Catholic lands. Yet even here the relationship of reformist energies to witch hunting was complex, for people rarely leveled accusations at members of other religious confessions. Catholics rarely accused Lutherans, Lutherans rarely accused Calvinists, and so forth. To some extent this is unsurprising. Witchcraft accusations were local affairs, and most people lived in religiously homogenous communities. As general propaganda, witchcraft theory could be deployed by religious authorities against opposing confessions. Catholic and Protestant leaders certainly did accuse each other of being in league with Satan, and charges of witchcraft but more so of promoting superstition flew back and forth between religious camps. Yet this polemic had little effect on how accusations were brought forward, and even religious officials tended to focus their concerns about witchcraft within their own communities rather than against other groups. For all that witches were typically marginal members of a community, they were rarely complete outsiders. Rather than an obvious threat from outside, witchcraft was the ultimate manifestation of the secret enemy within. Jews, for example, long associated in Christian minds with superstition and harmful magic, rarely figured in witch trials.

The animosity and religious hatred that the Reformation engendered between Christian confessions did not produce witch hunts. These energies were channeled into a long series of incredibly violent religious wars. Nevertheless, the Reformation surely did promote witch hunting by initiating an age of intense religious confessionalism in Europe. Confessionalism emerged not in the earliest days of the Reformation, when Luther and other Protestant leaders were convinced that they could supplant the Catholic Church, and Catholics were convinced that they could eradicate upstart Protestantism. Rather, it developed with the second generation of reform, when significant Protestant churches were clearly established in various regions of Europe, and the Catholic Church was redefining itself, in response to Protestant challenges, via the Council of Trent (convened in 1545 and meeting sporadically until 1563). While religious wars focused on external enemies, confessionalism directed its energies inward. Clergy worked diligently to instruct the faithful of their particular confession about the nature of proper religious belief and practice. Preachers railed against superstition and exhorted people to be increasingly vigilant about maintaining proper morality and religious zeal, both in their own lives and within their communities. In these efforts, diabolical witchcraft served as an image of dangerous religious deviance.

Confessionalism was in full force in Europe by 1560, when the resurgence of witch hunting also began. The next hundred years saw the most intense witch hunting, at least in central and western Europe (a later surge of trials in eastern Europe will be discussed in the next section). The absolute height of the hunts came in the fifty-year period from 1580 to 1630. Fully 90 percent of executions for witchcraft in German lands, which were the heartland of European witch hunting, occurred in these few decades. Publication of treatises on witchcraft also resumed, and, while these were by no means the sole medium for propagating concern over witches, their frequency provides a useful gauge. After being reprinted last in 1520, *Malleus maleficarum* was issued again in 1576. Already in 1572, however, the Calvinist minister and theologian Lambert Daneau (1530–1590) had written *Les sorciers* (The Witches). In 1580 Jean Bodin (1529/30–1596) published his *De la démonomanie des sorciers* (On the Demon-mania of Witches), which quickly surpassed the *Malleus* as the preeminent source on witchcraft for Catholic authorities. In 1589 the suffragan bishop of Trier, Peter Binsfeld (ca. 1540–1603), published *De confessionibus maleficorum et sagarum* (On the Confessions of Witches), based on a major series of trials in Trier. In 1595 the magistrate Nicholas Rémy (1530–1612) issued his *Daemonolatreiae* (Demonolatry), drawing on his extensive experience with witch trials in the Duchy of Lorraine. In 1598 the Scottish king James VI (reigned 1567–1625, also as James I of England, 1603–1625) wrote *Daemonologie* (Demonology) after he too had some direct experience with witch trials. In 1599 and 1600 the Jesuit Martin Del Rio (1551–1608) published his massive, multivolume *Disquisitiones magicae* (Investigations into Magic—see figure 5.3). Henri Boguet (ca. 1550–1619), a magistrate in Franche-Comte who personally executed many witches, published his *Discours des sorciers* (Discourse on Witches) in 1602.

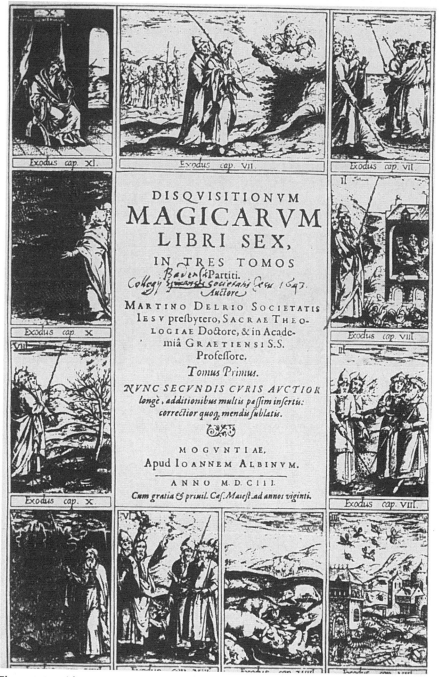

Figure 5.3 Title page of Martin Del Rio's *Disquisitiones magicae* (1599–1600).

In 1608 an Italian friar without any firsthand experience of witch trials, Francesco Maria Guazzo (dates unknown), wrote a *Compendium maleficarum* (Handbook of Witches), while the French judge Pierre de Lancre (1553–1631), with significant firsthand experience, wrote a *Tableau de l'inconstance de mauvais anges et demons* (Description of the Inconstancy of Evil Angels and Demons) in 1612. And these represent only the major treatises on witchcraft from this period.

Perhaps the most ominous publication was a mere pamphlet from 1563, *Warhafftige und Erschreckhenliche Thatten der 63 Hexen* (True and Horrifying Deeds of Sixty-Three Witches), recounting a group of executions at Wiesensteig, a small principality of around 5,000 inhabitants in the highly fragmented southwestern region of the German Empire. This pamphlet described the first major hunt in what would become the region of most intense witch-hunting activity in Europe. That same year, the English Parliament passed a new act making witchcraft a capital crime, and similarly harsh legislation was also approved in Scotland. Within only a few years, in 1566, Protestant England had its first known witch trial, although hardly a major hunt as had occurred in Wiesensteig. At Chelmsford, in the southeast of England, three women were accused and one was ultimately executed. In 1590 and 1591 Scottish officials in Edinburgh put on trial the North Berwick witches, so called because they supposedly gathered at regular sabbaths at North Berwick, some twenty-five miles east of the capital. The trials are particularly famous because these witches were accused of plotting to murder King James VI by raising storms while he journeyed across the North Sea. James observed portions of the trials, and they may have inspired the interest in witchcraft that led him to write his *Daemonologie*.

On the continent, numerous trials began in Lorraine in the 1570s, including some conducted by Nicolas Rémy, who claimed in his *Daemonolatreiae* to have personally condemned between 800 and 900 witches. This was no doubt a significant exaggeration, but still, from 1580 until 1620, local authorities executed close to 2,000 people in this duchy, giving Lorraine one of the largest known total numbers of witchcraft executions in Europe. Beginning in 1609, French and Spanish authorities conducted rather different hunts in the Basque lands on both sides of the Pyrenees. On the French side, the presiding judge again claimed hundreds of executions, although the actual known number was twenty-three. The Spanish prosecutions took a quite different course that will be discussed in the next section of this chapter. Between 1645 and 1646, the self-proclaimed "Witch-Finder General" Matthew Hopkins (died 1647) conducted the largest hunt on English soil in the regions of Essex and Sussex, in which nearly 250 people were tried and at least a hundred were executed, while the "great Scottish witch hunt," actually a series of trials held in various regions of that country, took place in 1661 and 1662, and totaled more than 300 victims.

The most terrible hunts, however, were those conducted by a handful of German bishops and prince-bishops. In the territory of Trier over 300 people were executed in the 1580s and 1590s. In Mainz, major hunts with victims running into the hundreds erupted every decade from the 1590s through the 1620s. From these Rhineland archbishoprics, witch hunting spread east along the Main River to the Franconian bishoprics of Bamberg and Würzburg, each of which experienced major hunts in the 1610s and 1620s, as did the Bavarian bishopric of Eichstätt along with the associated territory of the abbey of Ellwangen. The absolute worst hunt took place in the Rhineland in the territory of Cologne, the third of the great German archbishoprics. Here highly organized and efficient trials from about 1624 until 1634 resulted in the deaths of probably around 2,000 people. Among other major German hunts, only those in Mainz came close to matching this number, with clusters of trials spread out over a significantly longer period. All told, these German "superhunts" (as they have been called by the historian Wolfgang Behringer) accounted for almost a quarter of all executions for witchcraft in Europe in the century from 1560 until 1660.

Yet such gigantic hunts, claiming hundreds or even thousands of victims, were abnormalities. Most witch trials resulted in a handful of executions, usually of people implicated in the initial accusation. Even when a trial grew into a true hunt, with accusations feeding upon themselves and each new accused witch implicating several others, the process almost never escalated to claim hundreds of lives. Given the natural mechanisms by which a hunt could intensify—"guilty" witches naming others, and the potential use of torture to wring confessions from the accused—the fact that in most cases this destructive escalation did not occur, or at least was contained, is perhaps one of the most surprising aspects of the history of early modern witchcraft. To explain why something did not happen is a difficult task for historians, yet some reasons seem clear. Despite widespread notions of satanic cults and diabolical conspiracies, most accusations of witchcraft were rooted in specific cases of perceived harm believed to be wrought through *maleficium*. Thus the initial accusation was usually all that concerned the accuser, and clearly, given the number of trials that remained tightly contained, this was often all that concerned authorities as well. Once the malefactor or malefactors responsible for the supposed harmful magic were discovered, found guilty, and punished, justice was served, and the community could return to normal.

When trials escalated into major hunts, feeding on their own energies, the situation was different. Inspired by the initial trial, other people might come forward to make unrelated accusations, magistrates might become convinced that more witches were hiding in the community and press their own investigations, and of course accused witches themselves were pressed to name names. Yet even in these cases, a hunt might well end of its own accord after a certain number of trials and executions. Officials, comforted that they had uprooted evil from their region, might stop pursuing their investigations. The community as a whole, after an initial fearful wave, might grow calmer, and so accusations would subside. In other cases, of course, this happy release of tension did not occur. Instead, as accusations and convictions mounted, fear grew, paranoia might seize courts, and real panic might grip the entire community. In these situations, accusations multiplied and grew more indiscriminate. That is, people who did not conform to the stereotypical image of a witch were accused and arrested. This was certainly the case in Bamberg when the wealthy, socially respected (and, of course, male) *Bürgermeister* Johannes Junius was found guilty of witchcraft in 1628.

Yet even in severe cases, an end would come. Local authorities would eventually experience what has been termed a crisis of confidence.[3] Perhaps because of the convictions of socially respectable persons, perhaps from the sheer number of convictions mounting up, or perhaps most often because some more skeptical superior court had rebuked their decisions, they would acknowledge that the process of the trials had become corrupted and that they were, in fact, executing innocent people. If local officials did not put an end to their own hunts, outside authorities might step in. A classic example is that of the Salem hunt in colonial Massachusetts in 1692. For months, accusations mounted in Salem and spread through the colony with no sign of letup. The colonial governor finally intervened, however, when his wife was accused, and the seemingly out-of-control trials came to a screeching halt. Even more dramatically, officials of the German emperor terminated a hunt in the county of Vaduz in the eastern Alps that had lasted from 1678 to 1680. The territorial prince, Count Ferdinand Karl Franz von Hohenems, was stripped of his title and imprisoned soon thereafter. Following his death, his brother sold the rights to Vaduz and other territories to the House of Liechtenstein, forming the basis of the tiny state that still bears that name.

The reasons that a particular hunt might spiral out of control while another group of trials could remain perfectly contained can be addressed only in terms of specific situations, but some attempt can be made to explain the overall number of trials, especially in the century from 1560 to 1660. Legal developments that allowed for effective prosecutions had already converged with the developing notion of conspiratorial, diabolical witchcraft in the fifteenth century to produce the first real hunts. After a lull in the early sixteenth century, the forces of confessionalism worked to promote concern over religious and social deviance, exactly the sort of violations that witchcraft was seen to encompass. However, scholars have also advanced another compelling reason for the surge of trials after 1560.[4] Beginning around that time, and lasting for a century, Europe underwent a "little ice age." Climactic change was not dramatic—Europe suffered no widespread calamity—but conditions did deteriorate. In particular, harsher winters and wetter summers produced a greater number of localized crop failures, outbreaks of disease, and other hardships. People in early modern Europe were accustomed to such events, but they also seem to have had a fairly well-attuned sense of how often they should expect them. *Maleficium* was the explanation not for all misfortune, but for seemingly excessive misfortune, and all indications are that many Europeans were experiencing more misfortune more often during the crucial century from 1560 until 1660. Thus witch trials may have peaked during this period simply because more people were accusing their neighbors of *maleficium* at this time.

The Geography of Witchcraft

Many of the basic notions of witchcraft and operations of witch hunting described in the previous sections were common across much of Europe. Certainly, fear of the real power of *maleficium* was almost universal. Nevertheless, the legal prosecution of witchcraft and scope of witch hunting varied dramatically from region to region. As already indicated, the German-speaking regions of central Europe were clearly the heartland of witch hunting. Around half of all the executions in Europe occurred here, approximately 20,000–25,000 just in the lands of present-day Germany. These numbers swell by as many as 10,000 if other lands lying within the early modern boundaries of the German Empire (not all of them German-speaking) are included—Alsace, Lorraine, the Low Countries, parts of Switzerland, and others. The situation is even more severe when just the century from 1560 to 1660 is considered. The historian William Monter has estimated that during this period "Germany" in the wider sense absolutely dominated European witch hunting, with as many as three quarters of all witches executed being German speakers, and perhaps as many as six out of every seven dead coming from within the pre-1648 borders of the German Empire.[5]

To categorize "Germany," or even the German Empire, as the zone of witch hunting par excellence is, however, somewhat misleading. Although technically united under an emperor, at no point in this period was the empire a unified political entity. Rather, it was a patchwork of 82 principalities, 140 independent lordships, 75 imperial free cities, and hundreds of other tiny jurisdictions. Some of these jurisdictions executed hundreds or even thousands of witches; others, including some of the largest German states, executed few or none. The key difference seems to have been between smaller jurisdictions, where local courts had more autonomy or where the highest judicial authority remained essentially local, and larger states with strong systems of centralized governmental control over legal procedures. The former were far more likely to conduct major hunts than were the latter. Thus within the boundaries of the empire, the fragmented west, and especially the corridor stretching from the southern Low Countries along the Rhine to Switzerland, saw the most trials and the greatest hunts. The larger, more centralized German states to the east, as well as the Rhineland-Palatinate in the west, executed far fewer witches despite their much larger populations.

The situation in the Low Countries was exceptionally complex. The territories comprising present-day Belgium and the Netherlands initially lay within the German Empire, but in 1555, Emperor Charles V, who was also King Charles I of Spain, gave them to his son Philip II of Spain (reigned 1556–1598). Philip did not, however, succeed his father as emperor (that title going instead to Charles's brother Ferdinand I), so the Low Countries became Spanish rather than imperial territory. In the 1560s and 1570s these lands saw significant witch trials. Then in 1579, the northern provinces banded together as the United Provinces of the Netherlands, declaring their formal independence from Spain in 1581. These provinces also became predominantly Calvinist, while the southern Spanish Netherlands were Catholic. In 1592 Philip II issued a decree that extended the right to try witches to local authorities, and not surprisingly the number of trials in the south increased. In 1593, however, the highest court in the United Provinces effectively ended trials in Holland, the largest and most influential province, and other regions of the country soon followed suit. After 1610 there were almost no more witch trials in the north.

If patterns of witch hunting in the Low Countries were complex, no pattern whatsoever can be discerned for the region of Switzerland. This is because the Swiss Confederation was comprised of a bewildering array of independent cantons, territories, and jurisdictions that were, moreover, both religiously and linguistically heterogeneous. Some areas, such as German-speaking Basel or French-speaking Geneva, were wealthy and highly cosmopolitan. Others, such as those in the high Alps, were poor, rural backwaters. The lands of the western Alps had seen some of the first witch trials in the early fifteenth century, and the mountainous canton of Glarus saw Europe's last fully legal execution for witchcraft in 1782. The poor region of Vaud, ruled after 1536 by the city of Bern, executed close to 1,000 witches between 1580 and 1620, during the overall height of the European hunts. This is slightly less than half the number executed in the Duchy of Lorraine during these same years, but the Pays de Vaud had only one-third of Lorraine's population. On the other hand, the city of Geneva executed significantly less than 100 witches for the entire century from 1560 to 1660.

Unlike the German Empire, France had been a unified kingdom for centuries prior to the early modern period. It did not, however, have exactly the same boundaries as the modern French state. If we use present-day borders, then "France" had around 5,000 executions for witchcraft. But this figure shrinks dramatically if we exclude the eastern regions of Alsace, Lorraine, and Franche-Comte, which were French-speaking and had significant numbers of trials, but at this time nominally belonged to the German Empire and were in fact largely independent. Within its early modern borders, the Kingdom of France saw fewer than 500 recorded executions for witchcraft. Moreover, as in the German Empire, so within the Kingdom of France there were important regional variations. Most of the northern half of the kingdom was under the ultimate jurisdiction of the Parlement of Paris, a central court to which cases involving significant crimes, including witchcraft, could be appealed. The Parlement exercised considerable restraint in cases of witchcraft; of over 500 death sentences passed by lower courts and appealed to Paris, it executed barely 100 witches. Moreover, it grew increasingly cautious as time went on. In 1625 the Parlement expanded its control over lower courts by requiring that all cases involving witchcraft within its jurisdiction be appealed automatically to Paris. After this year, also, the Parlement passed no more death sentences for witchcraft (although as late as 1691 it did uphold death sentences for two shepherds accused of "so-called sorcery"). This marked the effective end of witchcraft as a capital crime, at least in those regions of France over which the Parlement of Paris had jurisdiction. In more outlying regions of the country, the situation could be quite different. Normandy, for example, had its own parlement, which upheld sentences for witchcraft at a much higher rate. While the region never saw a truly major hunt, witch trials and executions were endemic. Normandy was also one of the few regions in western and central Europe where the majority of accused witches, as many as three out of every four, were men.

One of the few major hunts to take place in France proper began in 1609 in the Pays de Labourd, a region with a primarily Basque population in the extreme southwest of the kingdom under the jurisdiction of the Parlement of Bordeaux. The hunt soon reached other Basque lands across the Pyrenees in Spain, and both sides of the Basque hunt present fascinating examples of the contrast between essentially local and more centralized judicial control. On the French side, the chief magistrate was Pierre de Lancre, who also wrote a treatise based on the trials he conducted. Although an outsider sent to the Pays de Labourd by the French king Henry IV, de Lancre quickly lost the caution that characterized his colleagues in Bordeaux, who seem to have followed the example of that city's favorite son, the humanist and witchcraft skeptic Michel de Montaigne (1533–1592). Instead, de Lancre became caught up in the intense local anxieties that were fueling the hunt. He was convinced that the region was rife with witches who would assemble, up to 2,000 at a time, at huge sabbaths. Deciding that virtually all the region's inhabitants were tainted by witchcraft in some way, he abandoned normal judicial procedures, accepting testimony from children, for example, which was legally inadmissible. In just four months in 1609, he executed at least twenty-three people before officials at Bordeaux released his remaining prisoners and apparently he executed no more witches thereafter. Frustrated by this professional snubbing, de Lancre took up the pen, authoring several demonological works over the next two decades. The Basque hunt represents the largest single cluster of legal executions ever recorded in France—the largest French hunt overall took place in Languedoc from 1643 to 1645, but executions were more spread out and many deaths resulted from illegal lynching directed by unofficial witch finders.

Refugees from de Lancre's hunt in the French areas of the Basque lands directly triggered the hunt that also developed in 1609 on the Spanish side of the Pyrenees. The first witch accused in these proceedings was a Basque woman who had spent several years in France and claimed to have become a witch there. She attracted the attention of local authorities and ultimately of the local tribunal of the Spanish Inquisition based in Logroño. An investigation begun in 1609 resulted in six executions in November 1610. Two of the tribunal's judges wanted to expand the hunt, but the third, Alonso de Salazar Frias (1564–1635), was far more skeptical, and his doubts were clearly shared by the *Suprema*, the central council of the Inquisition in Madrid. At the order of the *Suprema*, Salazar Frias alone undertook a careful investigation from 1611 to 1612 not so much of cases of witchcraft as of the procedures that local officials had used in their investigations and to obtain confessions. He composed a long report, stating that in his judgment there was no clear evidence of any witchcraft in the region. In 1614 the *Suprema* issued a letter to the Logroño tribunal ordering it to be more cautious when investigating cases of witchcraft and above all to adhere carefully to proper procedure in gathering evidence and applying torture. In 1623 the *Suprema* ordered all inquisitorial courts to adhere to these principles, and when witch trials were conducted under such centrally imposed restraints, they rarely resulted in convictions.

Throughout the major period of early modern witch hunting, in fact, convictions for witchcraft in both Spain and Italy remained remarkably low, largely due to the presence of standing inquisitions. This fact may seem initially surprising, given that in the late medieval period, ecclesiastical inquisitors had been instrumental in the development and spread of the idea of diabolical witchcraft, and also in the conduct of many early witch trials. Medieval inquisitors, however, were essentially autonomous figures, usually operating in close cooperation with local authorities, and they could easily be drawn into webs of local anxieties about witchcraft. The Spanish Inquisition, founded as an agency of the Spanish monarchy in 1478; the Roman Inquisition, established by the papacy in 1542 and having jurisdiction over many inquisitorial courts in Italy; and other standing inquisitions, such as those in Portugal or Venice, were permanent, highly centralized institutions. They imposed the same restraints on witch hunting as did the Parlement of Paris or other secular centralized judicial bodies—basic skepticism about many accusations, careful consideration of evidence, restraint in the use of torture, and above all, remoteness from local atmospheres of panic that could allow judicial proceedings to run amok.

The numbers in Mediterranean lands tell a remarkable story. Basic belief in magic was as widespread as anywhere else in Europe, as was fear of *maleficium*. Thus accusations and trials were common enough. In the critical century from 1560 to 1660, for example, the Spanish Inquisition tried close to 4,000 cases that involved witchcraft or some other type of magic, often love magic, which seems to have been more common in southern than in northern Europe. In Italy, the number of trials was probably significantly higher. Yet, for the entire period after 1526, when certain new guidelines were enacted, the Spanish Inquisition executed only about twenty-five people for witchcraft. After 1610, both the Spanish and Roman Inquisitions stopped executing witches altogether. The Portuguese and Venetian Inquisitions exercised similar restraint. Of course local secular courts outside the control of the inquisitions could and did still conduct witch trials and execute people for witchcraft. Yet all told, Spain saw only around 300 executions. Portugal had only about ten. Despite the presence of the centralized Roman and other inquisitions in the sixteenth and seventeenth centuries, Italy was politically fragmented throughout the early modern period. Moreover, a large number of the earliest witch trials from the fifteenth century had taken place in Italy. Thus the Italian peninsula saw significantly more executions than the Iberian, ultimately over 2,000. Still, one should note that a region the size of Italy executed over the course of centuries only slightly more witches than were killed in the small territory of Cologne in only a few years.

The British Isles executed even fewer witches than did Italy, although they also had barely half of Italy's population in this period. England and Scotland together put to death perhaps as few as 1,500 people for witchcraft. Ireland, with a total of four known witchcraft executions, figures in these numbers not at all. No thorough study exists of the lack of Irish witch hunting. In a land replete with magical beliefs, people surely accepted and feared the power of *maleficium*. One plausible explanation, however, is that the Irish resisted accusing their neighbors of this crime in the English-controlled courts. In England itself, many studies have stressed that the full conception of diabolical witchcraft never gained as much acceptance as in the continental heartland of witch hunting. That is, in England the crime of witchcraft remained more focused on simple *maleficium*, rather than on diabolism, sabbaths, and so forth. Many English accounts of witchcraft avoid descriptions of elaborate sabbaths. However, English records reveal a greater concern about witches possessing demonic familiars—demons bound to the witch, often taking the form of a small animal the witch would keep as a pet. Thus the English too certainly considered witchcraft to have its diabolical aspects.

In terms of limiting trials, far more important than the general concept of witchcraft under which the English operated was the kingdom's strongly centralized judicial system. Most cases were heard by royal circuit judges rather than purely local magistrates, and, very importantly, the use of torture was extremely limited in English courts, permitted only by the direct command of the Royal Privy Council. Trials could still occur, and even one major hunt. In 1645 and 1646 Matthew Hopkins put to death at least 100 people in the southeastern counties of Essex and Sussex. Hopkins, however, was a clearly deranged personality. Although he claimed to have been appointed by Parliament as the nation's "Witch Finder General," he in fact held no official position, instead looking to local communities to pay him for his services. He and his henchmen would then set out to find witches, freely (and illegally) employing torture to make them confess. Although he enjoyed a brief period of success, thanks mainly to the temporary breakdown of centralized legal structures that accompanied the English Civil War (1642–1649), his extreme methods soon aroused opposition. Due to this, and perhaps owing also to illness, he retired from witch hunting and died within a year, but not before publishing a pamphlet defending his methods. This aberrant episode represents the only truly major hunt ever to take place in England.

Scotland experienced significantly more intense witch hunting than did England. By fairly conservative estimates, Scotland saw three times as many executions among a population only one quarter the size of England's. Ideas of sabbaths and other elements of continental demonology seem to have been somewhat more present in Scottish than in English cases of witchcraft. Nevertheless, again the main factor affecting the scale of the prosecutions was the judicial structure under which trials were carried out. Like England, Scotland had a centralized system of royal circuit judges, but its system was less extensive. Many trials were conducted by local magistrates, with far higher rates of conviction and execution than in cases heard by Scottish circuit judges or in the central royal Court of Justiciary in Edinburgh. Another important aspect of the lower degree of centralized judicial control in Scotland was that restrictions on employing torture were less effectively maintained than in England.

Of course, Scotland also has the distinction of having been ruled by the monarch most closely associated with witchcraft and witch hunting, James VI. In 1590 and 1591 James observed the trial of a group of witches accused of attempting to kill him. In 1597 he wrote his *Daemonologie*, a work mostly derivative of continental treatises on witchcraft. After he succeeded Elizabeth I to the throne of England in 1603, he immediately ordered copies of Reginald Scot's skeptical *Discoverie of Witchcraft* burned throughout England, and in 1604 the English Parliament passed harsh new legislation against witchcraft. Nevertheless, neither in England nor in Scotland was witch hunting particularly more severe during James's reign than at other times. James did preside over the first of Scotland's two major periods of witch hunting, from 1590 to 1597, inaugurated by the trials of the North Berwick witches in which he had taken part. In 1597, however, the same year in which he completed his *Daemonologie*, James acted to restrict witch hunting, which he felt was beginning to escape centralized royal control. A second and even more intense period of trials, the so called "great Scottish witch hunt," produced over 300 executions in 1661 and 1662, but this occurred well after James's reign.

Shortly after the major Scottish hunts died down, the largest hunt in Scandinavian lands began. Given the small size of their populations, Scandinavian countries executed a significant number of witches. Denmark, with a population barely larger than Scotland, executed around 1,000 witches. Some 350 people were also put to death in Danish-ruled Norway, more than in the whole of Spain, which had over twelve times Norway's population. Over 400 witches were executed in Sweden and Swedish controlled Finland. Yet more than half of these executions occurred very late, in a wave of trials that spiraled out from a hunt in the northern Swedish parish of Mora. Beginning in 1668, several children began making accusations that women in the community were kidnapping them and transporting them to sabbaths held on the mythical mountain of Blåkulla. Authorities began to investigate in earnest the following year, and ultimately over twenty people were executed, often on the testimony of the hundreds of children who came forward with tales of being kidnapped. From Mora, accusations and trials spread out across Sweden and into Swedish areas of Finland, lasting until the mid-1670s and resulting in between 200 and 300 deaths.

The only major hunt in any European colonial territory in the Americas, the 1692 trials in Salem, Massachusetts, was also driven largely by the accusations of children. These trials, in which hundreds of people were accused and imprisoned, and twenty were directly killed (nineteen by execution and one dying under torture while refusing to plead to the charges against him), cast a long shadow, but in fact they represent one of the most aberrant hunts in the history of European witchcraft. In general, executions for witchcraft were almost nonexistent in European overseas colonies during the early modern period, and although several hundred trials did occur, they were rare. Only in British North America were witches tried in any real number, primarily in New England, where fervent Puritan religiosity and practical autonomy from centralized English control (especially in the crucial year of 1692) created an atmosphere in which accusations and trials could flourish. All told, there were under 400 accusations, slightly over 100 trials, and fewer than 40 executions in New England, which by the time of the Salem hunt had a population of nearly 100,000 people. This means that New England executed around twice as many people for witchcraft per capita as did England and Scotland. On the other hand, per capita execution rates in the central European heartland of witch hunting could be five to ten times as high as in New England. Moreover, in each category (accusations, trials, and executions), Salem accounts for over half of the New England totals, and the severity of this hunt produced such a backlash that no further legal executions for witchcraft were ever conducted in New England.

Even as witch hunting was ending in western Europe and its colonies, it was reaching its peak in eastern Europe. Poland, bordering on the German heartland of witch hunting, clearly imported much of its concern over witchcraft, which appeared first in the west of the country, in regions with large German urban populations and close connections to German lands. Significant witch hunting developed only in the late seventeenth century, however, and accelerated in the early eighteenth. There are several reasons for this late peak. In 1543 a royal edict placed witch trials in Poland entirely under the jurisdiction of ecclesiastical courts, which actually tended to be less severe in their prosecution of witchcraft than were secular courts. Although centralized royal control was weak in Poland, this edict was largely obeyed, and secular courts rarely conducted witch trials until the second half of the seventeenth century. Perhaps more significantly, throughout most of the Reformation period, Poland remained remarkably tolerant and avoided the excessive zeal of religious confessionalism. After 1648, however, Poland was aggressively re-Catholicized, and thus experienced all the tensions about maintaining proper religiosity and community morality that had fed earlier concerns over witchcraft in more western lands. Finally, from 1655 to 1660, war between Sweden and Russia ravaged much of Poland. As elsewhere, such devastation did not lead directly to rising accusations of witchcraft but created long-term social stresses that began to manifest in witch trials after the immediate calamity had passed.

Ultimately, although exact figures will probably never be known, Poland saw several thousand executions for witchcraft. Hungary, with a population almost as large, saw fewer than one thousand. As in Poland, however, the major waves of Hungarian witch hunting came late, developing only in the later seventeenth century, following the expulsion of the Turks and reassertion of Christian rule over most of the kingdom, and peaking in the 1710s and 1720s. Significant numbers of trials continued until Empress Maria Theresa (reigned 1740–1780) began to restrict them in the 1750s and virtually ended executions for this crime in 1768. Further east, Russia had as long a tradition of executing people for performing harmful magic as any European state. In fact, during the medieval period, the number of Russian executions for harmful sorcery was significant enough to arouse comment from western travelers in Russian lands. Ideas of witchcraft and witch hunting did not develop in Russia as they did in the rest of Europe, however, largely because of religious differences. Orthodox Russia never accepted the same image of diabolical witchcraft that developed in the West, and of course Russia did not experience the religious convulsions of the Reformation and ensuing confessionalism, although sectarian Old Believers who sought to preserve traditional forms of Orthodox religion appeared in the later seventeenth century. In the mid-sixteenth century, the tsar reclassified harmful sorcery as a crime for secular courts. Numbers of trials seem to have increased into the seventeenth century and lasted well into the eighteenth. Still, Russia experienced probably only a few hundred legal executions for witchcraft in the course of its history.

Skepticism and Decline

The wide variation in the intensity and nature of witch trials across Europe invalidates the notion of a generalized "witch hunt" that characterized the entire continent throughout these centuries. Moreover, the very notion of diabolical, conspiratorial witchcraft that underlay the hunts never went unchallenged at any point in this period. *Malleus maleficarum*, written in 1486, began with the declaration that anyone who denied the existence of witches or the reality of witchcraft as the *Malleus* presented it was guilty of heresy, a clear indication that such denials existed or at least were anticipated by proponents of witch hunting. As noted above, several humanist authors in the early sixteenth century doubted not so much the potential reality of witchcraft as the fact that the many poor old women being convicted of this crime in the courts were really participants in a powerful demonic conspiracy. The scholar Heinrich Cornelius Agrippa, himself a practitioner of learned magic, actually defended one such woman.

In 1563, the same year in which the pamphlet describing the execution of sixty-three witches at Wiesensteig was published, marking the beginning of the major period of witch hunting in German lands, Johann Weyer (1515–1588) published his *De praestigiis daemonum* (On the Deceptions of Demons). Weyer, a Dutch physician and scholar, and an erstwhile student of Agrippa, wrote not only the first major skeptical treatises against witchcraft but one of the most thorough attacks not just on witch hunting but on some of the basic ideas that supported it. As earlier skeptics, Weyer argued that many trials were deeply flawed and produced false convictions, but he went further to argue that many of the crimes attributed to witches were in fact impossible. He did not deny the power of demons, but he limited their power in the physical world and maintained that they could never be compelled by humans to perform the magical acts attributed to witches. Against the notion of the pact supposedly made between witches and the devil, Weyer advanced a legal argument that valid contracts required good faith (*bona fides*) on the part of both parties, and obviously, since the devil was incapable of acting in good faith, he was incapable of forming any valid contract. To explain the number of people, particularly old women, who believed themselves to be witches, or at least acquiesced when accusations were made against them, Weyer, the physician, suggested that they were deluded or simply senile.

An even more extreme attack on witchcraft was made by Reginald Scot (1538–1599), a university-educated English gentleman influenced by Weyer, in his *Discoverie of Witchcraft*, published in 1584. The most radical skeptical author until Balthasar Bekker over a century later, Scot denied that the devil or demons had any power in the physical world. All supposed *maleficium* could be explained by natural causes, and those witches who confessed to having magical powers did so only under torture or the threat of torture, or because they themselves were deluded. Some supposed witches might cause real harm, but they did so through the use of poisons or similar natural means. Other people claimed to have magical power, and might even perform tricks to fool the credulous into believing that they did, only for their own gain. Another skeptic, the Dutch scholar and Catholic priest Cornelius Loos (1546–1593), was also inspired by Weyer. Teaching in Trier during the major hunt there, he was commissioned by the driving force behind those trials, Bishop Peter Binsfeld, to compose a refutation of Weyer and a defense of witch hunting. Instead, Loos became convinced that Weyer was correct and, inspired by the injustice of the trials taking place around him, he produced the skeptical pamphlet *De vera et falsa magia* (On True and False Magic) in 1592. Imprisoned for the heresy of denying witchcraft, he was forced to recant his statements and was banished to Brussels, but he refused to remain silent for long and so was again arrested, dying in prison in 1593.

Like Loos, another important Catholic critic of witch trials who was directly inspired by the horrors of a major witch hunt was the German Jesuit Friedrich Spee (1591–1635). Beginning in 1627, Spee taught theology in Würzburg, then experiencing one of the greatest hunts in German lands, as was nearby Bamberg. Spee was appointed to hear the confessions of many of the accused in prison. He quickly realized that most of these people were entirely innocent, and in 1631 he anonymously published *Cautio criminalis* (A Warning on Criminal Justice). Beginning by accepting the position that witchcraft was real and that witches really existed and deserved punishment, he then proceeded to make the most extensive critique of the unjust, excessive, and often illegal procedures used in witch trials produced in early modern Europe. Systematically demolishing every means by which prosecutors obtained convictions, particularly the uncontrolled use of torture, Spee left little doubt that, while witchcraft might be real, hardly anyone who confessed to being a witch actually was one. Because his skepticism was more narrowly focused on the mechanism of trials, rather than on the essential notion of witchcraft, Spee's critique proved more widely acceptable and influential than Weyer's or Scot's. Within a few years, *Cautio criminalis* had been translated into several languages and was being read in both Catholic and Protestant lands.

By the end of the seventeenth century, Europe, or at least the leading circles of European thought, were ready for a broader skepticism of the type Weyer and Scot and prematurely promulgated. In the early 1690s, the Dutch clergyman Balthasar Bekker (1634–1698) published *De Betoverde Weereld* (The Enchanted World) in four volumes, which were soon translated into German, English, and French. A rationalist thinker following the model of René Descartes (1596–1650), who had argued for a sharp separation between the physical and spiritual worlds, Bekker denied the ability of demons to affect the physical world in any way, and thus eliminated the basis for any belief in the reality of witchcraft. A decade later, in *De crimine magiae* (On the Crime of Magic) of 1701, the Prussian legal scholar Christian Thomasius (1655–1728) also drew on Cartesian rationalism to argue that demons had no power over the physical world. He followed in the tradition of Spee as well (whose anonymous work he mistakenly believed to have been written by a Protestant), harshly criticizing the methods employed in witch trials.

By the time of Bekker and Thomasius, however, while some sporadic trials persisted, serious witch hunting was a thing of the past, at least for western Europe. A curious fact in the history of witchcraft is that trials tended to decline well in advance of any official legal changes. For example, in France, the Parlement of Paris did not execute anyone for witchcraft after 1625. Not until 1682, however, did Louis XIV (reigned 1643–1715) effectively eliminate witchcraft as a crime in France, at least as it had long been understood (no known French royal edict had ever officially criminalized witchcraft in a specific form). In England, witch trials largely petered out during the reign of Charles I (reigned 1625–1649), but the 1604 statute under which the crime was prosecuted was not officially repealed until 1736. The Spanish and Roman Inquisitions had not executed anyone for witchcraft since 1610, although this did not mean that all trials or even convictions ceased at that time. In Italy, trials gradually tapered off in the second half of the seventeenth century. In Spain, the Inquisition heard the case of a woman accused of witchcraft, including satanic pacts and attendance at sabbaths, as late as 1791, although this was by then an anomaly.

The situation in central Europe was complicated by the political and legal disunity of the German Empire. Various jurisdictions ceased to hunt witches at various times. The last major series of trials in German lands was the so-called Zaubererjackl (Sorcerer-Jack) trials in the territory of Salzburg from 1678 to 1680, which resulted in around 150 executions. These late trials were hardly typical of usual German patterns, however. They focused not on old women but on young beggar boys, putative followers of "Sorcerer-Jack," a beggar named Jacob (Jackl) Koller (born 1655) who was never captured and became a semimythic figure, supposedly teaching young boys to use sorcery against those who did not support their begging. The figure of Sorcerer-Jack continued to be invoked in trials in the region into the eighteenth century. Throughout German lands, smaller-scale trials continued intermittently throughout the 1700s but steadily declined. The last fully legal execution for witchcraft in German-speaking lands, and in Europe as a whole, was that of Anna Göldi in the Swiss canton of Glarus in 1782. In 1793 two women were executed in Posen, which at that time was passing from Polish into Prussian control. While this execution was carried out by a local court, evidence seems clear that if either Polish or Prussian authorities had been in full control of the region at the time, the death sentence would not have been allowed to stand.

The end of witch hunting came in two distinct phases, which can be tied to two types of skepticism. First, authorities became concerned about the means by which trials were conducted and the validity of the convictions obtained. Such skepticism had been evident from the early sixteenth century and achieved its fullest expression with Friedrich Spee in the early seventeenth, although already by Spee's time the Spanish and Roman Inquisitions had issued strict procedural controls for witch trials and the Parlement of Paris was deterring witch hunting in France. Later, acting on a more fully developed skepticism that had been present since the late sixteenth century but was only widely accepted in the later seventeenth, authorities began to modify or repeal the legislation against witchcraft. Such repeals were aimed not so much at ending witch trials, which had largely ceased already in most regions, but at denying the reality of the crime of witchcraft as it had long been conceived. In 1682, for example, in the wake of the so-called "Affair of the Poisons" that rocked the French court, Louis XIV issued a decree substantially altering the nature of magical crime in France. Actual poisoning, long associated with witchcraft, remained a capital crime, but henceforth French authorities were to regard (and punish) purely magical rites as superstitious and sacrilegious acts, but not as means to cause real physical harm. Hence two death sentences upheld by the Parlement of Paris in 1691 were for "so-called sorcery." Similarly, the English act of Parliament in 1736 that repealed the old witchcraft statute of 1604 established new penalties for those who continued to claim or pretend that they had real and effective magical powers, a possibility which the government now officially refused to allow.

After 1736, officials in the English government and church were effectively enjoined against expressing any credence in the now superstitious belief in witchcraft. Needless to say, widespread belief in witchcraft and other forms of magic did not vanish in England in this year, not in France in 1682, nor anywhere else in Europe as witch hunting came to an end. In some areas, other beliefs that might explain unexpected death or misfortune arose or took on renewed strength. For example, in the Hungarian region of Transylvania, belief in vampires may well have taken on new life even as central authorities became increasingly skeptical about witchcraft. Debates about vampires circulated around the Habsburg court in Vienna and may have influenced Maria Theresa's mid-eighteenth-century legislation effectively ending witch trials. Mostly, though, belief in witchcraft and magic simply endured, and continued to be expressed in local communities as it always had been. For despite all the sound and fury attached to the great witch hunts of Europe, witch hunts and witch trials were never the way most common people dealt with witchcraft.

The Scale and Significance of the Witch Hunts

No single aspect of the history of witchcraft and the period of the witch hunts has attracted as much attention as the possible total numbers of the dead. From various corners, and usually for various polemical reasons, wild figures are sometimes hurled—hundreds of thousands, as many as nine million dead; a concerted attempt to wipe out all unruly women from Europe. Precise numbers are of course impossible to attain. Even in the best-documented regions, records have been lost, and for many regions all we have are a few reports and then well-informed guesswork. Nevertheless, thanks to the careful work of many scholars studying many regions, reliable and widely accepted approximations have been achieved.[6] Such numbers have been given for many regions and specific hunts discussed above. Now is the time for totals, and the total number of those legally executed for witchcraft across Europe during three centuries of major witch hunting activity was probably between 40,000 and 50,000. So many lives taken, and tens of thousands more ruined by lesser punishments or simply by the horrors of the trials themselves or the suspicion that clung to anyone once accused, are by no means inconsequential. Yet, spread out over so many lands and several hundred years, these executions hardly constitute the greatest catastrophe Europe ever endured. During the period of the greatest hunts, the violence of religious wars and deprivation that followed in their wake could claim as many victims in a single year.

To compare legal executions to the devastation of war is perhaps unfair (although some do elevate witch hunting to that level). A different equation might contrast a maximum of 50,000 executed witches with approximately 5,000 people executed for religious heresies in the early modern period. These figures are deceptive too, however, because heresy was not typically a capital offense. Most courts sought to convert rather than to simply combust those who held improper beliefs. In France, for example, even in the harshest courts, execution rates in heresy trials seem never to have risen much above 10 or 12 percent. By contrast, the overall execution rate for cases heard by the Parlement of Paris, which dealt with an assortment of serious crimes, stood at around 25 percent in the mid-sixteenth century. In some regions, cases of witchcraft also yielded around 25 percent execution rates, although in many regions the rate was considerably higher. The Pays de Vaud had the most dismal record, executing around 90 percent of accused witches over an extended number of years, and certainly many of the major hunts attained such execution rates for brief periods. Across Europe, the average was probably on the order of 50 percent of all witch trials resulting in executions. With so much variation in witch hunting procedures, the idea of an "average" witch trial is largely meaningless. Still, these general figures indicate that, with the exception of truly massive hunts that could erupt to claim hundreds or even thousands of victims, witch trials were not some incomprehensible anomaly within early modern society. Rather, they represent the severe reaction of a harsh age to what was widely considered to be a very real and very serious crime.

Given the violent nature of early modern justice (in many jurisdictions, scores of crimes could receive capital punishment) and the magnitude of the supposed crimes entailed in witchcraft, the severity of legal response to accu-

sations is perhaps not surprising. More startling, given the presumed pervasiveness of witchcraft, is how few trials there were—probably under 100,000,
again for all of Europe and spread (very unevenly) over some three centuries.
Recent research has begun to highlight the fact that formal accusations
brought before legal courts were by no means the way that most Europeans
typically responded to witchcraft. Early modern people believed in magic,
they accepted the power of demons, and they certainly acknowledged the
harmful power of *maleficium*. Most people used magic themselves, simple
charms or incantations to protect and help them in their daily tasks, and so
they were perfectly ready to believe that some of their neighbors might wield
much greater power. The most typical response, however, was to try to pla-
cate, or simply to avoid, these dangerous individuals. Even when people felt
that they had been magically assaulted, the most common reaction seems to
have been to approach the witch herself and try to either importune or
coerce her to reverse her spell. Or people might turn instead to other magical
experts—magical healers or cunning folk—whose power could be expected
to overcome the bewitchment. Only rarely, and it seems usually as a last
resort, did people turn to legal authorities.

A telling feature of many trial records is the advanced age of accused
witches, along with testimony that they had been suspected or even known
to be witches for many years. Why, if people usually knew the witches in
their midst and believed in their terrible power, did they wait so long to bring
forward accusations? In the small, tightly knit communities in which cases
of witchcraft usually arose, formal accusations, let alone trials, could be
incredibly destructive. Intricate networks of family and friendship relations
that formed the very basis of society, which apparently could withstand the
fact that everyone in a given locale might "know" a certain person to be a
witch, would begin to dissolve once an actual accusation was made. This is
almost certainly why most accused witches were typically poor old women
who were either widows or never married. They were the people most lacking
in familial and community networks of support, from which retaliation—
above all in the form of credible counteraccusations—might be expected to
come. This basic social restraint on witch trials might seem gossamerlike, but
the fact remains that despite the universal belief in dangerous *maleficium*, the
existence of a legal system that readily accommodated witch hunting, and
secular and church authorities who actively encouraged people to identify
social and religious deviance in their midst, Europe did not erupt into a
wholly uncontrolled conflagration even during that period when witch trials
were at their most severe.

Notes

1. Translations from Junius's case here and below are from Alan Kors and Edward Peters, eds., *Witchcraft in Europe, 400–1700: A Documentary History*, 2nd ed. (Philadelphia: University of Pennsylvania Press, 2001), 349–53.

2. Carlo Ginzburg, *The Night Battles: Witchcraft and Agrarian Cults in the Sixteenth and Seventeenth Centuries*, trans. John and Anne Tedeschi (Baltimore: Johns Hopkins University Press, 1983).

3. H. C. Erik Midelfort, *Witch Hunting in Southwestern Germany 1562–1684: The Social and Intellectual Foundations* (Stanford, Calif.: Stanford University Press, 1972), 158. Brian P. Levack, *The Witch-Hunt in Early Modern Europe*, 3rd ed. (Harlow, England, and New York: Pearson Longman, 2006), 193, describes a "loss of confidence."

4. See, in particular, Wolfgang Behringer, "Weather, Hunger and Fear: Origins of the European Witch-Hunts in Climate, Society and Mentality," *German History* 13 (1995): 1–27; Behringer, "Climactic Change and Witch-Hunting: The Impact of the Little Ice Age on Mentalities," *Climactic Change* 43 (1999): 335–51.

5. William Monter, "Witch Trials in Continental Europe 1560–1660," in *Witchcraft and Magic in Europe: The Period of the Witch Trials*, ed. Bengt Ankarloo and Stuart Clark (Philadelphia: University of Pennsylvania Press, 2002), 16.

6. General figures are discussed by Monter, "Witch Trials," 12–16; Levack, *Witch-Hunt*, 21–23; and Wolfgang Behringer, *Witches and Witch-Hunts: A Global History* (Cambridge: Polity, 2004), 149–57.

CHAPTER SIX

✦

From Renaissance to Enlightenment, 1450–1800

Within the history of magic, the subjects of witchcraft and witch hunting dominate the early modern period, overshadowing in the historical imagination other forms of magical practice and concerns over superstition and improper belief that were also prevalent throughout this age. Yet in broader historical studies of this period, witchcraft and magic in general tend to be treated marginally, if not excluded altogether. The early modern era, as its name implies, is usually seen as encompassing the beginnings of European modernity. The history of the age can be presented as a succession of overlapping movements—the Renaissance, Reformation, Scientific Revolution, and Enlightenment—each of which has been depicted by historians as marking the birth of modern European cultural, intellectual, political, and religious systems, and forming modern Western conceptions of humanity and the universe. Although historians now just as often stress aspects of these movements and developments in these centuries that are not so obviously modern or protomodern, still the fires of the witch hunts do not cast the sort of light in which this period is typically viewed, and the prevalence of magical practices and beliefs during these centuries is still sometimes considered to be mainly a remnant of the medieval past, presented as a counterpoint to more progressive tendencies. Yet for people at the time, magic and superstition were critical issues lying very much at the center of developments that historians now associate with each of the major movements of this era.

This chapter shows how understandings of magic and concerns over superstition figured in the Renaissance, Reformation, Scientific Revolution, and Enlightenment. It explores how conceptions of magic changed and developed, how practices altered, and how they sometimes remained relatively static even in the face of considerable pressure to change. It argues that even the beginnings of modern science, rooted in this period, developed as much in concert with magical thinking and magical beliefs as in opposition to them. Lastly, it explains how magic finally faded from most serious intellectual thought (although hardly from European history) and how at least the more educated and elite classes of European society came to regard belief in any form of magic as foolish superstition. The chapter concludes by returning briefly to witchcraft and suggesting that, more than Renaissance thought or reformed theology or even scientific discovery, witch hunting may have played a crucial role in the ultimate decline of magic within the European consciousness. "Disenchantment" and a rejection of magic as a category of serious thought and action is a defining characteristic of the modern West. Yet that move toward disenchantment was largely rooted, I suggest, in the particular historical development of magical beliefs and practices in Europe and the concerns and responses they generated.

Renaissance Magic

"Renaissance" is a term to conjure with, its invocation calling up notions of a vast cultural awakening, the dawning of rational enlightenment, and the birth of modern Western culture. In fact, historians now generally agree that the Renaissance is best understood in a much more limited sense to describe specific intellectual currents that developed in Italy in the later fourteenth and fifteenth centuries. Above all, the Renaissance can be linked to humanism, an intellectual movement that arose in opposition to the then dominant medieval academic system of scholasticism. In the sixteenth century these currents spread north of the Alps and to the rest of Europe. The focus of the earliest humanists on classical languages, rhetoric, and literature gradually broadened out to affect political thought, art, and other aspects of European culture. Yet even these trends never fully superseded older medieval systems of thought, and they certainly did not, in and of themselves, comprise a complete cultural shift. Thus historians now rarely use the term Renaissance to describe a distinct historical period. Rather Renaissance trends are seen to flow through late medieval and early modern European society, manifesting more strongly in some times and places than in others, and significantly reshaping certain aspects of thought and culture while leaving others relatively untouched.

The basic feature of the Renaissance, the root from which all other developments grew, was the desire on the part of academics and intellectuals to recover ancient texts and through them ancient learning and culture. This desire was by no means new or unique to the Italian humanists of the fourteenth and fifteenth centuries. The return to and close scrutiny of authoritative ancient sources was characteristic of intellectual movements throughout the Middle Ages, and the medieval centuries were in fact marked by numerous renaissances. The most recent of these, prior to the Italian Renaissance, was the intellectual revival and rediscovery of many ancient texts, particularly works of Aristotle, that accompanied the rise of schools and universities beginning in the twelfth century. Chapter 3 outlined the importance of those developments for the learned magic of that period. The Italian Renaissance that began in the later fourteenth century to some extent simply continued the medieval intellectual tradition of recovering ancient sources. Yet Renaissance humanists saw themselves as deeply opposed to the intellectual system of scholasticism that had developed in medieval schools and universities, and some important differences separated Renaissance thought from its medieval antecedents. While medieval scholastics had focused above all on the works of Aristotle, humanists were more attracted to Platonic and Neoplatonic thought. Also, in terms of their recovery of past knowledge, Renaissance humanists set more comprehensive goals than their scholastic counterparts. While scholastics mined ancient texts for specific knowledge and information, humanists wanted to recapture, and in some sense to restore, the whole of ancient culture.

These general aspects of the Renaissance also characterize what I want to refer to as Renaissance magic. I do not mean this term to apply to all magical practices of the period; rather, it refers only to relatively limited, highly intellectualized forms of elite magic. Erudite Renaissance mages drew upon and continued many aspects of learned magical traditions from the twelfth, thirteenth, and fourteenth centuries, and yet they also typically considered themselves to be very different in their pursuits and approaches to magical power than medieval astrologers, alchemists, and necromancers, whom they liked to describe as simple and foolish in their methods. Renaissance mages felt that their own practices were based on a much fuller understanding and appreciation of ancient systems of philosophy and power. This knowledge was founded in many instances on newly discovered sources, in whose antiquity and authority they had great faith. From these sources they sought not just to gain knowledge of specific rites or actions they might use to wield power but also in many instances to revive what they believed to have been the lost magical culture of antiquity, which promised not only power but a fuller understanding of the universe and humanity's place in it. Such magic did have its more popular and popularized aspects, but it largely remained the purview of a relatively small cadre of highly learned magicians, and so its history can largely be traced by recounting the careers of some of its major practitioners. Although spread across Europe, many of these men knew one another, sometimes exchanging correspondence or even meeting directly, since as members of the European intellectual elite they often traveled widely. Moreover, because the advent of printing and increased literacy promoted a far more widespread diffusion of written treatises than ever before, the magical thought of a few men could now significantly shape more general conceptions of magic.

The history of Renaissance magic in this limited, specific sense might be said to begin in the 1460s, when a Byzantine monk brought a group of texts known as the *Corpus hermeticum* from the collapsing eastern empire to the Medici court in Florence. Here they were translated from Greek into Latin and eventually published by Marsilio Ficino (1433–1499), who could, for this reason, be considered the first Renaissance magician. These works of esoteric philosophy and spiritual magic were written in the second and third centuries, but tradition ascribed them to much deeper antiquity, for they supposedly derived from the Egyptian god of wisdom, Thoth, identified with the Greek god Hermes and often known as Hermes Trismegistus (Thrice-Great Hermes—see figure 6.1). Medieval scholars had known of these texts and actually possessed a Latin version of one Hermetic work known as *Asclepius*, but the main body of Hermetic writings only became available in the West through Ficino's translation. Although the influence of Hermetic thought on all aspects of learned magic in the Renaissance has often been overstated, the undeniable impact of this body of supposedly ancient texts nevertheless reveals much about the nature of Renaissance magic, as does the magical thought and career of Marsilio Ficino.

A major Florentine humanist working under the patronage of Cosimo de' Medici (1389–1464), Ficino was one of the principal proponents of Platonic thought in the fifteenth century, already engaged in translating works of Plato when the manuscript containing most of the books of the *Corpus hermeticum* came into Cosimo's possession. Mistakenly believing the Hermetic texts to be far older sources that had influenced Plato (in fact, the lines of influence ran the other way, the *Corpus hermeticum* being infused with Neoplatonic thought dating at least five centuries after Plato's death), Cosimo ordered Ficino to leave Plato aside and turn his attention to Hermes Trismegistus. Ficino probably translated the works before Cosimo's death in 1464; a

Figure 6.1 Hermes Trismegistus depicted in a floor mosaic in the Siena cathedral.
Source: Scala / Art Resource, NY

printed edition was first published in 1471. Then in 1489, Ficino wrote his own major work of magical thought, *De vita coelitus comparanda* (On Life Connected to the Heavens). It was actually the final part of a larger work, *De vita libri tres* (Three Books of Life), which was above all a treatise on medicine and the human body. The third book dealt mainly with the nature of astral forces, how these affected human beings, and how such forces might be manipulated for better health and other benefits.

That Ficino developed his magical system primarily in a medical context indicates the degree to which he conceived of his magic as being entirely natural rather than in any way demonic and how critically concerned he was to present it in that light. The key concept in Ficino's magical system was *spiritus*. This was not the human spirit or soul in a standard Christian sense. Rather, while *spiritus* was not entirely physical, it was a natural aspect of the human body and provided the medium though which ephemeral and occult forces radiating through the universe, above all astral forces, could affect the human body and mind. Ficino's active magic entailed manipulating the *spiritus* by various means to make it more susceptible to particular forces, the strong influence of which was desired at a particular time. For example, the *spiritus* could be attuned to the martial energies of the planet Mars before a battle, or to the energies of Venus in preparation for an amorous pursuit. Negative influences, such as those that caused disease or melancholy, could also be warded off by making the *spiritus* less susceptible to them and more receptive to countervailing forces. *Spiritus* might be attuned to a particular astral influence in many ways, including consuming certain types of food or drink, burning various kinds of incense, or surrounding oneself with materials that were naturally sympathetic to the desired planet's influence. Gold was naturally attuned to the beneficial energies of the sun, for example. Another major means of making the *spiritus* especially susceptible to specific influences was through music, as particular songs or melodies were believed to be (rather literally) in tune with certain astral emanations and would alter the *spiritus* subtly to be more influenced by these forces.

By conceiving of his magical rites as directly affecting only his own *spiritus* or that of others to make them more receptive to particular astral forces, rather than manipulating those forces directly, Ficino avoided a major pitfall. Christian authorities had for centuries condemned any attempts to control astral forces by words or rites, claiming that such actions were actually forms of communication with demons who then manipulated natural forces or otherwise produced the desired magical effects. One of Ficino's major goals was to present his magic as legitimate and compatible with Christian doctrine. By doing so he hoped to demonstrate how ancient magical practices could still be regarded as both effective and permissible within a Christian conception of the universe. In this endeavor, Ficino often walked a fine line, for example, regarding the use of talismans. He maintained, along with most Christian thinkers of his day, that some natural substances were particularly attuned to certain astral forces and could be used to attract or amplify these. Deliberately crafting figures from these materials, however, especially if they were inscribed with symbols or writing, was far more problematic, since these then seemed like a form of communication with some (demonic) intelligence. Church authorities since Thomas Aquinas had resoundingly condemned such practices. Ficino condemned talismans too, but in ambivalent terms, and he went to great lengths to argue that Aquinas's condemnation of astral magic was not as broadly focused as it seemed.

The degree to which Hermetic thought shaped Ficino's magic, as opposed to Platonic, Neoplatonic, or other influences, is still debated. Certainly after translating the Hermetic corpus, he must have been infused with Hermetic ideas. Yet he mentioned Hermetic writings directly only a handful of times in the whole of *De vita*. Basic ideas of the interconnectedness of the human body (the microcosm) with the natural forces of the larger universe (the macrocosm), as well as ideas regarding powerful emanations from higher astral spheres to the earth, were central to Neoplatonic thought. There is no need, then, to think of Hermeticism as the direct source of all of Ficino's magic. Yet Hermetic ideas, themselves largely reflective of Neoplatonism, certainly influenced his thought, and perhaps especially his desire to explain and justify supposed ancient magical practices in terms that could be acceptable to Christian theology. He was, for example, fascinated with an account in the Hermetic *Asclepius* of how Egyptian priests had fashioned statues and infused them with the power of demons. Ficino wanted to salvage this rite from condemnation by arguing that the priests actually used astral forces and so their practices were not in fundamental conflict with Christian doctrine.

Ficino has been discussed at such length because he can be considered the first of the major Renaissance magicians, and his writings introduce many of the typical characteristics and dilemmas of Renaissance magic. This magic, based in sources that supposedly stemmed from deepest antiquity and that were therefore, in the minds of Renaissance thinkers, profoundly admirable and authoritative, fostered and expressed a desire on the part of its practitioners not just to replicate ancient rites but to revive the supposed magical culture and philosophy of antiquity. Yet these men were also, for the most part, firmly Christian and orthodox in their beliefs, and many of them expended considerable effort in order to circumvent the obvious conflicts between ancient pagan rites and Christian doctrine by arguing, like Ficino, that their magic was entirely natural and uncorrupted by demonic forces.

Another major Italian humanist and a member of the Medici Platonic Academy in Florence, although by no means a pupil of Ficino or even a straightforward Platonist, was Giovanni Pico della Mirandola (1463–1494). Pico has been considered a quintessential humanist because of his famous *Oratio de hominis dignitate* (Oration on the Dignity of Man) of 1487, a defining statement of the value of individual human intellectual and spiritual capabilities and worth. Although he was opposed to many aspects of astrology, which he felt could become overly deterministic and detract from human achievement, he was deeply interested in magic. To the heady mix of Neoplatonism and Hermeticism already circulating in Italy, he added the study of Kabbalah, a Jewish system of mysticism that had developed mainly in medieval Spain but that, not unlike the *Corpus hermeticum*, Renaissance scholars thought was far more ancient. The essential Kabbalistic principle was that the entire universe existed as a continual emanation from the divine. Since in the Book of Genesis God created the universe by speaking, Kabbalah became centered on words and letters, particularly the twenty-two letters of the Hebrew alphabet and the ten sefirot (or sephiroth), names representing aspects of the power of God descending through the universe. Through the careful contemplation of these, one could ascend toward the divine. Since Hebrew could be conceived as the original language spoken by God, learned magicians had long believed that Hebrew words might carry particular power, and so the move from mystical contemplation to more active magical manipulations involving Hebrew words could be slight.

In his Kabbalistic magic, Pico focused on the use of Hebrew language and mystical systems to achieve the magician's own self-purification and refinement of spirit. By basing his system of magic on the manipulation of the human spirit so that it became more receptive to higher powers, Pico, like Ficino, endeavored to avoid charges of invoking and worshiping demons. He certainly would have wanted to stay clear of any such charges. In 1487 he had suffered a papal condemnation for some of his philosophical opinions. He had fled Florence, suffered imprisonment in France, and had only been released through the Medicis' intervention. Yet Kabbalistic magic was by no means entirely safe from accusations of demonic involvement, for Kabbalah posited spiritual forces, either angels or demons, depending on a given authority's attitude toward them, closely associated with the various levels of ascent toward the divine. As one ascended, one had to encounter, negotiate with, and manipulate these entities, which of course any suspicious authority could take as evidence of demonic magic. Moreover, Pico had related the levels of the sefirot to the ascending astral spheres of the Ptolemaic universe. Thus his Kabbalistic magic integrated easily with other Renaissance magical systems but also could be seen as raising many of the same concerns as those systems. Pico's contemporary, the German humanist Johannes Reuchlin (1455–1522), in his *De arte cabalistica* (On the Cabalistic Art), extended Pico's ideas and pushed them more openly in the direction of angelic (or demonic, in the minds of his critics) magic.

Another German who studied Kabbalah, as well as Neoplatonism and Hermeticism, was Heinrich Cornelius Agrippa von Nettesheim (1486–1535). Born and educated in Cologne, Agrippa was drawn to magical studies very early and had already compiled his compendium of magic, *De occulta philosophia* (On Occult Philosophy), by 1510, when he was scarcely twenty-four years old, although he did not allow this work to be published until 1533. Unlike most previous major Renaissance magicians, who tried diligently to present their magic as entirely natural and nondemonic, Agrippa freely admitted the angelic and/or demonic nature of much magic. He strove instead to distinguish essentially good and permissible forms of such magic from profoundly evil and corrupting forms. As seen in the previous chapter, in 1519, while serving as civic orator in the town of Metz, he had come to the defense of a woman accused of witchcraft, arguing that simple old women were not likely to be involved in any real demonic magic. Throughout his life, he was himself often suspected of being in league with demons, and many of the dark stories that first circulated around him later became incorporated into the legend of the most famous fictional Renaissance mage, Faust (himself based on a real figure, Georg, or Johann, Faust, a learned magician educated at the University of Krakow who moved through various parts of the German Empire in the early sixteenth century). Perhaps due to these pressures, even before the eventual publication of *De occulta philosophia*, Agrippa had backed away, or at least seemed to back away, from some of the positions he advocated there. The status of his actual opinion on various aspects of magic at particular points in time is thus difficult to determine, but his main importance was not as an original thinker. Rather, his *De occulta philosophia* served to transmit many basic elements of Renaissance magic to a much wider audience, especially north of the Alps.

Another major northern magus and near contemporary of Agrippa was Philippus Aureolus Theophrastus Bombastus von Hohenheim (1494–1541), who, mercifully for anyone obliged to refer to him by name, took the pseudonym Paracelsus after the ancient Roman physician Celsus. Paracelsus was a German-speaking Swiss physician who taught briefly at the University of Basel (1527–1528) before being removed for his unorthodox views and methods (he brazenly lectured in German, for example, rather than in Latin). Although he vigorously rejected all aspects of demonic magic, he strongly advocated natural magic, and he was an important alchemist and astrologer. Like Ficino, Paracelsus believed that astral forces exerted vital influence on the human body. Thus he felt that all physicians needed to be skilled astrologers and to some extent astral magicians. He also frequently employed alchemy in his medical treatments, experimenting with many chemical mixtures, drugs, and even metallic compounds, often to be taken internally. If Ficino and Pico reveal how magic was intimately connected to larger philosophical systems of the Renaissance, Paracelsus shows how magic was also linked to emerging strains of experimental medicine in this period.

Another major physician and astrologer was the Italian Girolamo Cardano (1501–1576), who was trained at Pavia and later became a professor of medicine at the University of Bologna. Like most educated men of his day, he firmly believed in the important connection between medicine and astral forces. In 1534 he moved fully into the realm of astrology, publishing his first collection of general prognostications, now a popular genre, thanks to the printing press. Cardano intended his astrological publications to spread his reputation and garner him new clients. Clearly his strategy worked, because his name became known across Europe, and he was summoned from as far away as Scotland in 1552 to treat the archbishop of Edinburgh. On his journey north, he spent time at many of the courts of France and England, encountering various important people. A minor celebrity in France at this time, who like Cardano was both a physician and an astrologer, was Michel de Nostredame (1501–1566), better known by his Latinate name, Nostradamus. He and Cardano do not appear to have met, but like Cardano he published prognostications to build his reputation and attract clients. He issued the famously obscure rhymed verse prophecies of his *Centuries* in 1555. Thanks to enduring interest in this work, he has earned a unique reputation in the modern world, yet in his own day there were many of his ilk, and he hardly ranked among the most important, successful, or influential Renaissance magicians.

A very important figure, and someone whom Cardano certainly met on his travels, was John Dee (1527–1608), probably the most significant sixteenth-century English mage. The son of a minor official in the court of Henry VIII (reigned 1509–1547), Dee took degrees at Cambridge and then traveled to the continent to continue his studies of mathematics and navigation at the University of Louvain in the Low Countries. In addition to pure mathematics and nautical knowledge, he became fascinated, in the course of his education, with alchemy, astrology, Kabbalah, and Hermetic magic. Returning to England, he turned down university posts in favor of direct noble patronage for his services, notably from Robert Dudley, Earl of Leister, but also from the royal family. Court magicians had been common since the Middle Ages, and such patronage allowed Renaissance mages (as well as other scholars and scientists) the advantage of more time for their own often esoteric studies than university positions permitted. Involvement with political figures and court intrigue carried risks as well, of course. During the brief reign of Mary Tudor (reigned 1553–1558), oldest daughter of Henry VIII, Dee was imprisoned on charges of sorcery—accused of forecasting the queen's death for her political rivals. When Mary did die and her younger sister Elizabeth ascended to the throne (reigned 1558–1603), Dee was restored to favor and provided Elizabeth with astrological services, as well as with his mathematical and navigational expertise.

Like many Renaissance mages, Dee suffered throughout his life with rumors that he was actually an evil sorcerer in league with demons. Such rumors were no doubt only exacerbated by the fact that, later in life, he did indeed come to focus on angelic magic, seeking to communicate with angels via a crystal ball. For this, Dee employed the services of young apprentices who would actually see the angels and report on what they said. Most notably among these men was Edward Kelly, whose exact status as honest assistant or opportunistic charlatan history has never been able fully to determine. In 1583 Dee and Kelly left England for the promise of better patronage on the continent. Dee's neighbors in England were clearly relieved at the departure of the suspected sorcerer and promptly burned down his house. On the continent, first in Poland and then in Bohemia, Dee never found patronage fully to his liking. He also seems to have grown disenchanted with magical pursuits and especially his attempts with Kelly to communicate with angels. Dee finally broke with his assistant and returned to England, where he died penniless. His remarkable career illustrates the heights to which a skillful Renaissance magician could rise as well as the risks this profession entailed and the depths to which one could fall.

Perhaps the most daring Renaissance magician, and certainly the one who came to the most notorious end, was Giordano Bruno (1548–1600). Born into a poor family in the town of Nola in southern Italy, he entered the Dominican order of the Catholic Church in Naples in 1563. Bruno possessed a brilliant mind but developed a profound hatred for the traditional, mainly Aristotelian scholastic learning that remained prevalent especially within the Dominican order (the order of Thomas Aquinas, after all). He was drawn, therefore, to virtually every other alternate system—Neoplatonism, Hermeticism, Kabbalah, and Copernicanism, to name a few. In his magical and occultist writings, he made no pretense of accommodating his thought to Christianity. Instead, he unabashedly declared that Christianity was a corrupt religion and that the pure, magical religion that he believed had existed in antiquity needed to be restored in Europe. Driven from Naples and then from Italy, he received noble and even royal patronage in England, France, and the German Empire, providing astrological and other magical services at aristocratic courts. He came to consider himself a messiah of sorts, and this may have prompted his return to Italy in 1591, where the following year he was arrested by the Venetian Inquisition, mainly for his belief in an infinite universe containing a multitude of worlds, all infused with life. He recanted those positions authorities deemed heretical, but his case was transferred to Rome, where it dragged on. Eventually in 1599 he refused to recant yet another list of errors and was condemned as a relapsed heretic. He was burned in 1600 in Rome's Campo de Fiori. In the modern era, Bruno came to be regarded in Italy as a martyr for free thought and science, and in 1889 a statue honoring him was erected in the Campo de Fiori, where it still stands (see figure 6.2).

Similar to Bruno, and in many ways even more extreme, was Tommaso Campanella (1568–1639), another southern Italian Dominican dedicated to the overthrow of Aristotelian scholasticism and convinced that magical and Hermetic systems could form the basis for religious and societal reforms. Coming to Naples in 1589, he soon found himself briefly jailed for his radical views, and thereafter he would spend much of his life in prisons. In 1592 he journeyed to Padua, where he met the young scientific radical Galileo (1564–1642). Imprisoned again in 1593 in Padua and in 1594 in Rome, Campanella was eventually exiled back to his native southern Italy. There, in 1598 and 1599, he became deeply involved in a serious revolt against Spanish rule of the Kingdom of Naples, inspired by millenarian religious hopes. Tortured severely for his involvement in this failed rebellion, he remained imprisoned in Naples for over twenty-five years, escaping execution only by feigning madness. While in prison, he wrote his best-known work, *Civitas solis* (City of the Sun) in 1602, a detailed account of a utopian state governed by Hermetic principles. Thanks to this and other works, his reputation actually grew during his long confinement. In perhaps the strangest twist

Figure 6.2 Nineteenth century monument to Giordano Bruno in the Campo de Fiori, Rome.

Source: Alinari / Art Resource, NY

of all, in the late 1620s Pope Urban VIII (reigned 1623–1644), a deep
believer in astrology and astral magic, became worried about omens portending his death. He consulted with Campanella, whom he had transferred to
Rome, and even engaged in protective magical rites with him. Finally
released from prison, Campanella enjoyed some brief success in Rome before
he again found his situation becoming dangerous. He fled in disguise to
France in 1634, where one of his last acts was to cast a horoscope for the
newly born French prince, who would grow to become the "Sun King," Louis
XIV (born in 1638).

Campanella might be considered the last of the Renaissance magicians,
since as he languished in prison in 1614 the classics scholar Isaac Casaubon
(1559–1614) correctly dated the *Corpus hermeticum* to the second and third
centuries C.E. Stripped of their great antiquity, these texts lost, to the Renaissance mindset, a good portion of their aura of authority. The tenets of Hermeticism and other aspects of learned Renaissance occultism certainly did
not fade immediately, remaining powerful intellectual forces for the rest of
the seventeenth century. Gradually, however (and just how gradually we will
see in a later section of this chapter), they lost influence to new scientific
methods and a mechanical natural philosophy that denied the presence of
occult forces and emanations in the universe.

Given the eventual displacement of Hermeticism, Kabbalistic magic, and
other forms of Renaissance occultism by newer systems of natural philosophy,
Renaissance magic could be viewed as a dead end, but in fact it was an important episode not just in the history of magic in Europe, but in the history
of Europe generally. Renaissance mages and occult thinkers, whatever the
differences in the exact systems they advocated, all sought to articulate more
precisely than ever before the relation between occult properties in nature,
the power of astral forces, and the presence of demons and angelic spirits
in the world. Unlike medieval learned magicians, who largely accepted the
Christian church's overarching conception of magical operations and the
nature of the universe in which they functioned, Renaissance mages often
challenged church doctrine and reigning scholastic cosmology and natural
philosophy, even while (except for Bruno) seeking to remain faithful Christians. Regardless of the disparate answers they provided, their coherent questioning of prevailing systems of thought provided an important foundation
for later scientific developments and raised a significant challenge to the
intellectual hegemony of Christian theology. Regardless of the disrepute into
which most of these ideas would later fall, systems of Hermetic, Kabbalistic,
astral, and alchemical magic fascinated some of the best minds in Europe for

several centuries by seeming to offer the best opportunity for understanding and mastering both the natural and the spiritual worlds.

Magic, Superstition, and Religious Reformation

While thanks to the personal communication and published treatises of Renaissance magicians, esoteric debate circulated among intellectual elites regarding Hermetic and Kabbalistic magic, astrology and astral forces, the potentials of alchemy, and the reality of angelic and demonic presences, most Europeans continued to interact with magic as they had in previous centuries. They relied on spells and charms handed down from their parents to heal illness, to ward off misfortune, and to protect from harmful witchcraft. They used traditional rites to ensure the well-being of crops and domestic animals, and they paid attention to any number of signs that could serve as omens or portents of the future. In cases of particular need, they might turn to healers, cunning folk, or professional fortunetellers who had special skills or knowledge of these arts. These common magical practices, while deeply rooted in folk wisdom and folk culture, were by no means utterly static, and in many cases they underwent considerable change in the course of the sixteenth and seventeenth centuries. They were affected less by the intellectual currents associated with the Renaissance than by the profound religious upheavals of the Protestant Reformation and the responding Catholic Counter-Reformation. For religious and secular authorities on both sides of the confessional divide that split Protestant from Catholic churches, magic and even more so superstition became central concerns, as legitimate beliefs and practices now needed to be defined ever more clearly in opposition to competing religious groups. Yet while the reformations drove some significant changes in certain magical practices, other practices endured, and common systems of magic in general proved remarkably resilient and adaptable to changing times.

The beginning of the Protestant Reformation is most commonly dated to 1517, when Martin Luther (1483–1546) circulated ninety-five theses for debate at the University of Wittenberg. Perhaps more appropriately, the real beginning of Luther's radical break with the Catholic Church should be dated to 1520, when he burned a papal bull that threatened him with excommunication unless he recanted his positions critical of Rome, or to 1521, when he stood before the imperial diet in the city of Worms and again refused to recant his positions. Kept from arrest and certain execution by the powerful territorial prince Frederick the Wise of Saxony (reigned 1486–

1525), Luther went into hiding. His writings, through their rapid and widespread popularization in printed pamphlets, quickly attracted a considerable following and ignited a mass movement. Within only a few years, other leading figures arose, such as Huldrych Zwingli (1484–1531) in Zurich and John Calvin (1509–1564) in Geneva. These men also broke with Rome along much the same lines Luther had, yet they by no means agreed with all of Luther's theological positions, such that Protestantism itself was from the beginning fragmented into various confessions. Calls for religious reform had been common throughout the Middle Ages, becoming particularly prevalent in the fourteenth and fifteenth centuries. Yet such calls usually focused on desires to eliminate corruption in the institutions of the church, to improve the moral and intellectual quality of priests, and to eliminate unorthodox popular practices and superstitions. Luther's motivations for reform, and those of later Protestant leaders, were based far more deeply on theological differences with fundamental church doctrine.

Luther's core position, to which all other Protestant groups essentially adhered, dealt with the central religious issue of salvation, and came to be known as justification by faith alone. Protestants believed that people were justified, that is, they received God's saving grace, solely through their personal faith and acceptance of Christ as savior. The medieval church, by contrast, had dictated that works also contributed to salvation, mainly the sacramental rites of the church that served to convey grace to their recipients, and this remained Catholic doctrine after the Reformation as well. From this position developed the Protestant opposition to a priestly caste ordained to perform sacramental rites (Protestant denominations had ministers to lead congregations, but these men had no special sacramental powers). Even more basically, Protestants came to conceive of all the rites and ceremonies of the Catholic Church as being utterly ineffective, at least in the ways that Catholics believed them to function. That is, these rites all became, for Protestants, superstitious. Protestant denominations retained some sacraments, of course, most notably the central sacrament of the Eucharist, but they reconceived of these in various ways as being salutary but largely symbolic actions that Christians should engage in as declarations of their faith rather than as directly efficacious rites that manipulated divine power to bestow grace or other blessings upon their recipients. This Catholic conception of sacramental and other ritual operation seemed to Protestants profoundly magical, and they objected to the implication that the Creator could be compelled by mere human action. On similar grounds, Protestants also dismissed the Catholic cult of saints and the efficacy of holy relics, along with a host of sacramentals—items associated with the liturgy or other ecclesiastical rites, such as blessed candles, salt, or holy water, which Catholics believed were infused with a certain degree of divine power that could be employed for various effects.

Stemming from basic Protestant salvational theology, these developments had profound implications for common magical practices. Most of the simple spells and charms used across Europe at the beginning of the early modern period, as in previous medieval centuries, were patterned after or incorporated elements of official liturgy, church rites, or prayers and blessings, in order to access the seemingly automatic power that most people conceived as adhering to these rites. In addition, the laity frequently used officially blessed or sacramental items in common magical practices, again with the notion that power clung to these items no matter the context in which they were used. The medieval church had long been concerned about such expropriations of ecclesiastical ritual, and opposition to this form of superstition grew markedly in the fifteenth century. Nevertheless, since the virtue and in some sense direct power of sacramentals and other ecclesiastical rites were officially acknowledged, common magical practices that appropriated them might be seen as functioning in entirely legitimate ways. Protestant authorities felt no compulsion to allow such leeway for a legitimized form of common magic. Instead of an immanent, active deity who continually exercised divine power in the world through sacraments, sacramentals, and the intercession of his saints, Protestant theologians emphasized a more transcendent creator. Human actions and, above all, human striving toward perfection and lives reflective of faith were required to carry out God's will, prayer was necessary and effective, and divine grace certainly operated in the world and in the lives of the faithful. Nevertheless Protestant theology and major elements of Protestant practice stressed that humans could not access divine power through mere ritual acts.

Of course, medieval authorities had long combated the notion that even official church rites, still less lay appropriations of these, somehow compelled divine action. God responded to prayers or ritual operations only as he willed and as the faith of the supplicant warranted, although in certain cases, notably the sacraments, God had covenanted with his church to respond regardless of the moral state of the ministering priest, thus giving these rites their seemingly automatic effectiveness. Despite profound disputes over doctrine, therefore, the difference between Protestant and Catholic conceptions of how divine power operated in the world was typically a matter of narrow definition and more basically of degree. Nevertheless, in the eyes of many faithful Catholics as well as Protestant opponents, Catholicism did allow more room for human operations to manipulate divine power. Catholic authorities throughout the sixteenth and seventeenth centuries, therefore, as medieval authorities before them, encountered great difficulties clarifying the precise boundaries separating legitimate rite from corrupt superstition for the average laity. Protestant ministers and magistrates could be somewhat more absolute in the distinctions that they drew. As we will see, however, Protestantism's more straightforward position on questions of ritual efficacy by no means eliminated the Protestant laity's reliance on a variety of rites, blessings, spells, and charms.

Although Protestantism posited a rather less immanent deity than Catholicism, and Protestants had (officially) less range of opportunity to access and manipulate divine power, Protestantism by no means banished all active supernatural, spiritual forces from the world. Instead, it conceived of such forces as necessarily demonic. For all that Protestant theology differed from Catholic, as seen in the previous chapter, Protestant demonology did not diverge markedly from its medieval roots. If anything, Protestant authorities exhibited more anxiety about the demonic than previous medieval or contemporary Catholic ones. Christian authorities had always maintained that demons ultimately acted in the world only according to God's will, to test the faithful and punish the faithless. Protestant reformers were deeply concerned with divine wrath, and they further emphasized the notion of demons as instruments of that wrath directed against human iniquity. Whereas Catholicism at least allowed an array of effective rites and ceremonies that the faithful could deploy to protect themselves from demonic power, Protestants could only pray for greater faith and fortitude or take direct action against the worldly agents of Satan. Indeed, such actions could be seen as a sign of a community's faith.

Given the right confluence of factors, Protestant states were capable of conducting witch hunts just as severe as any that occurred in Catholic lands. Moreover, since Protestant authorities largely denied the direct efficacy of ecclesiastical rites, they were all the more ready to see anyone who employed common spells or charms often based on these, even when for clearly beneficial purposes such as healing, as necessarily being in league with demons. Catholic officials too, although they had an intellectual and theological basis that could allow them to regard some such rites as drawing on divine power, were generally deeply suspicious of this sort of "white magic." Yet on the whole, Protestant authorities were even more inclined to regard healers, cun-

ning folk, and other practitioners of beneficial magic as being just as dangerous to proper godly society as supposedly maleficent witches.

There was of course popular resistance to these limitations and strictures
issuing from Protestant authorities. The majority of the Protestant laity, as
their Catholic counterparts, saw many magical protective and healing rites
as absolutely essential. In fact, in the absence of official ecclesiastical rites
performing the same functions, which Protestantism fairly effectively eliminated, the reliance of common people on cunning folk and popular healers
was probably even greater in Protestant lands than in Catholic ones. In some
cases, this popular resistance led to the survival of certain rites. For example,
Protestant authorities in Germany had sought to eliminate the mid-Lenten
celebrations that marked the end of winter and were believed to help ensure
agricultural success in the coming year, but they simply could not overcome
the widely felt need for such rites, which survived in many places into the
nineteenth century. More typically, however, resistance resulted in adaptations and accommodations. Again to take only one example, in the Middle
Ages important processional ceremonies had developed for the Rogation
Days celebrated on the three days before the Feast of the Ascension in which
village priests would process around the fields with a consecrated Eucharist
(or saints' relics) to ensure good crops. The beneficial power of this rite was
too critical to be eliminated entirely, but Protestant officials removed the
Eucharist as the ritual focus and inserted in its place hymns and prayers said
during the procession, which at least relocated power to God's word rather
than a sacramental item consecrated by a priest. By the seventeenth century,
even this ceremony seemed too superstitious, so instead of conducting pro-
cessions, ministers delivered special sermons, but these too came to be seen
by the laity as having some degree of automatically effective protective
power.

In their efforts to eliminate such perceived superstitions, ecclesiastical and
secular Protestant authorities faced much the same problem as had the
medieval church. They could shape belief and practice from the pulpit and
through other means of instruction, and they certainly could bring coercive
power into play on occasion, but they did not have the resources to police
and prevent all the multifarious and often relatively minor rites and practices
that enjoyed widespread support among the laity. Even among the clergy,
although both Protestants and Catholics tried to implement more effective
programs of clerical training in this period, many clerics were still drawn from
village society and essentially shared many of the common beliefs of their
parishioners. There is even some evidence that Protestantism's emphasis on

the direct relationship between faithful Christians and their God, rather than a relationship mediated through specially consecrated clergy and formal rites, along with the correspondingly somewhat reduced status of Protestant ministers as compared to Catholic priests, may have limited authorities' abilities to correct and control common beliefs. In one case in the 1640s, a Protestant clergyman instructed a farmer that he should not use a particular spell to quell fires. Rather than accepting his pastor's authority, the man immediately got his family Bible and demanded that the pastor show him where, in God's revealed word, such spells were explicitly forbidden. Here we see a wonderful example of how, if Protestantism could not fully eliminate common spells and charms, it certainly could transform the way in which people viewed and justified these rites. Even authorities clearly recognized the ways in which spells and charms became adapted to Protestant belief. In the early period of the Reformation, Protestant ministers tended to describe such superstitions as surviving elements of papism (much as the early church had regarded superstition as a survival of paganism). By the later sixteenth century and into the seventeenth, however, such descriptions fell away, and ministers seem to have regarded these practices as now fully Protestant superstitions.

Common spells and charms did in fact come to acquire decidedly Protestant forms in lands where the new confessions held sway. In Catholic regions, such spells continued to draw heavily on the rites of the church, incorporating elements of the liturgy or making use of sacramentals. Protestant authorities denied that these contained any real power, and so the Protestant laity largely ceased to use them. Instead, Protestantism stressed the need for a direct relationship between believers and God, unmediated by essentially empty rites, and on the need for all believers to have direct access to the word of God. Accordingly, Protestants came to incorporate Bible passages, prayers, and psalms into their spells and other magical formula. Catholics made use of such elements too, but in Protestant magic the focus came to be far more exclusive. Likewise, Protestants emphasized Bibles themselves, along with hymnals and prayer books, as objects of power. Instead of beseeching the power of Mary or the saints, as many Catholic spells might do, Protestant magic implored more exclusively the power of God, Christ, or the Trinity. Yet Protestantism could not do away entirely with a notion of powerful intercessors akin to the saints. As early as the 1520s and continuing well into the eighteenth century, qualities and powers previously associated with the saints in medieval and Catholic tradition were attributed to Martin Luther and other Protestant leaders. Images of Luther or items touched or used by him, for example, were believed not to burn, or might perform wondrous acts or provide magical protection in various ways. Such beliefs, decried by authorities but persistent among large numbers of Protestant laity, perhaps served as a partial response to Catholic challenges that, if Protestantism was in fact the true form of Christian faith, surely God would work wonders for Protestants just as Catholics believed he did for them.

Of course, Catholicism faced an equally harsh critique from Protestants in these centuries, that its rites thought to invoke divine power were in fact magical and superstitious. In response, the Catholic Church did not alter any of its basic doctrinal positions on how divine power might operate in the world or how human beings might effectively interact with and implore that power. It did, however, escalate its efforts, already developing since the fifteenth century, to delineate clearly the boundaries between legitimate rite and illicit superstition. In many cases, this involved formulating more precise definitions of how ecclesiastical rites operated, so that corruptions in these rites or illegitimate effects could more easily be discerned. For example, only at the Council of Trent (1545–1563), where the main lines of Catholic response to Protestantism were worked out, was a complete theory of the operation of sacramentals established. Their effective operation, Trent ruled, was not automatic, as was the case with full sacraments (*ex opere operato*, by virtue of the operation itself, was the standard formula), but depended on the status and intention of the user. This meant that if a sacramental such as holy water or blessed salt was taken by a layperson and employed for some nonsacral purpose, it would not automatically convey divine power and produce a real effect. Thus if the spell was deemed to have had some effect, authorities could clearly perceive that demonic power must have lain behind the operation. Nevertheless, while authorities might now be clearer in their own thought, the Catholic laity largely continued to see sacramentals as automatically efficacious. Efforts were made by the church to better train clergy so that they could dispense a clear message to the faithful, and this concern produced some results, but many village priests remained little better educated than their parishioners and shared many of their basic beliefs. There is ample evidence that, despite the best efforts of the church, Catholics continued to use spells and charms frequently, as well as the services of priests, cunning folk, and even suspected witches in very pragmatic ways depending on which method or combination of methods seemed to offer the best chance for obtaining the desired magical result.

What then was the overall effect of the reformations of the sixteenth and seventeenth centuries on the common magical practices of Europe?

Although these movements were centrally concerned with magic and superstition, the degree of actual change they brought about was relatively undra-
matic. Certainly the efforts of reform-minded authorities and more basically
the spread of reformist doctrines caused various conceptions of common
magic to change and adapt to new systems of belief, more significantly in
Protestant than in Catholic lands. Thus the history of the reformations demonstrates clearly that common magic was never locked in place by some unal-
terable bedrock of folk culture impervious to all historical developments.
Neither, however, did the reformations of Europe bring about any absolute
break with the magical traditions of previous centuries. Certainly the Protestant Reformation did not mark, as the German sociologist Max Weber
asserted at the beginning of the twentieth century, the "disenchantment of
the world" and the birth of modern, rational European culture. What the
reformations show, above all, is the extent to which magical traditions could
change, adapt, and largely survive even in the face of the most dramatic religious and social upheaval Europe had undergone since the emergence of
Christianity to dominance over the pagan world of antiquity.

Magic and the Scientific Revolution

Magic and the systems of belief surrounding magic were important aspects of
both the Renaissance and the Reformation. Renaissance mages often
opposed older, medieval, scholastic conceptions of how magic might function, or at least proposed alternative methods through which magicians
could operate, and reforming Protestant authorities especially redrew older
medieval boundaries between legitimate and effective rites and empty or corrupt superstition. But neither movement resulted in anything like a complete
break in European magical traditions or rejected the reality of magic per se.
The Scientific Revolution was different in that, ultimately, it did produce a
system of thought and a conception of the universe that differed significantly
from, and in many ways denied, the basic principles on which European systems of magic rested. In the seventeenth century, so called mechanical philosophy maintained that inert matter and mechanical motion could provide
a sufficient explanation for all natural occurrences. It largely denied the need
for active divine power, angelic or demonic intelligences operating in the
world, or occult forces radiating from material bodies and affecting other
bodies at a distance. Yet in the sixteenth century, many important developments in the Scientific Revolution were deeply influenced by magical and
occult systems of thought, and even throughout the seventeenth century

magical and scientific thought continued to overlap and interact in significant ways. Even "pure" mechanical philosophy had at least this in common with more occult systems: they both developed in opposition to medieval, scholastic Aristotelianism as ways to understand the natural universe.

Throughout much of European history, as we have seen, learned forms of magic had usually been regarded as areas of serious intellectual endeavor—potentially illicit and condemnable, to be sure, but serious nonetheless. Since the twelfth century, aspects of magic, especially astrology, had made inroads into the philosophical and medical curricula of the schools and universities of Europe. Renaissance magic, with its overriding focus on explaining magical operations in terms of natural properties and powers of the physical world, was very closely related to such fully legitimate academic subjects as natural philosophy, mathematics, and astronomy. Virtually all of the major Renaissance magicians could also be considered scientists. John Dee, as noted above, studied mathematics and navigation as well as practicing astrology and seeking to communicate with angels. Girolamo Cardano was a physician as well as an astrologer, and his reputation in both areas of practice spread across Europe. Giordano Bruno became a proponent of Copernicus's heliocentric theory because it fit better with his Hermetic notion of an unbounded universe filled with infinite worlds than did the standard Aristotelian and Ptolemaic conception of a closed universe with the earth at its center. When Renaissance ideas of Hermeticism, Kabbalah, or occult astral forces encountered opposition from university faculties, this opposition arose not because of these ideas' perceived "magical" nature, in contrast to some clearly emerging "scientific" point of view, but rather because they stood in direct opposition to long-established Aristotelian conceptions of the natural world and its operations, which still dominated many university faculties in these centuries. These academics also often rejected, for precisely the same reason, such "scientific" theories as heliocentrism or the emerging mechanical philosophy.

If Renaissance magicians could also be practicing physicians, astronomers, and natural philosophers, then it should come as no surprise that physicians, natural philosophers, and astronomers could be deeply influenced by Hermetic or other aspects of Renaissance occult thought. The publication of Nicholas Copernicus's *De revolutionibus orbium coelestium* (On the Revolution of the Heavenly Spheres) in 1543 is often regarded as inaugurating the Scientific Revolution (that year also saw the publication of Andreas Vesalius's empirical study of human anatomy, *De humani corporis fabrica* (On the Fabric of the Human Body)). Educated at universities in both his native

Poland and in Italy, Copernicus (1473–1543) studied astronomy and medi-cine, as well as Greek, but of course it was in astronomy that he made his reputation, both in his own day and for posterity. Already in 1514 he was well enough known as an astronomer to be invited to Rome to participate in a reform of the calendar (he declined the invitation and remained in Poland). He developed his heliocentric theory over many years but refused to let it be published until the very end of his life. This theory utterly over-turned the basic premise of the Aristotelian and Ptolemaic conception of the cosmos that had been universally accepted in Europe during the Middle Ages, namely, that the earth stood immobile at the center of the universe and all the heavenly bodies revolved around it. Copernicus argued that the earth, like all other heavenly bodies save earth's own moon, revolved around the sun.

Because all the later major figures of the Scientific Revolution came to accept Copernicus's theory (and, of course, because it proved to be correct), heliocentrism is often regarded as completely "scientific" in a modern sense. Yet Copernicus made no significant new empirical observations to justify his theory. He used mostly old data gathered by others and previously interpre-ted in a solidly Ptolemaic framework. There were certain empirical problems with the earth-centered conception of the universe—for example, the retro-grade motion of the planets (because of the earth's own movement, planets sometimes appear to move backward in the night sky)—however, the Pto-lemaic system had explained these inconsistencies by relatively complex but not essentially implausible means (certainly no more implausible than the notion that the earth, which so clearly seems to be immobile under our feet, is in fact whizzing through space at tremendous speed). Retrograde motion, for example, was explained by the introduction of epicycles, series of lesser revolutions within the steady revolution of the planets around the earth that caused their occasional backward movement. In fact, Copernicus's own sys-tem was riddled with problems that took several generations to resolve. It was no more accurate than the Ptolemaic system at predicting and accounting for the observed movements of heavenly bodies and offered no satisfying expla-nation for planetary motion. So the Copernican heliocentric theory cannot be regarded simply as the replacement of a poor theory with an unquestion-ably superior, more empirically supportable one.

The underlying reasons for Copernicus's rejection of the Ptolemaic theory of the universe remain obscure, but he seems to have been motivated to some extent by a Neoplatonic and ultimately Pythagorean conviction in the mathematical simplicity and mystical harmony of the universe, in contrast to the inelegant, although completely workable, complexity that centuries of corrections and accretions had imposed on the Ptolemaic system. Copernicus was also clearly driven to some extent by Neoplatonic and Hermetic notions of the importance of the sun. From Ficino to Campanella, almost all Renaissance mages inspired by Hermeticism regarded the sun as the dominant and deservedly central astral body, associated with the Neoplatonic and Kabbalistic divine from which powerful forces radiated out to the rest of the universe. What could make more sense than that this ruling astral body should in fact be located at the center of the universe? Consider the manner in which Copernicus himself justified his theory in one section of *De revolutionibus*: "In the middle of all sits the Sun enthroned. In this most beautiful temple could we place this luminary in any better position from which he can illuminate the whole at once? He is rightly called the Lamp, the Mind, the Ruler of the Universe; Hermes Trismegistus names him the Visible God."[1]

Not exactly Copernicus's successor, since he did not accept the heliocentric theory of the universe, but certainly the next important figure in the advancement of European astronomical science was the Danish astronomer Tycho Brahe (1546–1601). He was actually far more empirical in his efforts than Copernicus ever was. Where Copernicus had relied mostly on previously collected astronomical data, Brahe undertook rigorous new observations of the heavens from his island observatory of Uraniborg. His empiricism affected other areas of his intellectual activity as well. As a physician he was an avowed Paracelsian, and also like Paracelsus he was a serious alchemist. In addition to housing an astronomical observatory, Uraniborg also contained several alchemical furnaces in which Brahe could conduct experiments just as rigorous as his heavenly observations. Copernicus's actual successor, Johannes Kepler (1571–1630), who worked out the mathematics of the heliocentric universe in much more detail, was also deeply influenced by Neoplatonic traditions of cosmic harmony and mathematical simplicity and elegance. In addition, Kepler believed that magnetic forces emanated from astral bodies, and he was a firm believer in astrology. His famous controversy with the Englishman Robert Fludd (1574–1637), who espoused a more traditionally Neoplatonic and Hermetic vision of the universe, of microcosm and macrocosm reflecting and bound to each other via spiritual forces and harmonies, was less a conflict between "scientific" and "occult" thought than an example of the different conclusions reached by natural philosophers grounded to some extent in very similar notions. Kepler was connected to the "magical" aspects of his society in another way as well. His mother, Katherina, was tried as a witch later in her life, and her son, then the imperial astronomer of Germany, had to come to her defense in 1620, securing her survival only with some difficulty.

In all areas of natural philosophical inquiry, not just astronomy, the Scientific Revolution came to overturn the older systems of logic and the observation and categorization of the natural world associated with Aristotelian thought. In their place arose more modern, predominantly mathematical rationalism, primarily associated with the Frenchman René Descartes (1596–1650), and more modern forms of empiricism and the advancement of knowledge based on careful experimentation and observation of results, mainly associated with the Englishman Francis Bacon (1561–1626). Although Bacon had some interest in alchemy, he derided most magicians and criticized magical and occult systems of thought because they operated according to principles that were not readily apparent or observable. Yet even the empirical method of systematically exploring and uncovering the secrets of nature advanced by Bacon in such works as his famous *Novum organum* (The New Instrument) in 1620 had certain roots in older occult forms.

In the Middle Ages, "books of secrets" had professed to disclose the hidden properties of natural substances, as well as providing instructions on how to unlock and employ these powers. Far from being complex theoretical treatises, these were mostly practical handbooks aimed at offering basic medical treatments for illness and injury as well as other homey recipes for practical purposes. To justify their knowledge, the authors of these works claimed simple experience—they had observed that the various concoctions, potions, and mixtures they recommended were actually effective, or they had at least heard so from reliable witnesses or had knowledge based on long tradition. Already a fairly popular genre by medieval standards, after the advent of printing in the later fifteenth century books of secrets, or, as was often the case, slimmer pamphlets of secrets, flourished. The most popular such book in the early modern period, Alessio Piemontese's *Secreti*, was issued in over one hundred different editions from the mid-sixteenth to the end of the seventeenth century.

While such handbooks and pamphlets may seem a long way from "real science," as compendiums of wondrous and marvelous properties found in nature, they did bear a direct relation to the "cabinets of wonders" that also began to proliferate in this period. To some extent these assemblages of natural oddities and curiosities were an entertaining diversion for the nobility, who often collected or at least funded them. But for natural philosophers of the period they were important tools of observation and classification; modern natural history museums have their roots in such collections. Of course, books of secrets promised only to expose certain occult properties in nature and to explain how these could be used to attain specific, practical ends; their authors did not seek to derive any systematic understanding of nature from the cases on which they expounded. In order to attract systematic study, wonders and marvels in general had to undergo an important shift—rather than being typically regarded as singular portents intended to reveal God's will, they needed instead to be viewed as unfamiliar but usefully illustrative examples of normal natural processes. This shift was to occur during these years.

Baconian-style empiricism in general can actually be seen not so much as rejecting occult aspects of nature as, in a way, making them central to its conception of the natural world. Aristotelian natural philosophy had also been based on the observation of the world, but it worked essentially by categorizing animals, materials, and natural effects according to their immediately observable properties. The new philosophy held that nature did not so easily reveal her true aspect, and therefore carefully crafted observations and deliberate experimentation were required to uncover her actual workings. Like changing understandings of "wonders," this new method can also be seen as resting on an important shift away from the idea that occult properties in nature were essentially mysterious, differing from normal natural properties, to the notion that such "secrets," properly uncovered, would reveal understandable elements of the natural universe. Such shifts in mentality and purpose were important, to be sure, but they represent a progression, not an absolute rupture between older magical and newer scientific systems of thought.

The career of Robert Boyle (1627–1691) demonstrates well how "magical" and "scientific" practices and systems of thought continued to interact during the seventeenth century. Boyle's "scientific" credentials are impeccable. He wrote on numerous subjects, from chemistry to physics to medicine, he was a founder of the Royal Society, and he is often called the father of modern chemistry. One of his major accomplishments was to raise the intellectual and social status of chemistry, which because of its sometimes dangerous, frequently dirty, and odorous experimental requirements was often regarded as more of a craft than a learned pursuit like astronomy, natural philosophy, or pure mathematics. In his most influential work, *The Skeptical Chymist* (1661), he attacked the positions of some other contemporary chemists and alchemists, either for being too narrow and pragmatic in their approach or for deriving overly grand cosmological systems from their experiments. The work was not an attack on alchemy per se, however, nor could it be; Boyle was an alchemist himself, who supported the traditional pursuit of producing silver or gold, who sought to communicate with angels by alchemical means, who was involved with a number of alchemist groups and societies, and who exchanged alchemical secrets with other luminaries like John Locke (1632–1704) and Isaac Newton (1642–1726).

Newton was, of course, the greatest and in many ways the culminating figure of the Scientific Revolution, whose 1687 *Principia mathematica* (Mathematical Principles of Natural Philosophy) might be seen as the ultimate triumph of mechanical philosophy, explaining the workings of the entire universe in terms of physical and mathematically measurable operations. Yet for advocates of pure seventeenth-century mechanical philosophy, there was a tremendous problem lying at the very center of the *Principia*: Newton's concept of gravity, the force that kept the entire universe in motion. Mechanical philosophy rejected as magical and occultist any idea that forces might emanate from natural bodies and affect other bodies at a distance. Yet this was precisely what Newton posited with gravity. The fact that Newton was deeply interested in alchemy as well as natural philosophy for much of his life is well known. Although there is no entirely conclusive evidence showing direct links between the various areas of his thought, some scholars have argued that Newton's interest in alchemy, with its stress on attractive forces and natural sympathies between materials, must have played some role in inspiring him to move beyond the restraints of pure mechanical philosophy and argue for an attractive force emanating between bodies and binding the universe together.

As with heliocentrism, the theory of gravity has become so central to modern scientific thought that it is difficult to realize how unscientific certain other thinkers of Newton's day regarded his theory. The German philosopher, mathematician, and scientist Gottfried Wilhelm Leibniz (1646–1716), for example, ridiculed the notion of gravity as a positively "occult" principle. Musing on the actual context from which Newton's thought arose, the twentieth-century British economist and onetime don at Newton's alma mater of Cambridge, John Maynard Keynes (1883–1946) declared that "Newton was not the first of the age of reason" but "the last of the age of magicians."[2]

The Enlightenment of Europe and the Disenchantment of the World

Keynes's statement on Newton captures the continued importance of magical systems of thought and their influence on major figures in the Scientific

Revolution down to the very end of the seventeenth century. Yet it also expresses the notion that such influence was diminishing, that the "age of magicians" was drawing to its close, and indeed that this era would have to end before the modern "age of reason," implicitly a radically different age, could dawn in Europe. In the eighteenth century, the era of the Enlightenment, magical practices and beliefs did undergo a remarkable repositioning within European culture, or at least within the culture of Europe's intellectual and ruling elites. All forms of magic were judged to be empty and foolish superstitions devoid of real power and incapable of producing real effects. Superstition also became redefined not as an essentially religious error, a belief or action that contradicted religious tenets or relied on demons, but as a scientific error, a belief or action that could not be justified by accepted systems of rationality or empirical demonstration. Through such a definition, religious belief itself could be labeled as superstitious. This wholesale rejection of all the magical systems of previous centuries, along with some of the basic systems of thought that underpinned magic and had made it, in those earlier periods, an entirely rational element of European culture, was a dramatic development and did indeed help to usher in the modern era in the West.

For most of the seventeenth century, as we have seen, the new mechanical philosophy, which stripped away spiritual forces, harmonic connections, and natural sympathies between objects and materials from the operations of the universe, interacted and competed with Neoplatonic and Hermetic systems, which stressed precisely such emanations and harmonies. By the eighteenth century, however, mechanical philosophy had largely won out, so much so that the possible alchemical roots and occult aspects of Newtonian physics, for example, were simply forgotten and gravity was accepted as a part of the natural physical operation of the universe. Enlightenment thinkers, inspired by the degree to which Newton had been able to explain the motion of both terrestrial and heavenly bodies in a single system that was now judged to be entirely scientific and rational, sought to apply principles of Cartesian rationalism and Baconian empiricism not just to the natural world but to human society as well. Finding no place for magic in their conception of the natural world, they determined that the foolish belief in magic was one of the major superstitions limiting human advancement, and they determined to contest it in all its forms. As enlightened thought came to dominate the upper classes of society, Europe underwent a major, although by no means a complete, "disenchantment" that still largely characterizes the serious thought of the modern West.

The German sociologist Max Weber (1864–1920) first used the phrase "disenchantment of the world" (*Entzauberung der Welt*; literally, "removal of magic from the world") in a lecture in 1917 and then incorporated the concept into the revised edition of his seminal work *Die protestantische Ethik und der Geist des Kapitalismus* (The Protestant Ethic and the Spirit of Capitalism). He meant to refer to the stripping away of what he regarded as magical systems of salvation in Europe that he judged had culminated during the Reformation with the Protestant rejection of any real power in Catholic sacramental rites. Weber saw this process (not necessarily an entirely positive one) as a major factor leading to rationalism and modern European society and consciousness. For over a century, Weber's basic notion of disenchantment has been refined, contested, and reinterpreted, yet it still remains essential to any conception of Western modernity. That disenchantment leads to rationalism is, in historical terms, simply an untenable formulation. Rationality is not universally constant across time and cultures. Rather, in any given culture it is rational to believe anything that can be justified on grounds that culture holds to be true. As we have seen, while authorities throughout European history have judged certain aspects of magic to be erroneous, ineffective, or foolish, at no time was belief in the reality of at least some kinds of magic regarded as irrational. At no time, that is, until the Enlightenment.

In order to achieve this startling break, Enlightenment thinkers needed not only to deny magic, but also to deny the premises on which rational belief in magic rested, above all, belief in the real power of demons and ultimately divine action in the world. The eighteenth century may be said to mark the disenchantment of Europe because the Enlightenment, building on the Scientific Revolution, effected the radical separation of the spiritual from the physical realm, the removal not just of magic from the world but of miracle as well. Throughout European history there had always been criticism and skepticism about aspects of magic, rejection of the existence of occult qualities in nature, and doubts about the nature and extent of demonic power. Yet skeptics needed to be careful to express their doubts without conflicting, or appearing to conflict, with essential elements of Christian belief. Proponents of witch hunting, for example, frequently argued against those who professed skepticism about the reality of witchcraft that to deny the possible existence of witches was to deny the existence of demons and the devil, and to deny the existence of the devil was to deny the existence of God and sink into atheism. Yet this was precisely the line of thought that some Enlightenment thinkers pursued.

The roots of such thought are found in the seventeenth century. Already in 1651, in his *Leviathan*, the radical English political thinker Thomas Hobbes (1588–1679) raised questions about the reality of miracles, although he still allowed the possibility of divine action in the world. In 1670 Baruch Spinoza (1632–1677) published his *Tractatus theologico-politicus*. In a chapter "On Miracles," he argued that since God had created the natural, physical laws of the universe to suit his will, there was no logical reason to assert that he would ever need to exceed those laws himself. That is, there could never be a need for miracles. Spinoza's philosophy was a major influence on the Enlightenment thinkers of the eighteenth century. The Scottish philosopher David Hume (1711–1776) picked up directly on this argument in his own chapter "On Miracles" from his *Enquiry Concerning Human Understanding* (1748). He argued that maintaining a belief in miracles actually served to undermine religious faith—understood as belief in the establishment by God of absolute and firm natural laws for the universe. Such notions were central to deism, which characterized much Enlightenment religious thought. Deists could maintain a belief in God, and so avoid complete atheism, but held that God only revealed himself and acted through the natural laws that he had established. Thus they could still adhere to a strictly rational—as conceived in the eighteenth century—understanding of the universe as being without magic and without miracles or any other elements of active divine intervention.

The eradication of superstition in all its forms became a battle cry for Enlightenment thinkers, especially the French philosophes. Men such as Denis Diderot (1713–1784), who wrote that "superstition is more injurious to God than atheism" in his *Pensées philosophiques* (Philosophical Thoughts) in 1746, and Voltaire (1694–1776), who directed his famous call to "crush infamy" (*ecrasez l'infame*) mainly against superstition, led the final charge. By superstition, these men understood not only common beliefs in magic, demons, ghosts, and spirits, but also organized religion, especially the Catholic Church, with its claims of effective ritual drawing down active divine power into the world. Of course, not everyone, not even all enlightened thinkers, agreed with this radical rejection of the potential for divine action and miracles in the world. Historians are only just beginning to appreciate how important theological and particularly demonological thought remained in the eighteenth century. Yet the major authorities of the Enlightenment all rejected magic, that is, the notion that human beings could affect the natural world in any way through symbolic ritual actions, invocations of spiritual entities, or operations that drew on occult sympathies or harmonies lying outside the increasingly agreed-upon scientific understanding of nature.

They were, moreover, able to disseminate their rejection of such beliefs and practices widely, not to all levels of society, but fairly thoroughly among the upper and middle classes, thanks to broad literacy and widespread publications. Enlightened thought was espoused not just in books and treatises, but in pamphlets, newsletters, and newspapers, which did much to create and shape accepted and acceptable mentalities among middle- and upper-class Europeans, as well as colonial elites such as the founding fathers of the United States.

That this intellectual shift occurred and came to dominate and define European culture is clear. Why it occurred, and why at this point in history, is less certain. In many ways, radical disenchantment in the eighteenth century appears to have been the natural culmination of a long historical process. Ever since the high Middle Ages, European thinkers had struggled to understand the operations of demons and other spiritual entities and occult forces in ways compatible with their conception of the physical world and the laws of nature. Demons might be preternatural for medieval scholastics such as Thomas Aquinas, but they were not supernatural, that is, operating entirely outside of natural laws. When they produced physical effects, whether it be impregnating a human woman or deceiving human senses with an illusion, they had to do so through physical means (a sort of demonic mechanical philosophy, if you will). These attempts to explain magic within the terms of Aristotelian physics might themselves be regarded as comprising a kind of disenchantment. The magic of the Renaissance, although opposed to Aristotelianism, could be seen as the continuation of this trend, especially insofar as Renaissance magicians attempted to remove the demonic entirely from the realm of elite magic in favor of natural forces, or to conceive of demons and angels themselves fully as natural forces. Protestant reformers, although allowing for demonic action in the world and human interaction with demons through witchcraft, raised questions about the means of human access to and manipulation of divine power. The Scientific Revolution then introduced the mechanical philosophy that did away with the need for direct divine action within the universe and became the basis for so much Enlightenment thought.

Yet as I have argued throughout this chapter, while magical beliefs and practices altered and adapted to Renaissance, Reformation, and scientific thought, many magical traditions remained vibrant and provided serious competition to mechanical philosophy until the very end of the seventeenth century. The intellectual respectability of magic did not fade because new "scientific" systems provided categorically superior explanatory models that precluded the need for or proscribed the possibility of magical operations. Instead, European intellectuals seem largely to have abandoned their belief in magic first and then set about developing other modes of understanding the universe that fully excluded "magical" forces. Thomas Kuhn, in his classic book *The Structure of Scientific Revolutions*, rejected the notion that scientific progress invariably proceeds through steady, incremental advances.[3] Small advances can be made as new knowledge and information about a given subject gradually accumulates, he argues, but this information is always interpreted within some overarching paradigm that governs basic understandings about the field in which the advancement is being made. These paradigms do not alter gradually under the weight of accumulated evidence; indeed, they cannot, since all evidence is interpreted within their structure. Paradigms themselves change only through relatively sudden, dramatic ruptures.

Every dominant paradigm has certain problems, certain information that it cannot easily accommodate. Normally these are either explained in some not wholly satisfying fashion or else they are simply ignored. The Ptolemaic, earth-centric conception of the universe, for example, could only accommodate planetary retrograde motion by the introduction of complex epicycles. Occasionally, however, radical suggestions of alternate paradigms emerge, and sometimes, as with Copernican heliocentrism, they come to supplant the earlier paradigm, producing a major revolution. Kuhn maintains, however, that new paradigms do not triumph because they objectively provide a better interpretive system than the old paradigm, at least not immediately. For example, while Copernicus's heliocentric theory did explain some of the observed properties of astral bodies in simpler and more elegant ways than did the older Ptolemaic system, the better part of a century was to pass before the details of a heliocentric model that was objectively superior to the Ptolemaic system were worked out. During this transition, experts did not throw their support behind heliocentrism because of the weight of accumulated evidence, but, Kuhn suggests, more out of aesthetic impulse and intuition than anything else. The complexities and inelegance of the Ptolemaic system, despite its continued accuracy, had caused many learned people to lose confidence in its basic correctness. Conversely, despite numerous problems and failures of the Copernican system to prove accurate, its supporters were confident that these problems would be resolved and its basic correctness eventually demonstrated.

Whether or not Kuhn provides a fully accurate and comprehensive model of scientific change, aspects of his theory of paradigm shifts can be applied to the history of magic. Here too we have encountered the issue of confidence in a system, namely in the area of witchcraft and particularly with witch hunting. In the course of the sixteenth and seventeenth centuries, many authorities lost confidence, not initially in the basic systems of thought that supported the idea of witchcraft, but in the ability of legal institutions to identify and prosecute witches fairly and effectively. The previous chapter suggested that this judicial dilemma eventually led to a broader skepticism about the reality of witchcraft in general. To rephrase this process in Kuhnian terms: the inability of courts to prosecute witches effectively was, if not an inherently incompatible anomaly, certainly a problem in an intellectual and moral paradigm that held witchcraft to be a real and terribly threatening crime. The solution of simply curtailing witch trials resolved the immediate problem but would have been intellectually unappealing and inelegant because it meant that there were horribly dangerous and destructive malefactors in the world against whom legal authorities could provide no protection. The rise of skepticism about the very existence of witches provided a more comprehensive solution. Yet because the idea of witchcraft was only one facet of European conceptions about magic, and more basically about demonic and divine power operating in the world, denial of the reality of witchcraft entailed a major shift in prevailing systems of thought and required that something like a new paradigm be accepted.

Full skepticism about witchcraft, about magic in general, and even about miracles began to take hold in Europe in the later part of the seventeenth century, before becoming firmly established in the eighteenth century. The standard argument claims that this was in response to developments in the Scientific Revolution, mainly the triumph of mechanical philosophy, and more fully in response to Enlightenment thought. Yet it seems more logical to argue that, rather than simple consequences of these other developments, skepticism about magic and witchcraft, and loss of confidence in the overall paradigm that supported the idea of witchcraft, were important causes of them. The new paradigm took about a century to form fully, and even then there were problems and dissenters; but overall the dominant Enlightenment position on magic did elegantly resolve the crisis of confidence generated by witchcraft and the dilemmas of witch hunting. Authorities did not need to worry about their inability to prosecute witches effectively because witches did not exist and their harmful magic was not real. Those who tried to prosecute witches became evil persecutors of the innocent; those who persisted in their belief in witchcraft, or in spells or charms of any sort, became superstitious fools. The modern Western mindset regarding magic—Weberian "disenchantment"—was established.

Never before had any society so radically distanced itself from basic belief in the potential reality of magic. While I have argued in the previous chapter that the witch hunts of Europe were neither so massive nor so sustained as often believed, still, no previous society had ever attempted such a systematized and legally rationalized response to the problem of maleficent magic. Western Christian conceptions of demonic power and magical operations, as well as legal systems that owed as much to the medieval church as to secular development, had created the image of the diabolic witch that fueled the hunts, and when the system of the hunts failed, those larger conceptions were called into question. Far from standing in dark and dismal contrast to the progressive forces of the Renaissance, Reformation, and Scientific Revolution, in terms of the history of magic and the history of emerging modernity, the major witch hunts of the sixteenth and seventeenth centuries may have been a key factor contributing to the ultimate eighteenth century disenchantment of Europe.

Notes

1. Quoted in Thomas S. Kuhn, *The Copernican Revolution: Planetary Astronomy in the Development of Western Thought* (Cambridge, Mass.: Harvard University Press, 1957), 131.

2. John Maynard Keynes, "Newton, the Man," in *Newton Tercentenary Celebrations* (Cambridge: Cambridge University Press, 1947), 27.

3. Thomas S. Kuhn, *The Structure of Scientific Revolutions* (Chicago: University of Chicago Press, 1962).

CHAPTER SEVEN

Magic in the Modern West from 1800

The Enlightenment radically shifted the place of magic in European culture, establishing "disenchantment" as a cornerstone of the rational, scientifically informed society that European elites now sought to construct. Yet the history of magic in Europe in no way came to an end during the eighteenth century. Although enlightened thinkers sought to reshape the whole of their society, the great majority of Europe's population long remained essentially untouched by Enlightenment thought and continued to live in a world infused with and shaped by magical beliefs and practices. While throughout the course of European history political and intellectual elites had held views, and indeed often inhabited cultural worlds, that could be quite different from those of ordinary people, and while different perceptions and understandings of magic had often been important markers of this separation, probably never before had Europe's elites been so fully separated from the common beliefs and basic worldview that continued to characterize most of society. So strange and foreign did the great majority of Europe's people now seem to the educated classes that intellectuals began to engage in ethnographic studies of various social groups, and especially of rural populations, within European lands. The study of folklore (and even the word itself) was a nineteenth-century invention, and the cataloging of folk customs, including magical practices and superstitions, became a major undertaking.

Yet the history of magic in the modern era is not just, as nineteenth-century folklorists believed, a matter of the survival of outmoded practices and habits of thought among the most backward elements of European society. As always throughout history, magical beliefs and practices changed once more with the times. Certainly, elements of traditional magic endured, often most strongly among rural populations more distant from the advances of a modern European society increasingly associated with urban centers. Even this traditional magic, however, adapted to new social and cultural conditions. Moreover, beginning in the nineteenth century new forms of magic and occult activity began to appear among the middle and upper classes, the groups most directly affected by the Enlightenment. Although these new magical systems were based, in reality or at least putatively, on older traditions, they were also very much a reaction and response to Enlightenment thought and the modern culture that it fostered. While this magic was in many ways a critique of modern rationality and the limits some people saw it as imposing, it was not a rejection of modernity. Both the ritual magicians and occultists of the nineteenth century and the modern witches and neopagans of the twentieth and twenty-first are best understood as part of modern Western culture, not anachronistic holdouts against it.

Throughout European history, as we have seen, the categories of magic and superstition have served to set the boundaries separating certain rites, rituals, and practices that given societies have deemed acceptable and legitimate from those judged to be immoral, antisocial, or, particularly in the modern world, irrational. The labels of magician, sorcerer, and especially witch were typically assigned to individuals, whether by powerful religious or secular authorities acting through legal courts, or by neighbors acting through equally effective systems of village gossip and community opinion. Many people, indeed most, engaged in actions that some others might well have considered magical, but few judged their own personal practices to be magic, at least not in the sense that magic was transgressive and illicit. In the modern West, however, with its stress on individual freedom (and, critically, freedom from legal punishment for performing previously illicit forms of magic), certain people began to prove very willing if not eager to take on the title of magician, and later also of witch, in no small part because these titles and the practices associated with them have been considered to transgress limits imposed by the structures of modern society. Yet in the very act of transgressing and to some extent attempting to transforms these limits, these individuals actually behave in a very modern, at times perhaps postmodern, fashion.

The Perseverance of Common Magic

The Enlightenment was the creation of European intellectual elites. These men and women (for some enlightened thinkers certainly were women) strove to change the whole of society through the means and mechanisms of intellectuals and academics—books and treatises, pamphlets and journals, and even personal correspondence. General literacy had advanced notably in Europe during the eighteenth century, and such publications circulated more widely than ever before. Written materials were now able to shape a broad segment of opinion more immediately than in any previous age. Still, there were considerable limits to the effects of enlightened thought. Enlightenment philosophes and other progressive reformers were largely unconcerned with addressing directly the lower levels of society that constituted the great majority of Europe's population. Once the ruling classes were swayed to accept enlightened beliefs, it was reasoned, they could institute centralized policies, above all educational reforms, that would serve eventually to raise these people, or at least their children, into the light of modern thought. This process, however, proved far slower and less complete than many optimistic reformers imagined.

Because political power interacted with magic mainly through law codes criminalizing certain types of magical practices, legal change in the status of magic was the most immediate consequence of the Enlightenment to affect all levels of European society. The practical effects of this change, however, were in most cases probably very slight. As we have seen already in chapter 5, primarily in the eighteenth century, governments across Europe removed witchcraft as a crime from their legal codes. Moreover, many new laws were introduced that made it a crime for people to accuse others of witchcraft, or to claim to be a witch or to have magical powers of any sort themselves. Legal authorities now typically regarded people who continued to assert such claims as committing fraud. Yet as we have also seen, by the time such legislation was enacted, most states in Europe had already, for other reasons, ceased prosecuting witches in any significant numbers. Moreover, among common people recourse to legal action appears never to have been the initial or principal reaction to suspected witchcraft. Thus the removal of a legal option simply caused people to rely all the more on the traditional resources they already typically used to deal with witchcraft—above all, counterspells and protective magic.

Throughout the nineteenth century and well into the twentieth, people across Europe continued to employ spells and charms, observe signs and omens, and rely on herbal and other folk remedies. And diviners, traditional healers, cunning folk, and witch-doctors (experts in identifying and removing bewitchments) continued to practice their craft. The threat of being charged with fraud for engaging in these actions was surely little deterrent compared to the previous danger such people faced of possibly being charged with witchcraft. Knowledge of common spells and charms continued to circulate in the modern era, as it long had in premodern Europe, through local tradition and oral culture. Many people might acquire some knowledge of such arts from parents, grandparents, or older practitioners. Some could develop a local reputation for special skill in certain areas, such that neighbors would seek them out for particular remedies, to provide love charms, or to perform other services. Moreover, a small number of people have always provided such services as their primary occupation, often moving itinerantly around a given region seeking clients. In the nineteenth century this occupation became, if anything, increasingly professionalized. For example, a literature developed collecting traditional charms, remedies, and methods for undoing witchcraft, and some cunning folk and witch-doctors now learned their craft, or at least augmented their skills, through this literature. As these people operated among a largely rural population that was only partially literate, the books they employed became symbols of authority and, just like more learned magical tomes in previous centuries, were often regarded as being imbued with their own special powers.

The survival of common magical practices in the modern era, which has only recently begun to attract significant attention from historians, has often been presented mainly as a rural phenomenon. This view is based largely on the approach taken by nineteenth-century folklorists, themselves members of the urban middle classes who regarded the rural hinterlands as preserving unchanged age-old traditions, including magical practices and superstitions. Since rural society as a whole underwent less change in the nineteenth century than industrializing urban centers, there is some validity to this approach. Yet to declare the countryside to be the sole domain of magic in modern Europe would be false. If traditional cunning folk and healers remained more common in rural areas, astrologers and other varieties of diviners flourished in the cities, in a division not unlike early modern patterns. The presence of astrologers, palm readers, and tarot card readers in any major Western city at the outset of the twenty-first century testifies that urban centers still support their own particular forms of magical or occult occupations.

Of course, such modern manifestations of magic as newspaper horoscopes, tarot decks, and ouija boards could be seen merely as entertainments or diversions, not the serious forms of magic people believed in and used for practical effects in previous eras. Such an analysis would support the complacent Enlightenment conviction that modern scientific rationality and technological developments would gradually displace superstitious thought and eliminate any real need for recourse to magic. In many ways, certainly, technology has eroded the place of magic in the modern West. For example, reliable postal systems and the telegraph in the nineteenth century, to say nothing of the nearly instantaneous telecommunications possible in the twenty-first, have largely eradicated any need for divinatory practices intended to obtain information about faraway events. And increased understanding and applications of the mathematical functioning of probabilities, for example, in actuarial tables, have to some degree replaced reliance on divination intended to reveal future events.

There are, however, no indications that technology has completely replaced magic in the modern West. People now enjoy far more mobility and opportunity, and thus in some ways confront more uncertainty, than most premodern Europeans ever experienced, and the number of people who continue to patronize astrologers, psychics, or other experts in divination shows that a basic need to discern future or hidden events has not abated. In medicine, too, scientific and technological advances have greatly reduced the need for magical healing, yet such practices have by no means disappeared from modern Western societies. Folk and faith healers still flourish, and many areas of so-called alternative medicine have actually become more popular in recent decades. Such practices are most often used not to the exclusion of professional medicine but in conjunction with it, as people try whatever methods seem to offer the best results, just as was commonly done in the past. Most people employing various forms of alternative medicine probably do not regard what they are doing as in any way magical or superstitious, but that would also not be significantly dissimilar from common conceptions in previous centuries.

Some evidence also indicates that belief in demonic possession and the practice of exorcism may be rising in the Western world. The Catholic Church has maintained an official rite of exorcism since the Middle Ages but in the modern period has tended to stress physical or psychological causes for aberrant behavior rather than possible possession. Nevertheless, in parts of Asia, Africa, and Latin America, where the Church is actually growing rather than declining, as it is in Europe and North America, fear of demonic attack and responses to it remain far more active, and these beliefs are now returning to some extent to the United States and Europe through immigration. Moreover, in the West, particularly the United States, certain Protestant groups are now again stressing belief in active demonic power in the world, including demonic possession, and they practice their own forms of exorcism against it. These believers would of course not consider their rites to be "magic"; Christianity has always strictly separated the magical from the religious. Yet however they are categorized, these developments certainly represent a reversal of intellectual and spiritual trends coming out of the Enlightenment.

One of the major factors for change and the real withering of many magical beliefs must be the profound alteration in concerns about fertility that has occurred in the modern West. A great number of common magical practices in the premodern world existed to protect and ensure the precarious fertility of human beings, essential domestic animals, and crops. Of course children still die in the modern world, and Western nations face certain social and economic consequences due to the small number of children their citizens are now choosing to have, but thanks to scientific, technological, and medical advances, the need to ensure basic sexual fertility against natural or supposed magical impediments has essentially vanished. Likewise, farmers still face inclement weather and even occasional catastrophic crop failures, and their economic survival can be precarious. But, thanks to massive overall production, modern methods of storing and shipping food, and a much more diversified agricultural base, communities as a whole no longer need to fear major catastrophes resulting from specific shortfalls or failures; the threat of famine is nonexistent in Western nations. In light of these conditions, the rites and ceremonies that for centuries served to ensure healthy crops and abundant harvests have melted away.

Leaving aside the development of modern witchcraft or Wicca, which will be treated in a later section of this chapter, traditional belief in witches might be seen as having undergone significant change in the modern world, but here we must be careful to specify what is meant by "witchcraft." Certainly the idea of diabolical cults of witches gathering secretly to worship demons and work maleficent sorcery against their neighbors faded from common conceptions of witchcraft in the seventeenth and eighteenth centuries (although it endures to some extent in modern fantasies about satanic conspiracies). This notion, however, had never been a deeply embedded element of common belief. Rather, authorities constructed the image of the witches' sabbath and superimposed this idea onto more generally held conceptions of how people responsible for performing *maleficium* conducted themselves. When elite support for the idea of a conspiratorial, diabolical cult of witches was withdrawn, this belief quickly evaporated from common consciousness as well, as ordinary people returned to the idea of the witch as an individual practitioner of harmful magic. This pre-diabolic notion of witchcraft did endure into the modern era, along with the counterspells and professional witch-doctors that concern over such witches had long supported.

Evidence of continued belief in traditional forms of witchcraft can be found throughout the twentieth century in Europe, and even some cases of lynching of suspected witches. In the 1920s, for example, newspapers reported cases of witchcraft in England, France, Germany, Italy, and elsewhere across Europe, although these newspapers, as agencies of essentially Enlightenment thought, regarded such cases as exotic traces of traditional superstition not yet wiped away by the advance of modernity. In 1954 a professional witch-doctor from Sarzbüttel, north of Hamburg in Germany, was put on trial. The court, as an enlightened institution, saw itself as prosecuting fraud, but the man's successful career revealed a considerable level of continued popular belief in witches and concern over their supposedly harmful activities. In 1976 a British court awarded damages (admittedly only fifty pence) in a case in which the defendant had used the royal mail to send the plaintiff a chicken's heart impaled with needles as part of a harmful spell. General surveys conducted in Germany in the last decades of the twentieth century consistently reported that between 10 and 15 percent of the population professed believing in the reality of some kind of witchcraft. A survey in France in the mid-1980s yielded a figure of 18 percent. Especially in Mediterranean lands, belief in the power of the "evil eye" remains widespread, as does the use of charms to ward off its effects. The idea that wicked people can work harm through magical means has by no means vanished from Europe in the twenty-first century.

There can be little doubt, of course, that had a survey regarding the reality of witchcraft been possible during the early modern period, the percentage of those avowing a belief in witches would have been far higher. To the extent that traditional belief in witches has faded, many scholars have suggested that a principal cause is not the slow diffusion of Enlightenment thought to all levels of European society, but rather the social effects of the steady industrialization of Europe. The industrial revolution began in England in the eighteenth century and spread to most other European nations in the course of the nineteenth, but its effects only permeated many rural areas in the twentieth century. Industrialization, this argument runs, worked to reduce belief in witches not so much through technological or economic advances, but by disrupting the tightly knit social fabric of preindustrial agricultural communities in which traditional belief in witchcraft functioned as a mechanism for expressing community tensions. Recent research on witchcraft in modern Africa, however, might seem to militate against this explanation. Forms of witchcraft in Africa are of course different from witchcraft in Europe, but they appear to perform many similar social functions, and African witch beliefs were influenced by European ones especially during the period of colonialism. Nineteenth-century colonial authorities also sought to impose enlightened disenchantment on African societies. In the postcolonial period, however, belief in witches appears to be on the rise in many regions of the continent, and some governments are even recriminalizing witchcraft. Concern over witches actually flourishes in many large, modern urban centers, often precisely because of the social dislocation that the development of these cities has produced.

The reality may be that widespread belief in witchcraft depends not so much on the social context of small rural communities per se, but on the notion, perhaps more easily sustained in such communities but not necessarily limited to them, that otherwise inexplicable misfortunes result from individual maleficence. Supposed witches can be blamed for any number of personal or societal ills, and by providing a focus for blame they help communities deal with the tensions arising from those problems, but only if people accept that such problems stem from evil individuals within the community itself. The modern Western mentality, however, tends to see many societal problems, and a number of individual ones as well, as caused by essentially impersonal economic, social, or cultural forces. To the extent that these forces still need to be personalized, the malefactors are not wicked people within the local community but members of vast, shadowy conspiracies from outside—government agencies flying black helicopters, the occult operations of the Council on Foreign Relations or the Trilateral Commission, the evil machinations of all-powerful Yale undergraduates in Skull and Bones. For some people in the modern West, conspiracy theories involving such groups have taken over some of the explanatory roles that witches once played in Europe. Perhaps early modern authorities' notions of a vast, conspiratorial cult of witches striking at all of society rather than localized maleficent individuals practicing harmful magic, which was only problematically accepted in that period, was simply a concept that emerged before its true time.

While I have stressed here the continued existence of magical beliefs and practices in the modern era, my point is not that they survived unaltered into the world of Enlightenment and industrialism. Historically, magical beliefs have never been static but have always responded to larger cultural changes, and the modern West has been characterized by more sustained, rapid change than any other historical culture has ever experienced. Nor am I subverting the conclusion of the previous chapter, that the disenchantment associated with the Enlightenment was probably the greatest single cultural shift to affect magic in over a millennium. Yet even that shift was far from absolute. Traditional forms of magic did survive into modern Europe, to continue their long process of change and adaptation to society's needs (see figure 7.1). Moreover, as we will see, specifically modern forms of magic arose in the course of the nineteenth and twentieth centuries. Their creators and practitioners claimed that they too were either survivals or at least revivals of older practices, and they certainly had complex relationships with historical magical traditions. Nevertheless, they were clearly new creations, creatively modeled on older systems (or imagined older systems), but responding to fully modern conditions.

The Renaissance of Ritual Magic

Even during the height of the Enlightenment, serious interest in magical or occult practices never fully disappeared among the upper levels of European society. In the 1770s, the Catholic priest Johann Joseph Gassner (1727–1779) conducted numerous exorcisms and healings of various sorts in southern Germany. As his fame spread, something like a popular religious revival began to sweep through German lands. He aroused considerable opposition, but also garnered support from both secular and ecclesiastical officials, and he sparked tremendous debate, remarkably among Protestant as well as Catholic authorities, about the nature of his activities and the powers he claimed to wield. Meanwhile, the German physician Franz Anton Mesmer (1734–1815) was enjoying major success with at least quasi-occult healing practices. Educated at the University of Vienna, he developed and employed the hypnotic, therapeutic practices that would come to bear his name, mesmerism, first in Vienna and after 1778 in Paris, the capital of enlightened thought. Mesmer based his practices on the theory of animal magnetism, that is, the belief that all living bodies produced and were infused by magnetic energies, and he developed various devices to manipulate this energy for healing purposes. The most elaborate of these was the *baquet*, a tub filled with water and metal filings, and also fitted with iron bars that patients would touch as they sat around, and sometimes in, these tubs. Mesmer's cures became extremely popular, but he also faced a great deal of academic skepticism and professional opposition from physicians and scientists, and in 1784 the medical faculty of the University of Paris formed a commission to investigate his practices. This commission, which included Benjamin Franklin, then an American minister to the French court and by this time world famous for his scientific discoveries and inventions, determined that Mesmer's theories were

Figure 7.1 Goya's *The Witches' Sabbath* (1797–98) presents a more modern imagining of a premodern theme.

Source: Scala / Art Resource, NY

unfounded. The following year Mesmer left Paris and eventually died in relative obscurity.

While Mesmer typically stressed the medicinal and scientific nature of his treatments, others took his ideas in more overtly magical directions. By the mid-1780s mesmerists operated throughout France, often combining mesmerism with other esoteric spiritual or magical practices. The mesmerist society in Lyon, in particular, had associations with alchemy, Hermetic magic, and Kabbalism. Other occultist groups also flourished. In the 1770s in Lyon, a nobleman, Jean-Claude de Saint-Martin (1743–1803), had founded the Martinist Order, a society dedicated to understanding the spiritual world through a mix of Christian and Kabbalistic mysticism. The order was based on the teachings of Martines de Pasqually (1727–1774), whom Saint-Martin met in Bordeaux in the late 1760s, joining his Masonic order of *Elus Coën*, or "elect priests" (*coën* being the French form of the Hebrew *cohen*). Later, the Martinists incorporated other occult systems and techniques, including mesmerism. Another follower of Martines de Pasqually was Jean-Baptiste Willermoz (1730–1824), and he and Saint-Martin were both important influences on the magical thought of Eliphas Lévi (discussed below).

While others were more influential, perhaps the most famous occult figure of this age was a Sicilian conman and adventurer, Giuseppe Balsamo, who styled himself Alessandro, Conte di Cagliostro (1743–1795). When he was twenty, having cheated a local silversmith out of a good deal of money, he fled his native Palermo and visited Greece, North Africa, and the Near East. He then traveled through Europe for two decades posing as an alchemist, mesmerist, and sorcerer, peddling cures and magical elixirs. Cagliostro found his greatest success in Paris, until he was implicated in the famous "Affair of the Diamond Necklace" at the court of Louis XVI (reigned 1774–1792). A conniving courtier, the Comtesse de La Motte, schemed to acquire a fabulously expensive necklace fashioned by Parisian jewelers, ostensibly for Queen Marie Antoinette but in reality for herself. Cagliostro, with his supposed talents for divination, figured in the complex machinations by which this was accomplished. Although acquitted of direct criminal action, he was banished from France. Returning to Rome in 1789, he was arrested for sorcery and heresy by the Roman Inquisition and spent the rest of his life in prison.

In the nineteenth century, a major surge of interest in spiritualism, that is, the belief in ghosts and the ability of certain people to communicate with the spirits of the dead, swept across both Europe and the United States, seizing mainly members of the urban middle class. Spiritualist rites most typically took the still familiar form of the séance, in which a group of people would gather in a specially prepared, darkened room with a medium who would communicate with the spirits of the dead. Such practices, actively patronized by members of the same social groups that had most thoroughly accepted the Enlightenment rejection of magic, have been taken by historians as evidence of a growing dissatisfaction with the limits imposed by enlightened rationalism and a desire to believe that the universe contained more aspects and levels of existence than official science would allow. The success of spiritualism was also a consequence of the failure of mainstream Protestant religious denominations, which had largely accommodated themselves to the principles of post-Enlightenment scientific rationalism, to satisfy what for some people was clearly an essential need for an active and immanent spiritual and supernatural world. Even the Catholic Church, whose doctrines concerning the possibilities of both divine and demonic operations in the world remained fixed by the sixteenth-century Council of Trent, increasingly accepted an "enlightened" and "scientific" view of the world in practice. Catholic officials had opposed many of Father Gassner's exorcisms in the 1770s, after all, and in 1835 the works of Copernicus, Kepler, and Galileo supporting the heliocentric theory had been taken off the Index of Prohibited Books. Some middle- and upper-class Europeans wanted less science and more spirituality, however, and the popularity of spiritual mediums and séances was only one aspect of a broader occult and magical revival.

In the mid-nineteenth century, a highly intellectualized form of ritual magic began to develop in Europe, based in large part on the learned magical systems of the Renaissance. Its most important figure was Eliphas Lévi (1810–1875), the pseudonym of the Frenchman Alphonse Louis Constant. Born in Paris, Constant trained to become a Catholic priest, but stopped after attaining only the preliminary rank of deacon in the late 1830s. He was drawn increasingly to the world of magic and occult studies, and he adopted Eliphas Lévi as the Hebrew forms of his first and middle names. In 1855 he published his major work, *Dogme et ritual de la haute magie* (translated as *Transcendental Magic: Its Doctrine and Ritual*). In this and later writings, he synthesized Hermetic, Kabbalistic, and alchemical traditions. He also innovated, constructing rites and symbolic systems of his own devising. Based on concepts of animal magnetism, he developed a theory of astral light, a fluid force that permeated the universe and that magicians could learn to control. Lévi is perhaps most famously associated with the image of

Baphomet, the devil as a half-human–half-goat creature. The name Bapho-met, possibly a corruption of Mahomet (itself a corruption of the name of the Islamic prophet Muhammad), was known in the Middle Ages. Among the reasons for suppressing the Knights Templar in the early fourteenth cen-tury, French authorities accused them of worshiping a demonic image named Baphomet, although the medieval image was not that of a satanic goat. Lévi constructed his image from the depiction of the devil in tarot card decks (he felt that the tarot was linked to Kabbalistic systems) and an ancient goat-deity supposedly worshiped at Mendes in Egypt (hence his image is some-times called the "Baphomet of Mendes"). He gave his Baphomet a goat's head, a human torso with female breasts and great bat wings, and the lower body and hooves of a goat, all surmounted with mystical symbols. It has become one of the most famous depictions of the devil and a symbol of mod-ern occultism and Satanism, and has also been frequently (if falsely) associ-ated with modern witchcraft.

Lévi's writings proved extremely influential. Other ritual magicians drew on his images and ideas for the rest of the nineteenth century and into the twentieth, and Paris remained an important center of occultism. The next major step in the development of nineteenth-century magic, however, came with the emergence of magical and occult societies, and this was above all an English phenomenon. Since the eighteenth century, the upper and mid-dle classes of British society had been dominated by clubs and fraternal orga-nizations. The largest of these, whose rites and organization became the model for many others, was Freemasonry. Masonic lodges had developed out of actual craft guilds of stonemasons in Scotland in the late sixteenth cen-tury, and the oldest current lodges in Edinburgh and St. Andrews can trace their history continuously back to around 1600. After the Grand Lodge of England was established in London in 1717, Freemasonry developed much more elaborate rituals, often drawing on mystical, alchemical, Hermetic, or Kabbalistic imagery and symbolism. Despite its use of these symbols, Freema-sonry was not itself dedicated to the study of magic or the occult, although some Masons clearly did become interested in these topics and some of the most important occult organizations of the nineteenth century were Masonic spin-offs. Freemasonry as a whole did come to regard itself as related to an older and decidedly occult society, or supposed society, the Brotherhood of the Rosy Cross.

The first mention of the Rosicrucians dates from the early years of the seventeenth century. Their order, a mysterious brotherhood supposedly founded in the fifteenth century by a German knight named Christian

Rosenkreutz (Rosycross), was described in two pamphlets, *Fama fraternitatis*
. . . (Discovery of the Fraternity of the Most Noble Order of the Rosy Cross),
printed in 1614, and *Confessio fraternitatis* . . . (Confession of the Laudable
Fraternity of the Most Honorable Order of the Rosy Cross) in 1615. Its members were dedicated to exploring alchemical, Hermetic, and Kabbalistic
knowledge. The third major piece of Rosicrucian writing was a German-
language romance entitled *Chymische Hochzeit Christiani Rosenkreutz* (The
Chemical Wedding of Christian Rosenkreutz), published in 1616. Its author
was anonymous but has been identified as the Lutheran theologian Johann
Andreae (1586–1654), who probably had a hand in the earlier pamphlets as
well. As described in these works, the Brotherhood of the Rosy Cross was a
group of Renaissance magi dedicated to bringing about spiritual and social
reform according to Hermetic and other occult, magical principles. The society never actually existed, but was widely accepted as a reality, and when
later Masons sought a more exotic history than their actual origins in medieval craft guilds, they eagerly linked themselves to the Rosicrucians. Life then
imitated art. When certain groups of Masons began to delve more directly
into occult matters, they naturally further emphasized their direct connections to the Rosy Cross. For example, the first major fully occult group established in England was the Societas Rosicruciana in Anglia, founded in 1865
by Masons and largely following Masonic patterns.

A major organization without Masonic roots, but one of the most remarkable creations of nineteenth-century occult culture, was the Theosophical
Society, founded in New York City in 1875 by the American journalist and
lawyer Henry Steel Olcott (1832–1907) and a Russian émigré who had come
to New York in 1873, Helena Petrovna Blavatsky (1831–1891). From the
start, Madame Blavatsky (as she is usually known) was the Society's leading
personage and guiding light. Preaching the limitations of the modern, strictly
scientific understanding of the universe, she asserted instead that the world
was animated by mystical forces that could be better understood through
older, esoteric systems of knowledge. Blavatsky was an admirer of Eliphas
Lévi, and the Theosophical Society initially concentrated on the study of
European traditions of Hermeticism and Kabbalah but soon shifted its focus
to reflect Blavatsky's interest in the religions and philosophies of Asia as a
source of wisdom. She claimed that during a supposed sojourn in Tibet during her peripatetic early life she had encountered ancient masters of wisdom,
the Mahatmas, who thereafter communicated with her. They had dictated
to her, she asserted, her major work *Isis Unveiled* (1877), although the heavy

influence (some would say plagiarism) of Lévi is evident throughout the book.

In 1878 Blavatsky left New York for India, eventually establishing a head-quarters for the Theosophical Society outside of Madras. Branches were also established in many American and European cities. Members were generally progressive, middle-class intellectuals. Like most occult organizations of the time, the society allowed powerful roles for women, and the organization as a whole was interested in pursuing both spiritual and social reform. For example, after Blavatsky, the society's second major female figure was Annie Besant (1847–1933). A proponent of women's rights and member of the socialist Fabian Society, she embraced Theosophy in 1889 and became president of the Theosophical Society in 1907. Moving to India, she continued to work for social reform and became involved in national politics, founding the Indian Home Rule League in 1916 and becoming president of the Indian National Congress in 1917 before a later split with Mohandas Gandhi. In the 1920s she toured the United States and Europe with Jiddu Krishnamurti (1895–1986), whom she claimed was a divine avatar and messiah.

While the Theosophical Society enjoyed considerable success, like other occult organizations it also experienced internal dissension as members advocated different paths to wisdom and more basically struggled for power, and it also aroused external skepticism. In 1882 a group of Cambridge dons founded the Society for Psychical Research to examine supposed paranormal phenomena in a rigorous fashion. This group attracted such notable members as the physicist Oliver Lodge, philosopher Henri Bergson, politician (and British prime minister from 1902 to 1905) Arthur Balfour, psychologist William James, and author Arthur Conan Doyle. On the continent, psychologists Sigmund Freud and Carl Jung were supporters of the society and contributors to its journal, as was Mark Twain in the United States. Although it achieved early fame for debunking many of the claims of Madame Blavatsky and the Theosophical Society, the Society for Psychical Research should not be considered an organization opposed to occultism; rather, its members were dedicated to applying scientific methods to evaluate occultist claims precisely because they were interested to know whether these claims were true. In this way, the group was emblematic of the essentially modern character of nineteenth-century occultism and of occult societies themselves. Although occult groups were often critical of the limitations they saw being imposed on human understanding of the world by Enlightenment rationality, they generally accepted the principles of modern science and the scientific method, and believed that the knowledge they advanced could be validated by such methods.

Until well into the 1880s, organizations such as the Theosophical Society and various quasi-Masonic groups promoted occult learning as a means to spiritual knowledge and greater understanding of one's self and the universe, but their members typically did not engage in actual magical practices. The premier Victorian magical society, the Hermetic Order of the Golden Dawn, founded in London in 1888, was, or came to be, quite different. Still basically Masonic in its structure, with various levels for its members and initiation ceremonies and rites to advance through them, the Golden Dawn was dedicated to Hermetic and Kabbalistic magic. Its founding members were William Wynn Westcott (1848–1915), a doctor, a Mason, and a member of the Theosophical Society; William Robert Woodman (1828–1891), also a doctor, Mason, and leading member of the Societas Rosicruciana in Anglia; and Samuel Liddell Mathers (1854–1911), who came to style himself "Count MacGregor of Glenstrae" and so is often known as "MacGregor Mathers." Like other groups, the Golden Dawn originally stressed the study of magical and occult systems as a means for self-realization and spiritual advancement. Its founders claimed to have discovered and decoded the initiation rites of an eighteenth-century German society of Rosicrucians. Westcott further claimed to have come into contact with a German woman, Anna Sprengel of Nuremberg, a member of this society who authorized him to establish a branch in England, thus securing the occult pedigree of the Golden Dawn. In fact, the rites of the order were largely Mathers's creation.

The Golden Dawn was immediately successful. In addition to the principal Isis-Urania Temple in London, other temples were founded around England and also in Paris. Luminaries were attracted, including the actress Florence Farr and, most notably, the poet William Butler Yeats. In 1891, news supposedly arrived from Germany that Anna Sprengel was dead, and with her all connection to the (equally supposed) Germanic Rosicrucian tradition was severed. In that same year, Madame Blavatsky also died. The Golden Dawn had maintained cordial relations with, and been influenced by, the Theosophical Society. Now Mathers, heading the temple in Paris, claimed that with Blavatsky's passing he was in contact with her secret masters, the mysterious Tibetan Mahatmas. On their authority, he established a second elite order within the Golden Dawn, known as the Order of the Red Rose and the Cross of Gold. This group was to admit only adepts and be dedicated to the active practice of ritual magic. The ever-creative Mathers fashioned most of the magical rituals this group was to use from an amalgam of Hermetic, Kabbalistic, and supposedly ancient Egyptian rites drawn largely from the magical systems of Eliphas Lévi.

Mathers's imperious style created serious rifts within the order. In 1900, to promote his own authority, he accused Westcott (who had resigned from the Golden Dawn in 1897 after government officials made clear to him that membership in such an organization was unacceptable for a medical examiner in the service of the royal government) of forging the foundational German Rosicrucian rites and inventing his communication with Anna Sprengel. Many members remained loyal to Westcott's tradition, however, or simply opposed Mathers and his attempt to seize absolute leadership, and the order eventually fractured. Yet during its decade-long heyday, the Golden Dawn had quickly established itself as the most important occult organization in Europe.

Other magical societies arose at this time, such as the French Martinist Order, claiming connections to the original eighteenth-century Martinists but actually founded in 1891 by the writer Gérard Encausse (1865–1916), known as Papus. He had briefly been a member of the French Theosophical Society but was really a student of Eliphas Lévi and a major popularizer of Lévi's magical ideas. Around the turn of the century the Austrian Mason Karl Kellner (1851–1905) initially conceived of an organization to be known as the Ordo Templi Orientis (Order of the Temple of the East—a reference to the Knights Templar), established after his death by his associate Theodor Reuss (1855–1923), who had already helped establish the Bavarian Illuminati and founded a German branch of the Martinist Order. Nevertheless, the Golden Dawn remained preeminent. It exerted a wide influence both during this period and afterward, and the magical rites developed by Mathers became an important basis for many later ritual magicians.

Certainly the most infamous legacy of the Golden Dawn came through its admittance, to an admittedly rather brief membership, of Aleister Crowley (1875–1947), the most famous and arguably most influential ritual magician of the twentieth century. In his own day and down to the present, Crowley has been as much admired by some as he has been reviled by others. Born Edward Alexander Crowley, the son of a brewer and strict Christian preacher in Warwickshire, England, he later changed his name to Aleister as a Celtic variation of Alexander. He attended Trinity College, Cambridge, but left without a degree. Instead he dedicated himself to the study of magic, moving to London and joining the Golden Dawn in 1898. Rising quickly through the regular levels of the order, he set his sights on admission to the elite second order, where magic was actually practiced. The London leadership of the Golden Dawn resisted, because he already had a reputation for experimenting with sinister rites, but from Paris Mathers overruled them and initiated Crowley into the second order in 1900. Crowley then supported Mathers when he challenged the legitimacy of the other leaders of the order. Yet Crowley's burning ambition and pride in his own magical skills also led him into rivalry with Mathers. Within a few years he had left the Golden Dawn and began developing his own magical rites and systems of thought.

In 1903 Crowley married Rose Kelly, who soon began receiving visions, and in 1904 she informed him that he was to receive *The Book of the Law* from a spirit named Aiwass. In this book, Crowley formulated the so-called Law of Thelema: "Do what thou wilt shall be the whole of the law." Not simply a statement of hedonism, this principle encapsulated the critical importance of the powerful and individualistic will of the magician in Crowley's thought (*thelema* being Greek for will). Certainly, though, he was enough of a hedonist. He incorporated drugs and sex abundantly into his magical rites. In 1909, he undertook a series of sexual-magical rituals with his apprentice Victor Neuburg (1883–1940) in the deserts of North Africa that seem to have shaken even the indomitable Crowley's will. He also kept a number of "scarlet women," lovers with whom he conducted magical rites, throughout his life. The most significant of these was Leah Hirsig (1883–1975), known as the "Ape of Thoth." In 1912 he became a member of the German Ordo Templi Orientis, whose rites involved tantric sex, and he founded a branch in London. In 1922 he rose to be head of the entire OTO. By that time, he was residing in Sicily, where in 1920 he had founded the Abbey of Thelema, intended as a sort of magical commune. It was in Sicily that he performed a ritual with Hirsig through which he claimed to have achieved the highest possible level of magical enlightenment, becoming in his own description like a god (see figure 7.2). Crowley cheerfully referred to himself as the Beast 666 and was sometimes called the most evil man in the world, so he rarely found himself welcomed by his immediate neighbors. In 1923 he was forced to leave Sicily. His later years were plagued by drug addiction, deteriorating health, and constant financial problems. In 1945 he finally settled in relative obscurity in southern England, and died there two years later.

Crowley in many ways embodies both the culmination of the remarkable occult revival of the later nineteenth century and its disintegration in the first half of the twentieth century. Practitioners of ritual magic continue to exist in modern Europe and North America, often following basic rites developed by Lévi, Mathers, or Crowley. And occult societies still exist—the

Figure 7.2   La Rocca in Cefalu, Sicily, site of some of Aleister Crowley's most notorious rites.

Source: Photo by David Hollander

Theosophical Society, Order of the Golden Dawn, and Ordo Templi Orientis—but they have lost the prominence they enjoyed in their prime. In the late nineteenth and early twentieth century, these groups and their members interacted in specific ways with then dominant strains of Western modernism. Like previous learned mages, they explored the boundaries between the physical and spiritual realms, regarding themselves as scientists and philosophers as much as magicians. Also, in a decidedly modernist bent, they explored the nature of consciousness. This aspect of their activity is perhaps best exemplified by Crowley's lifelong, and ultimately shattering, exercises to develop and test magical will. Modern learned ritual magic of the sort he practiced was very much centered on exploring the limits of the human mind, the nature of identity, and the perception and place of the self in the surrounding world.

Such concerns were not foreign to other areas of developing modern culture. Sigmund Freud (1856–1939), who expressed some interest in occultism, was keenly aware that certain aspects of his psychological systems could appear occult, especially the significance he placed on the interpretation of dreams. Other psychologists recognized the narrow boundaries separating their emerging discipline from some elements of occult endeavor and strove to reinforce them, usually by sharp criticism of occult thought. Freud's great successor and rival, Carl Jung (1875–1961), however, openly stressed more spiritualized notions of self-consciousness and self-realization, and after breaking with Freud he studied both Christian Gnosticism and Hermeticism.

The occult revival and the ritual magic of the late nineteenth and early twentieth centuries, then, cannot be dismissed simply as an outbreak of anachronistic antiquarianism, and they certainly were more than just a playful diversion for wealthy Victorian and Edwardian gentlemen and ladies. That it was to some extent, but it was also an important manifestation of some of modern European culture's deepest concerns. In their discomfort with the strict rationalism inherited from the Enlightenment, and in seeking for ways to move beyond its perceived limitations, practitioners of ritual magic and students of occult thought were very much a part of European modernism. That culture, however, would founder on the catastrophe of the First World War and would be largely swept away by the horrors of the second. The major magical movements of the second half of the twentieth century, neopaganism and above all modern witchcraft or Wicca, would similarly be reflections of their specific times, and of the increasingly postmodern Western culture of the late twentieth and early twenty-first centuries. Before turning to those movements, however, we should briefly explore the remarkable place of magic, witchcraft, and the occult in the watershed between the two halves of European history in the twentieth century, the Nazi regime in Germany.

Hitler and the Magicians

German-speaking central Europe shared in the late nineteenth- and early twentieth-century craze for occultism. Berlin and especially Vienna became major occult centers, and numerous occult societies emerged in central European lands, often with international connections. The Ordo Templi Orientis, for example, had links through Theodor Reuss to the French Martinist Order and even to the Golden Dawn. Another important figure, the Austrian Rudolf Steiner (1861–1925), headed the German section of the Theosophical Society in the early twentieth century before breaking off to form his own, related, Anthroposophical Society. The Nazis would later portray fascination with the occult as an aspect of underlying decadence that had weakened Germany, contributed to the German defeat in World War I, and utterly undermined the viability of the interwar Weimar Republic. Theosophy, Anthroposophy, Rosicrucianism, and international Freemasonry were all regarded as threats to the German state and Germanic culture. Once the Nazis came to power in the 1930s, occult groups faced harsh repression. Yet, in one of the numerous ironies surrounding the Nazi regime, its claims, and its realities, Nazi ideology and even the party itself had certain decidedly occult roots.

While most occult organizations in the late nineteenth and early twentieth centuries explicitly regarded themselves as international and open to anyone willing to accept their principles, some groups incorporated the profound nationalism that also infused this era of European history. This was particularly true in Germany, where the modern German state had only come into existence in 1871, fused together from various principalities and provinces of the former Holy Roman Empire, itself utterly fragmented and finally, formally done away with by Napoleon in 1806. Issues of nationalism and national identity were, then, especially prevalent in central Europe, and occultists in these lands often focused their explorations on the dim traditions of the ancient past, not in order to achieve esoteric wisdom applicable to all humanity, but to reveal and restore some kind of putatively original, authentic, and popular (völkisch) Germanic culture. Perhaps most famously the Austrian Guido von List (1848–1919) combined a fascination with the supposed pagan roots of German culture and interest in occultism in his study of early Germanic runes. His Guido von List Society was an important influence on the Bavarian Thule Society, an occultist organization founded in 1918 and dedicated to reviving völkisch German culture. The Thule Society was also politically active, mainly in resisting international communism. From the society in 1919 emerged a political arm, the German Workers' Party, which in 1920 expanded its name to the National Socialist German Workers' Party (Nationalsozialistische Deutsche Arbeiterpartei, abbreviated as Nazi). Its new party chief, Adolph Hitler (1889–1945), was influenced in his search for an appropriate emblem to choose a pagan and occult symbol, the swastika.

Nazi racial policies were doubtless somewhat influenced by specifically Germanic, völkisch occultism, but certainly no more than they were by nineteenth-century racial science, and of course by a more generalized and deeply rooted European anti-Semitism. Some members of the Nazi Party were very attracted to occultism and magic, most notably the deputy party leader Rudolf Hess (1894–1987) and Heinrich Himmler (1900–1945), head of the SS and Gestapo. The SS's famous deaths-head symbol, for example, had clear occult overtones, as did Himmler's selection of Wewelsburg Castle as its ceremonial headquarters, the setting for *völkisch* and occultist rites designed to emphasize the Aryan purity of the SS. Hitler and other Nazi leaders dabbled in astrology and other occult practices in minor ways. Yet on the whole, the Nazi leadership remained suspicious of occultism and opposed to most occult organizations and societies, which they regarded as dangerously international and tinged with Judaism. The importance of Jewish Kabbalah for many occult traditions constituted a serious argument against them in Nazi minds. The powerful propaganda minister Joseph Goebbels (1897–1945), in particular, loudly derided occult and magical systems.

One aspect of Europe's historical magical tradition that Goebbels was happy to appropriate for Nazi ends, however, was witchcraft, although he had to ignore much of the historical reality of witchcraft in order to do so. By the mid-twentieth century, the notion that medieval and early modern witches had actually been practitioners of a pre-Christian, pagan religion (which will be explored in more detail in the next section) had gained considerable credence. The Nazi leadership decided that witches would make useful symbols of northern European *völkisch* culture, in opposition to essentially Mediterranean Christianity, which was, moreover, rooted in Judaism. Women proclaimed to be witches were incorporated into many of the great Nazi celebrations and party rallies orchestrated by Goebbels in the 1930s. Himmler did his part as well, creating a *Hexen-sonderkommando* (Special Witch Unit) within the SS. As the Third Reich expanded to encompass all of the lands of the First Reich, the medieval and early modern German empire that had been the heartland of the witch hunts, this unit conducted impressively thorough surveys of judicial records, noting all witch trials. The most likely intent was to provide a basis for propaganda unmasking supposed Christian oppression and attempted extermination of true Germanic culture. These case files, which despite many errors and omissions comprise the most systematic survey of witch trials ever made over a large area, survived the war (while many actual archive records did not) but lay forgotten in Poland until a German historian, Gerhard Schormann, discovered and used them as the basis of a study of early modern German witch hunting in 1981—a strangely useful contribution from the dark Nazi era to the history of European witchcraft.[1]

As Europe's first and only "pro-witch" government, the Nazi regime has also exerted some lasting influence on popular understandings of witchcraft and on some forms of popular magical practices in the second half of the twentieth century. Most modern witches, or Wiccans, would be horrified at the thought of any connection between the Nazis and themselves. Yet there is no denying that the Nazi leadership accepted and promoted the notion of historical witchcraft as a pagan religion that proved so vital for the early development of modern witchcraft in the 1950s, 1960s, and 1970s. Nazi support of this idea had no direct influence on Wicca, or on most other forms of modern neopaganism. Yet some neopagan groups, particularly those that emphasize Nordic paganism, see themselves as continuing the Nazi struggle to promote "authentic" Germanic culture in opposition to Judeo-Christianity through their beliefs and their magical practices.

The connection between Nazism and certain groups of neopagan skinheads is obvious but marginal within the broader spectrum of neopaganism. There is a thread, however, connecting Nazism to certain conceptions of historical witchcraft that have become quite central to much modern neopagan and especially Wiccan thought, and even to popular conceptions of European witchcraft and witch hunting in general. Beginning especially with the rise of the feminist movement and important feminist scholarship in the 1960s and 1970s, many people came to see the historical European witch hunts as an example of the deliberate repression of unruly women by patriarchal authorities. There is no doubt that all the authorities who conducted the witch hunts were men and that a large majority of those convicted and executed for witchcraft were women. While most experts now reject the interpretation that witch hunts were primarily driven by, or are best understood as, male attempts to control women, the idea of witch hunting as woman hunting and woman hating has gained considerable acceptance in the popular imagination. Few people realize, however, that the earliest widespread articulation of a form of this idea occurred during the Nazi period.

Nazism advocated its own peculiar form of feminism, which asserted the superiority of Aryan woman over the men of degenerate races (though not, of course, over Aryan men). Nazi feminists saw the historical witch hunts as an example of Christian, and therefore ultimately Jewish, attempts to destroy Aryan womanhood. An otherwise unknown author, Friederike Müller-Reimerdes, offered a twisted Nazi conception of its own supposed near-holocaust by claiming in her 1935 pamphlet *Der christliche Hexenwahn* (The Christian Witch-Craze) that the hunts were an attempt to exterminate all woman carrying Aryan racial features, as a means to eliminate the Aryan race entirely from Europe. A year earlier, in 1934, Mathilde Ludendorff (1877–1966), an early follower of Hitler and a leader of the German pagan movement in the 1930s, asserted in her pamphlet *Christliche Grausamkeit an Deutschen Frauen*

(Christian Cruelty to German Women) that some nine million women had been killed in the course of the witch hunts.[2]

The figure of nine million women killed as witches has proved to be a remarkably enduring feature of the mythology that has grown up around historical witchcraft. Despite the best efforts of now several generations of historians to provide accurate statistics, it gets trotted out every now and then by uninformed people and is grimly maintained as accurate by a few (it must be stressed, a very few) determined feminist and neopagan authors—all of whom would no doubt be mortified to learn that they are, in this claim, echoing Nazi propaganda. The German historian Wolfgang Behringer has traced the origin of this utterly bogus figure to an eighteenth-century scholar, Gottfried Christian Voigt (1740–1791), who estimated the total number of witchcraft executions in Europe from some twenty cases recorded over fifty years in the archives of the town of Quedlinburg. Voigt decided that this data provided a universally applicable ratio of witch trials for a given population over a given period, and so simply enlarged the numbers to account for the entire population of Europe and for the full 1,800 years of Christian history, during the whole of which time he apparently assumed witch hunts were being conducted with equal ferocity. The number he arrived at was then rounded off to nine million by a Viennese professor of church history, Gustav Roskoff (1814–1889), in his 1869 book *Geschichte des Teufels* (History of the Devil). From there, while never accepted as definitive, this imaginary figure entered mainstream German historical discourse about witchcraft, ultimately infusing Nazi rhetoric.[3]

The Rise of Modern Witchcraft

In the second half of the twentieth century, and particularly since the 1970s, a spectrum of so called neopagan movements has developed in Europe and North America. Conceived by their practitioners as revivals or at least imaginative recreations of ancient, pre-Christian systems of belief, they focus mainly on nature worship. Many emphasize female spirituality and the feminine divine, which neopagans typically feel Christianity has historically repressed. A number of neopagan belief systems focus on a single goddess-figure, usually conceived as a fertility deity and universal mother and referred to as the Great Goddess, or simply the Goddess. Most neopagans also claim to believe in and practice magic in some form. By the end of the twentieth century, the groups comprising this movement had become numerous and varied, so here I will focus only on the development of modern witchcraft, also commonly known, especially by its adherents, as Wicca. Although now also quite diverse in their practices and organizations, Wiccans do share basic traditions, and they comprise the largest single component of the neopagan spectrum. Moreover, Wicca is the oldest of the modern neopagan movements, and is the root, or at least the inspiration, from which many others have sprung. Finally, while by the end of the twentieth century the United States had become the inarguable heartland of neopaganism, Wicca originated in Europe. One scholar has called it the only religion that England has ever given to the world (which is true in terms of fully unique religious systems, although this discounts such major Christian confessions as Anglicanism or Methodism).[4]

A historian approaching modern witchcraft confronts two significant problems. The first is that much of the early history of Wicca is known only through the accounts of its founders, which are often inconsistent and unreliable (a fact that certainly also applies to other religions such as Christianity or Islam). The second is that the founders of Wicca had a very specific notion of historical witchcraft in Europe and of their movement's relationship to it. This myth, it must be said, profoundly distorted the actual history of witchcraft, but it played a major role in the early development of Wicca. Of course all religions construct nonhistorical narratives in the interest of belief, which historians of religion must then take seriously as expressions of faith. My account, however, is not intended primarily as a history of Wicca as a religion, but rather as an examination of the movement as the most recent and currently most significant development in the long history of magic in Europe. For this reason, Wicca's relationship to historical witchcraft and other past magical traditions, real and imagined, must be clarified.

Modern witchcraft initially arose in England primarily through the efforts of Gerald Gardner (1884–1964), who in 1954 published the book that essentially launched the Wiccan movement, *Witchcraft Today*. Gardner claimed that the witchcraft supposedly existent in his day was no different from, and was in fact a direct continuation of, the witchcraft that had existed in early modern Europe. He asserted that witchcraft was and had always been an ancient, pre-Christian pagan faith surviving through unbroken chains of practice and family traditions down through the ages. Gardner was not himself from a lineage that maintained this ancient tradition. He had been born into a thoroughly modern and well-off family near Liverpool, had entered government service, and had spent most of his career stationed in Asian outposts of the British Empire. In 1936 he retired and moved back to England, settling two years later in the New Forest region on the southern coast near the Isle of Wight. There he became involved in a theater group that staged plays on occult and Rosicrucian themes. Through this group, he claimed to have met a woman he called Old Dorothy, to whom he later ascribed the last name Clutterbuck. She supposedly was a hereditary witch, the inheritor of ancient traditions preserved and handed down through her family, who initiated Gardner as a witch himself in 1939. In fact there was a wealthy lady, Dorothy Fordham, nee Clutterbuck (1880–1951), who lived in this area at the time. According to all independent accounts, however, she was an utterly respectable member of society, profoundly conservative in her deportment and activities. She had no involvement with the somewhat outré Rosicrucian Theater, and portions of her diaries that have been made available for examination present no trace of evidence that she led a secret double life as a witch.[5] Rather than "discovering" modern witchcraft, Gardner assembled it from various sources.

Already in the Far East, Gardner had been drawn to the study of world religions, and once back in England he pursued amateur anthropological studies, joining the Folk-Lore Society, an important ethnographic group at the time. He was also clearly interested in magical practices and the occult, as his association with the Rosicrucian Theater indicates. He pursued magical studies seriously enough to seek out Aleister Crowley, meeting him in 1947 and being initiated into the Ordo Templi Orientis. Gardner appears to have had some ambition to found an OTO temple himself, yet for unknown reasons his interest in established ritual magic traditions had faded by the early 1950s. He later referred to Crowley as a "charming charlatan." Gardner's interest in magical systems in general was not fading, however; instead, he focused increasingly on developing his system of modern witchcraft. But from where did Gardner's idea of witchcraft as a ritualistic magical religion come?

As the previous section indicated, the idea of historical European witchcraft as a pagan religion had gained many adherents by the middle of the twentieth century. The origins of the idea actually lie in nineteenth-century scholarship. Informed by Enlightenment ideals, historians of the nineteenth century typically considered historical belief in witchcraft to have been a delusion fostered mainly by clerical authorities, whom they blamed for promoting the murder of thousands of innocents through witch hunting. In 1828, however, Karl Ernst Jarcke (1801–1852), a young legal scholar at the University of Berlin with pro-clerical leanings, suggested that witchcraft had actually represented the remnants of pre-Christian paganism in Europe. Thus Christian authorities had had at least some real justification for seeking to repress these practices and the people who engaged in them. A well-established historian, Franz Josef Mone (1796–1871), took up this argument in 1839. Then in 1844 the famous philologist and folklorist Jakob Grimm (1785–1863), now best known along with his brother for their collection of fairytales, but a leading light of the German academic world in the nineteenth century, also supported the notion that some elements of traditional witchcraft were based on pre-Christian Germanic traditions.[6] Only in 1862, however, did the French historian Jules Michelet (1798–1874) argue in his book *La sorcière* (The Witch, translated into English as *Satanism and Witchcraft*) that historical witchcraft had been an active pagan religion in the medieval and early modern periods, rather than simply the residue of earlier pagan practices. Michelet was profoundly anticlerical, and his purpose was the opposite of Jarke's: rather than justifying Christian opposition to witchcraft, he sought to depict a cruel and intolerant church using the witch hunts to eradicate a vibrant, popular religion.

Serious historians dismissed Michelet's work on witchcraft and it had little impact within academia. He was broadly read by the general public, however, on both sides of the Atlantic. In the United States, his work was cited by one of the founding mothers of the woman suffrage movement, Matilda Joslyn Gage (1826–1898), who saw the witch hunts as a classic example of male repression of women.[7] Michelet also influenced a wealthy American amateur ethnographer, Charles Leland (1824–1903), who was educated in Paris and lived most of his life in Florence. There he met a woman named Maddalena who claimed to practice exactly the sort of witch religion that Michelet described. The roots of her folk religion, she maintained, extended into deep antiquity, even to the pre-Roman Etruscan period. Leland eagerly collected her beliefs and practices, publishing them in 1899 as *Aradia, or the Gospel of the Witches*. In fact, Leland probably worked with Maddalena, or at least strongly encouraged her to construct her beliefs in a certain way. The witchcraft described in *Aradia* largely mixed Michelet's historical ideas with more recent mythographic notions of the sort promoted by James Frazer (1854–1951) in his famous work *The Golden Bough*, first published in 1890.[8] Frazer argued that beneath the myths of various ancient cultures lay an essentially unified religious system focused on natural fertility cycles and on fertility gods and especially goddesses.

Entering the twentieth century, we encounter the most important name in the construction of the myth of witchcraft as an ancient pagan fertility religion, Margaret Murray (1863–1963). She was a remarkable woman, a major Egyptologist trained at the University of London, with a successful academic career at a time when English higher education was hardly welcoming to women. Hers is now, however, a name that causes all serious historians of European witchcraft to grimace. In addition to her professional expertise in ancient Egypt, she wrote on many subjects connected with the study of ancient religions and belonged to the English Folk-Lore Society. It was probably through this group that, around the time of the First World War, she was exposed to the idea of a pagan witch religion. Her first publications on this matter were in the journal of the Society beginning in 1917. In 1921 she published *The Witch-Cult in Western Europe*, a full-blown but poorly researched and argued academic history of witchcraft as an ancient pagan fertility religion opposed by the Christian church in Europe. Although her book was immediately dismissed by historians, Murray was committed to advancing her ideas. In 1929 she wrote the article on witchcraft for the fourteenth edition of the *Encyclopedia Britannica* (it remained through subsequent editions until 1968), and in 1931 she published *The God of the Witches*, presenting her basic theories and claims for a more popular audience. After World War II her theories achieved even further popularity, and remarkably also began to gain some academic acceptance, more so in Europe than in the United States, before being debunked again, this time definitively, by a series of scholars mainly in the 1970s.[9] In 1954 Murray made her most farfetched claims in *The Divine King of England*. Here she presented a vast, premodern conspiracy theory in which every king of England from William the Conqueror in the eleventh century to James I in the seventeenth had been a member of the witches' cult, and many major events in English history were tied to the ritual operations of this secret group. Murray served as the primary historical source for Gerald Gardner. The two had collaborated on an early paper on historical witchcraft for the Folk-Lore Society, and Murray wrote a brief introduction to *Witchcraft Today* when it appeared in 1954.

Claiming to have been initiated into a coven of witches whose traditions and practices stretched unbroken back through the centuries, Gardner maintained that these magical rites were ancient. In fact, they blended Rosicrucian, Hermetic, and other ritual magic as practiced by Aleister Crowley and groups like the Golden Dawn, elements of nature worship and fertility ceremonies influenced by Frazerian theories and Gardner's own study of world religions, along with elements purely of Gardner's creation. By the early 1950s, he had systematized these rites and ceremonies, assembling them into a collection evocatively referred to as the Book of Shadows. This book then went through significant revisions over the course of the decade by Gardner and his chief assistant and high priestess, Doreen Valiente (1922–1999).[10] In fact, Valiente may have been as important as Gardner himself in the creation and early codifications of Wiccan rites. She particularly disliked the influence of Crowley and his systems of ritual magic on earlier versions of the Book of Shadows and excised many of these passages. She also began to emphasize the central figure of the Goddess in Wiccan belief. Even with Crowley's influence muted, Wiccan rites remained highly sexualized. Gardner stressed the need for both priests and priestesses as well as male and female practitioners when performing rites so that sexual energies could be exploited. Rites were to be performed nude, and while these did not involve actual ritualized intercourse, Gardner suggested that priests and priestesses might have sex privately before or after the ceremonies to heighten their powers.

Aside from creating a new system of belief and ritual structure, Gardner was also a tireless promoter and publicist. An old act against witchcraft and vagrancy made it a crime in Great Britain to claim to be a witch. Parliament finally repealed this act in 1951, and almost immediately Gardner went public with his beliefs, partnering in his early publicity efforts with Cecil Williamson (1909–1999), who had formerly worked in the movie industry and since 1947 had operated a witchcraft museum as a tourist attraction. Using this museum as a base (Gardner was declared to be the "witch in residence"), the promotion of modern witchcraft was achieved mainly through press coverage and Gardner's own publications, including his necessarily novelized account (since it was first published in 1949, before the repeal of the witchcraft act) High Magic's Aid and then Witchcraft Today. It was in this latter work that Gardner designated modern witchcraft as Wica, now commonly spelled Wicca, from the Anglo-Saxon word for sorcerer or male witch (the female form would be wicce).

Wiccan groups, or covens, spread throughout the 1950s and 1960s, sometimes established by followers of Gardner and sometimes emerging independently. The first documented coven in the United States appeared in 1963. Gardner in no sense controlled these groups, but insofar as they adhered to the rites and practices he established, they can be said to comprise the Gardnerian tradition. There were soon defections from this tradition, however. As early as 1957, Doreen Valiente, Gardner's chief assistant, grew tired of his dominance, formed her own group, and began to develop her own traditions, although still along essentially Gardnerian lines. In the mid-1960s, Alex Sanders (1926–1988) emerged as a major figure on the English witchcraft scene, arguably eclipsing Gardner. Sanders claimed that his grandmother was a witch and that she had initiated him into witchcraft while he was still a young boy. Thus he was a hereditary witch in whose family the old religion had passed down unbroken. Claims to such hereditary knowledge became a standard way to challenge the authority of Gardner's rites and systems of witchcraft. In fact, Sanders drew heavily on Gardner's Book of Shadows, as well as on earlier systems of ritual magic such as those developed by Eliphas Lévi. Seeking publicity even more assiduously than Gardner, Sanders was soon styling himself the "King of the Witches" in Britain. His Alexandrian tradition became a major rival to the Gardnerian strain of Wicca. Further fragmentation ensued, until by the late 1960s and early 1970s many Wiccans began claiming that personal experimentation and entirely individualized versions of the Craft (as it was coming to be called) were as valid as any more systematic tradition.

Also in this period, the center of modern witchcraft began shifting from England to the United States, where Wicca also became more clearly feminist in nature. In 1968 a group calling itself the Women's International Terrorist Conspiracy from Hell (WITCH) formed in New York City, fully appropriating historical witchcraft for the modern women's movement. WITCH issued a manifesto claiming that historical witchcraft had been not just a pagan religion but a protofeminist one, in opposition to patriarchal Christianity. The group also publicized the figure of nine million women dead in the witch hunts, which had been introduced to American feminist thought by Matilda Joslyn Gage in her 1893 work *Woman, Church, and State*. WITCH soon disbanded, but their use of witchcraft was taken up by major feminist writers in the 1970s, including Mary Daly in *Beyond God the Father* (1973) and *Gyn/Ecology* (1978) and Andrea Dworkin in *Woman Hating* (1974).[11] Their concern was less with witchcraft as a modern religion than as a supposed counterpoint to the historical dominance of men and an example of the supposedly genocidal horrors men could inflict on women. The witch, in both her historical and modern guises, became a symbol of female empowerment. The fullest incorporation of such ideas into the actual system of Wicca was achieved by the highly influential Californian Wiccan writer Starhawk (born 1951 as Miriam Simos). Her 1979 book *The Spiral Dance*, a poetic meditation on the meaning of Wicca and its rites, became for many, especially in the United States, the most essential statement of Wiccan beliefs. In this and other works, Starhawk helped to establish the central role of feminism, as well as environmentalism and related political concerns, in Wicca, particularly as it exists in North America.

Starhawk's approach to Wicca was largely philosophical and poetic. She uncritically accepted the myth of witchcraft as a pagan religion popularized by Murray and Gardner, and she repeated the venerable fable of nine million women executed during the witch hunts in *The Spiral Dance*. The tenth anniversary edition of this work included a note stating that this figure was an estimate that was "probably high," but Starhawk continued to defend her conviction in the essential reality of most of Murray's theory of historical witchcraft. In the same year as the original publication of *The Spiral Dance*, however, the journalist and practicing Wiccan Margot Adler (born 1946) published *Drawing Down the Moon*, which took a serious look at the origins of Wicca and other neopagan movements. She recognized that many of Gerald Gardner's claims about how he gained his knowledge of the rites and ceremonies of modern witchcraft were obviously false, and more basically that the idea of historical witchcraft as a pagan religion was untenable. She also recognized, however, that such facts were irrelevant to Wicca's authenticity or value as a belief system. While some modern witches still cling adamantly to the historical accuracy of their myths about the "burning times," most now recognize that theirs is actually a new religion and a new magical tradition formed from complex roots. But if Wicca's connection to historical witchcraft is not what its founders claimed, its blurring of any distinction between concepts of religion and magic and even its misconceptions and misappropriations of the past very much reflect certain persistent tendencies recurring over the long course of Europe's magical history.

Just as the occultist and magical groups of the late nineteenth and early twentieth centuries cannot be dismissed an mere antiquarians, so Wiccan and other neopagan groups in the late twentieth and early twenty-first centuries cannot simply be explained as misinformed attempts to resuscitate ancient pagan beliefs. All these modern groups are best seen as drawing on magical traditions and employing magical rites in profoundly presentist ways in order to confront and criticize aspects of contemporary culture. If nineteenth-century occultists were fully imbued with the spirit of modernism that pervaded Europe until the First World War, the origins and early success of modern witchcraft were shaped by the dilemma faced by mainstream European religious and philosophical systems in the aftermath of the horrors of World War II. Wiccans and other neopagans were then influenced by, incorporated, and responded to aspects of the counterculture of the 1960s, the feminism of the 1970s, the environmentalism of the 1980s, and the gender and identity politics of the 1990s and beyond. Perhaps most basically, the neopagan association of magic with nature, instinct, emotion, and especially with playfulness as well as with serious power can be seen as elements of a

postmodernist reaction to the absolute value of intellect and scientific rationalism that has dominated Western culture since the Enlightenment.

From its emergence in the 1950s, modern witchcraft has attracted a great
deal of attention. At the beginning of the twenty-first century, even the
highest estimates assumed that there were no more than around 400,000
Wiccans and other neopagans in the United States (alongside over one and a
half million Muslims, nearly four million Jews, and over two hundred million
Christians). Their numbers are certainly much smaller in Europe. Yet
witches of a more or less Wiccan variety have figured in far more popular
movies and television shows than, for example, America's over 800,000 Uni-
tarians. Especially because of their claims that they practice real and effective
magic, modern witches have often been regarded with great interest, but also
with fear and suspicion. In particular, they have frequently been branded as
Satanists, just as other magicians and occultists throughout the modern
period. In fact, as non-Christians, neopagans by definition cannot be Satanists because they do not acknowledge the existence of the Christian devil.
Even self-proclaimed Satanist groups like the famous Church of Satan
founded in 1966 in San Francisco by Anton Szandor LaVey (1930–1997) do
not believe in or worship the Christian devil. Rather, they advocate personal
freedom and carnal pleasure, and pursue both through ritual magic in the
style of such precursors as Aleister Crowley. Of course, Western authorities
have a long tradition of maintaining that people can be guilty of inadvertently or unintentionally summoning and worshiping demons, or more simply of hiding such activity behind claims of innocence. Yet none of the
numerous scares over alleged satanic cults that have regularly erupted in
modern Europe and the United States, usually centered on the supposed discovery of animal or even infant sacrifices, has ever produced any evidence
connecting such practices to occultist or neopagan groups. Indeed, once the
initial claims have been examined carefully, there has typically been no credible evidence of such activity at all.

So the history of magic, both as a source of presumed power and as a
source of fear, continues in Europe and in the Western world generally into
the twenty-first century. Wiccans and neopagans practice magical rites, as do
groups of ritual magicians, as do traditional healers and cunning folk. And
numerous people who would never think of themselves as practicing magic
consult astrologers or psychics, read horoscopes, avoid black cats, or throw
salt over their shoulders, all with greater or lesser degrees of seriousness.
Since the Enlightenment, Western culture as a whole has looked on the possible real power of such practices with far greater skepticism than during any

other historical era, but some level of skepticism has always been present in the history of magic, no matter what period is considered. Throughout the centuries, there has been constant disagreement and debate about whether, and how, magic really functions, and more basically about what constitutes magic.

Happily, historians do not need to treat magic as an objectively definable set of actions that operate, or claim to operate, in some particular way. Rather, we can describe how the ever shifting categories of magic and superstition have been used to label various actions and beliefs at different times. Generally throughout history, religious or secular authorities have labeled as "magic" practices they wish to condemn by casting them as sacrilegious and threats to social order. Increasingly in the modern period, with the threat of legal punishment removed, certain groups have labeled their own actions as magic, often as a way to criticize or challenge established authorities or social structures. Whatever specific conceptions and meanings of magic or superstition prevail in any given period, in general these categories have always had to do with the realm just beyond human beings' clear understanding and straightforward control. They have been used throughout history to construct and to contest the limits of culturally approved belief and socially acceptable action. They have also been used to demarcate the unknowable and to give shape to the known. Shadowy as they are, their force throughout history has been very real.

Notes

1. Gerhard Schormann, *Hexenprozesse in Deutschland* (Göttingen: Vandenhoeck & Ruprecht, 1981).

2. Mathilde Ludendorf, *Christliche Grausamkeit an deutschen Frauen* (Munich, 1934); Friederike Müller-Reimerdes, *Der christliche Hexenwahn* (Leipzig, 1935).

3. Wolfgang Behringer, "Neun Millionen Hexen: Entstehung, Tradition und Kritik eines populären Mythos," *Geschichte in Wissenschaft und Unterricht* 49 (1998): 664–85. See also Behringer, *Witches and Witch-Hunts: A Global History* (Cambridge: Polity, 2004), 157–58, 233–35.

4. Ronald Hutton, *The Triumph of the Moon: A History of Modern Pagan Witchcraft* (Oxford: Oxford University Press, 1999), vii.

5. The diaries have been examined by Ronald Hutton. See Hutton, *Triumph of the Moon*, 211.

6. K. E. Jarcke, "Ein Hexenprozess," *Annalen der deutschen und ausländischen Criminal-Rechts-Pflege* 1 (1828); F. J. Mone, "Über das Hexenwesen," *Anzeiger für Kunde der teutschen Vorzeit* 8 (1839). The importance of these two scholars was first identified by Nor-

man Cohn, *Europe's Inner Demons: The Demonization of Christians in Medieval Christendom*, rev. ed. (Chicago: University of Chicago Press, 2000), 148–49. Jacob Grimm, *Teutonic Mythology*, trans. J. S. Stallybrass, 4 vols. (London: George Bell and Sons, 1882–88), 3: 1044–93.

7. Matilda Joslyn Gage, *Woman, Church, and State: A Historical Account of the Status of Women through the Christian Ages* (New York: Kerr, 1893).

8. See now James Frazer, *The Golden Bough: A Study in Magic and Religion*, 3rd ed., 12 vols. (London: Macmillan, 1913–1920); or the single volume abridgement *The Golden Bough* (New York: Macmillan, 1927).

9. In particular, see Cohn, *Europe's Inner Demons* (originally published in 1975).

10. While Gardner published some extracts from the Book of Shadows, and pirated versions later appeared in print, there has never been a fully official published version. But see Janet Farrar and Stewart Farrar, *The Witches' Way: Principles, Rituals, and Beliefs of Modern Witchcraft* (London: Hale, 1984).

11. Mary Daly, *Beyond God the Father: Toward a Philosophy of Women's Liberation* (Boston: Beacon, 1973), and Daly, *Gyn/Ecology: A Metaethics of Radical Feminism* (Boston: Beacon, 1978); Andrea Dworkin, *Woman Hating* (New York: Dutton, 1974).

Sources and Suggestions for Further Reading

Chapter One

Abusch, Tzvi. *Babylonian Witchcraft Literature: Case Studies.* Atlanta, Ga.: Scholars Press, 1987.

———. *Mesopotamian Witchcraft: Toward a History and Understanding of Babylonian Witchcraft Beliefs and Literature.* Leiden: Brill Styx, 2002.

Abusch, Tzvi, and Karel van der Toorn, eds. *Mesopotamian Magic: Textual, Historical, and Interpretive Perspectives.* Leiden: Brill Styx, 2000.

Ankarloo, Bengt, and Stuart Clark, eds. *Witchcraft and Magic in Europe: Ancient Greece and Rome.* Philadelphia: University of Pennsylvania Press, 1999.

———. *Witchcraft and Magic in Europe: Biblical and Pagan Societies.* Philadelphia: University of Pennsylvania Press, 2001.

Asirvatham, Sulochana R., Corinne Ondine Pache, and John Watrous, eds. *Between Magic and Religion: Interdisciplinary Studies in Ancient Mediterranean Religion and Society.* Lanham, Md.: Rowman and Littlefield, 2001.

Betz, Hans Dieter, ed. *The Greek Magical Papyri in Translation, Including the Demotic Spells.* 2nd ed. Chicago: University of Chicago Press, 1992.

Bremmer, Jan N. "The Birth of the Term 'Magic.'" In *The Metamorphosis of Magic from Late Antiquity to the Early Modern Period,* edited by Jan N. Bremmer and Jan R. Veenstra, 1–11. Leuven: Peeters, 2002.

Brenk, Frederick E. "In the Light of the Moon: Demonology in the Early Imperial Period." In *Aufstieg und Niedergang der römischen Welt* II.16.3, edited by Wolfgang Haase, 2068–2145. Berlin: Walter de Gruyter, 1986.

Ciraolo, Leda, and Jonathan Seidel, eds. *Magic and Divination in the Ancient World.* Leiden: Brill Styx, 2002.

Cryer, Frederick, *Divination in Ancient Israel and its Near-Eastern Environs: A Socio-Historical*

Investigation. Sheffield, England: Journal for the Study of the Old Testament Press, 1994.

Dickie, Matthew W. *Magic and Magicians in the Greco-Roman World.* London: Routledge, 2001.

Faraone, Christopher A. "An Accusation of Magic in Classical Athens." *Transactions of the American Philological Association* 119 (1989): 149–60.

———. "Binding and Burying the Forces of Evil: Defensive Use of 'Voodoo' Dolls in Ancient Greece." *Classical Antiquity* 10 (1991): 165–205.

———. *Ancient Greek Love Magic.* Cambridge, Mass.: Harvard University Press, 1999.

Faraone, Christopher A., and Dirk Obbink, eds. *Magika Hiera: Ancient Greek Magic and Religion.* Oxford: Oxford University Press, 1991.

Finkel, Irving L. "Necromancy in Ancient Mesopotamia." *Archiv für Orientforschung* 29–30 (1983–84): 1–17.

Frankfurter, David. "The Magic of Writing and the Writing of Magic: The Power of the Word in Egyptian and Greek Traditions." *Helios* 21 (1994): 189–221.

Gager, John G., ed. *Curse Tablets and Binding Spells from the Ancient World.* Oxford: Oxford University Press, 1992.

Graf, Fritz. *Magic in the Ancient World.* Translated by Franklin Philip. Cambridge, Mass.: Harvard University Press, 1997.

Janowitz, Naomi. *Magic in the Roman World: Pagans, Jews, and Christians.* London: Routledge, 2001.

Janssen, L. F. "'Superstitio' and the Persecution of Christians." *Vigiliae Christianae* 33 (1979): 131–59.

Jeffers, Ann. *Magic and Divination in Ancient Palestine and Syria.* Leiden: Brill, 1996.

Johnston, Sarah Iles, and Peter Struck, eds. *Mantikê: Studies in Ancient Divination.* Leiden: Brill Styx, 2005.

Martínez, Florentino García. "Magic in the Dead Sea Scrolls." In *The Metamorphosis of Magic from Late Antiquity to the Early Modern Period,* edited by Jan N. Bremmer and Jan R. Veenstra, 13–33. Leuven: Peeters, 2002.

Luck, Georg. *Ancient Pathways and Hidden Pursuits: Religion, Morals, and Magic in the Ancient World.* Ann Arbor: University of Michigan Press, 2000.

Luck, Georg, ed. *Arcana Mundi: Magic and the Occult in the Greek and Roman Worlds.* Baltimore: Johns Hopkins University Press, 1985.

Martin, Dale B. *Inventing Superstition: From the Hippocratics to the Christians.* Cambridge, Mass.: Harvard University Press, 2004.

Meyer, Marvin, and Paul Mirecki, eds. *Ancient Magic and Ritual Power.* Leiden: Brill, 1995.

Mirecki, Paul, and Marvin Meyer, eds. *Magic and Ritual in the Ancient World.* Leiden: Brill, 2002.

Noegel, Scott, Joel Walker, and Brannon Wheeler, eds. *Prayer, Magic, and the Stars in the Ancient and Late-Antique World.* University Park: Pennsylvania State University Press, 2003.

Ogden, Daniel. *Greek and Roman Necromancy.* Princeton, N.J.: Princeton University Press, 2001.

———. *Magic, Witchcraft, and Ghosts in the Greek and Roman Worlds: A Sourcebook.* Oxford: Oxford University Press, 2002.

Pinch, Geraldine. *Magic in Ancient Egypt.* Austin: University of Texas Press, 1994.

Reiner, Erica. *Astral Magic in Babylonia.* Philadelphia: American Philosophical Society, 1995.

Rollins, S. "Women and Witchcraft in Ancient Assyria (c. 900–600 B.C.)." In *Images of Women in Antiquity,* edited by Averil Cameron and Amélie Kuhrt, 34–45. Detroit: Wayne State University Press, 1983.

Russell, Jeffrey Burton. *The Devil: Perceptions of Evil from Antiquity to Primitive Christianity.* Ithaca, N.Y.: Cornell University Press, 1977.

Salzman, Michele R. "'Superstitio' in the Codex Theodosianus and the Persecution of the Pagans." *Vigiliae Christianae* 41 (1987): 172–88.

Schäfer, Peter, and Hans G. Kippenberg, eds. *Envisioning Magic: A Princeton Seminar and Symposium.* Leiden: Brill, 1997.

Ward, John O. "Women, Witchcraft, and Social Patterning in the Later Roman Law-codes." *Prudentia* 13 (1981): 99–118.

Chapter Two

Aune, D. E. "Magic in Early Christianity." In *Aufsteig und Neidergang der römischen Welt* II.23.2, edited by Wolfgang Haase, 1507–57. Berlin: Walter de Gruyter, 1980.

Barb, A. A. "The Survival of the Magic Arts." In *The Conflict Between Paganism and Christianity in the Fourth Century,* edited by Arnaldo Momigliano, 110–25. Oxford: Clarendon Press, 1963.

Brown, Peter. "Sorcery, Demons, and the Rise of Christianity: From Late-Antiquity into the Middle Ages." In Peter Brown, *Religion and Society in the Age of St. Augustine.* New York: Harper and Row, 1972, 119–46.

Flint, Valerie I. J. *The Rise of Magic in Early Medieval Europe.* Princeton, N.J.: Princeton University Press, 1991.

Garrett, Susan R. "Light on a Dark Subject and Vice Versa: Magic and Magicians in the New Testament." In *Religion and Science in Concert and in Conflict,* edited by Jacob Neusner, Ernest S. Frerichs, and Paul Virgil McCracken Flesher, 142–65. Oxford: Oxford University Press, 1989.

Graf, Fritz. "Augustine and Magic." In *The Metamorphosis of Magic from Late Antiquity to the Early Modern Period,* edited by Jan N. Bremmer and Jan R. Veenstra, 87–103. Leuven: Peeters, 2002.

Griffiths, Bill. *Aspects of Anglo-Saxon Magic.* Hockwold-cum-Wilton, England: Anglo-Saxon Books, 1996.

Hen, Yitzhak. *Culture and Religion in Merovingian Gaul A.D. 481–751.* Leiden: Brill, 1995.

Janowitz, Naomi. *Icons of Power: Ritual Practice in Late Antiquity*. University Park: Pennsylvania State University Press, 2002.

Jolly, Karen Louise. *Popular Religion in Late Saxon England: Elf Charms in Context*. Chapel Hill: University of North Carolina Press, 1996.

McClusky, Stephen C. *Astronomies and Cultures in Early Medieval Europe*. Cambridge: Cambridge University Press, 1998.

Meens, Rob. "Magic and the Early Medieval World View." In *Community, the Family, and the Saint: Patterns of Power in Early Medieval Europe*, edited by Joyce Hill and Mary Swan, 285–95. Turnhout, Belgium: Brepols, 1998.

Meyer, Marvin, and Richard Smith, eds. *Ancient Christian Magic: Coptic Texts of Ritual Power*. San Francisco: HarperSanFrancisco, 1994.

Murray, Alexander. "Missionaries and Magic in Dark-Age Europe." *Past and Present* 136 (1992): 186–205.

Russell, Jeffrey Burton. *Satan: The Early Christian Tradition*. Ithaca, N.Y.: Cornell University Press, 1981.

Schäfer, Peter. "Jewish Magical Literature in Late-Antiquity and the Early Middle Ages." *Journal of Jewish Studies* 41 (1990): 75–91.

Scragg, D. G., ed. *Superstition and Popular Medicine in Anglo-Saxon England*. Manchester: Manchester University Press, 1989.

Thee, Francis C. R. *Julius Africanus and the Early Christian View of Magic*. Tübingen, Germany: Mohr, 1984.

Ward, John O. "Witchcraft and Sorcery in the Later Roman Empire and the Early Middle Ages: An Anthropological Comment." *Prudentia* 12 (1980): 93–108.

Wood, Ian N. "Pagan Religions and Superstitions East of the Rhine from the Fifth to the Ninth Century." In *After Empire: Towards an Ethnology of Europe's Barbarians*, edited by G. Ausenda, 253–68. Woodbridge, England: Boydell and Brewer, 1995.

Chapters Three and Four

Ankarloo, Bengt, and Stuart Clark, eds. *Witchcraft and Magic in Europe: The Middle Ages*. Philadelphia: University of Pennsylvania Press, 2002.

Bailey, Michael D. "The Medieval Concept of the Witches' Sabbath." *Exemplaria* 8 (1996): 419–39.

———. "From Sorcery to Witchcraft: Clerical Conceptions of Magic in the Late Middle Ages." *Speculum* 76 (2001): 960–90.

———. "The Feminization of Magic and the Emerging Idea of the Female Witch in the Late Middle Ages." *Essays in Medieval Studies* 19 (2002): 120–34.

———. *Battling Demons: Witchcraft, Heresy, and Reform in the Late Middle Ages*. University Park: Pennsylvania State University Press, 2003.

———. "The Disenchantment of Magic: Spells, Charms, and Superstition in Early European Witchcraft Literature." *American Historical Review* 111 (2006): 383–404.

Bailey, Michael D., and Edward Peters. "A Sabbat of Demonologists: Basel, 1431–1449." *The Historian* 65 (2003): 1375–95.

Boureau, Alain. *Satan the Heretic: The Birth of Demonology in the Medieval West.* Translated by Teresa Lavender Fagan. Chicago: University of Chicago Press, 2006.

Broedel, Hans Peter. *The Malleus Maleficarum and the Construction of Witchcraft: Theology and Popular Belief.* Manchester: Manchester University Press, 2003.

Burnett, Charles. *Magic and Divination in the Middle Ages: Texts and Techniques in the Islamic and Christian Worlds.* Aldershot, England: Ashgate, 1996.

Cohn, Norman. *Europe's Inner Demons: The Demonization of Christians in Medieval Christendom.* Rev. ed. Chicago: University of Chicago Press, 2000.

Davidson, L. S., and J. O. Ward, eds. *The Sorcery Trial of Alice Kyteler: A Contemporary Account (1324) Together with Related Documents in English Translation, with Introduction and Notes.* Binghamton, N.Y.: Medieval and Renaissance Texts and Studies, 1993.

Fanger, Claire, ed. *Conjuring Spirits: Texts and Traditions of Medieval Ritual Magic.* University Park: Pennsylvania State University Press, 1998.

Herzig, Tamar. "Witches, Saints, and Heretics: Heinrich Kramer's Ties with Italian Women Mystics." *Magic, Ritual, and Witchcraft* 1 (2006): 24–55

Jones, William R. "The Political Uses of Sorcery in Medieval Europe." *The Historian* 34 (1972): 670–87.

Kelly, Henry Ansgar. *The Devil, Demonology, and Witchcraft: The Development of Christian Beliefs in Evil Spirits.* Rev. ed. New York: Doubleday, 1974.

Kieckhefer, Richard. *European Witch Trials: Their Foundations in Popular and Learned Culture, 1300–1500.* Berkeley and Los Angeles: University of California Press, 1976.

———. *Magic in the Middle Ages.* Cambridge: Cambridge University Press, 1989.

———. "Erotic Magic in Medieval Europe." In *Sex in the Middle Ages: A Book of Essays,* edited by Joyce E. Salisbury, 30–55. New York: Garland, 1991.

———. "The Holy and the Unholy: Sainthood, Witchcraft, and Magic in Late Medieval Europe." *Journal of Medieval and Renaissance Studies* 24 (1994): 355–85.

———. "The Specific Rationality of Medieval Magic." *American Historical Review* 99 (1994): 813–36.

———. "Avenging the Blood of Children: Anxiety Over Child Victims and the Origins of the European Witch Trials." In *The Devil, Heresy, and Witchcraft: Essays in Honor of Jeffrey B. Russell,* edited by Alberto Ferreiro, 91–109. Leiden: Brill, 1998.

———. *Forbidden Rites: A Necromancer's Manual of the Fifteenth Century.* University Park: Pennsylvania State University Press, 1998.

———. "Mythologies of Witchcraft in the Fifteenth Century." *Magic, Ritual, and Witchcraft* 1 (2006): 79–108.

Klaniczay, Gábor. *The Uses of Supernatural Power.* Edited by Karen Margolis. Translated by Susan Singerman. Princeton, N.J.: Princeton University Press, 1990.

Kors, Alan, and Edward Peters, eds. *Witchcraft in Europe 400–1700: A Documentary History.* 2nd ed. Philadelphia: University of Pennsylvania Press, 2001.

Kramer, Heinrich. *Malleus maleficarum*. Edited and translated by Christopher S. Mackay. 2 vols. Cambridge: Cambridge University Press, 2006.

Mammoli, Domenico, ed. *The Record of the Trial and Condemnation of a Witch, Mattueccia di Francesco, at Todi, 20 March 1428*. Res Tudertinae 14. Rome: n.p., 1972.

Mormando, Franco. *The Preacher's Demons: Bernardino of Siena and the Social Underworld of Early Renaissance Italy*. Chicago: University of Chicago Press, 1999.

Page, Sophie. *Astrology in Medieval Manuscripts*. Toronto: University of Toronto Press, 2003.

———. *Magic in Medieval Manuscripts*. Toronto: University of Toronto Press, 2004.

Peters, Edward. *The Magician, the Witch, and the Law*. Philadelphia: University of Pennsylvania Press, 1978.

Rider, Catherine. *Magic and Impotence in the Middle Ages*. Oxford: Oxford University Press, 2006.

Rose, Elliot. *A Razor for a Goat: Problems in the History of Witchcraft and Diabolism*. 1962. Reprint, Toronto: University of Toronto Press, 2004.

Russell, Jeffrey Burton. *Witchcraft in the Middle Ages*. Ithaca, N.Y.: Cornell University Press, 1972.

———. *Lucifer: The Devil in the Middle Ages*. Ithaca, N.Y.: Cornell University Press, 1984.

Thorndike, Lynn. *A History of Magic and Experimental Science*. Vols. 1–4. New York: Columbia University Press, 1923–34.

Chapter Five

Anglo, Sydney, ed. *The Damned Art: Essays in the Literature of Witchcraft*. London: Routledge, 1977.

Ankarloo, Bengt, and Stuart Clark, eds. *Witchcraft and Magic in Europe: The Period of the Witch Trials*. Philadelphia: University of Pennsylvania Press, 2002.

Ankarloo, Bengt, and Gustav Henningsen, eds. *Early Modern European Witchcraft: Centres and Peripheries*. Oxford: Oxford University Press, 1990.

Apps, Lara, and Andrew Gow. *Male Witches in Early Modern Europe*. Manchester: Manchester University Press, 2003.

Barry, Jonathan, Marianne Hester, and Gareth Roberts, eds. *Witchcraft in Early Modern Europe: Studies in Culture and Belief*. Cambridge: Cambridge University Press, 1996.

Behringer, Wolfgang. *Shaman of Oberstdorf: Chonrad Stoeckhlin and the Phantoms of the Night*. Translated by H. C. Erik Midelfort. Charlottesville: University of Virginia Press, 1998.

———. *Witchcraft Persecutions in Bavaria: Popular Magic, Religious Zealotry and Reason of State in Early Modern Europe*. Translated by J. C. Grayson and David Lederer. Cambridge: Cambridge University Press, 1998.

———. *Witches and Witch-Hunts: A Global History*. Cambridge: Polity, 2004.

Bostridge, Ian. *Witchcraft and its Transformations c. 1650–c. 1750*. Oxford: Clarendon Press, 1997.

Boyer, Paul, and Stephen Nissenbaum. *Salem Possessed: The Social Origins of Witchcraft.* Cambridge, Mass.: Harvard University Press, 1974.

Brauner, Sigrid. *Fearless Wives and Frightened Shrews: The Construction of the Witch in Early Modern Germany.* Edited by Robert H. Brown. Amherst: University of Massachusetts Press, 1995.

Briggs, Robin. *Witches and Neighbors: The Social and Cultural Context of European Witchcraft.* New York: Viking, 1996.

Caro Baroja, Julio. *The World of the Witches.* Translated by O. N. V. Glendinning. Chicago: University of Chicago Press, 1965.

Ciruelo, Pedro. *Pedro Ciruelo's A Treatise Reproving All Superstitions and Forms of Witchcraft.* Translated by Eugene A. Maio and D'Orsay W. Pearson. Rutherford, N.J.: Fairleigh Dickinson University Press, 1977.

Clark, Stuart. *Thinking with Demons: The Idea of Witchcraft in Early Modern Europe.* Oxford: Clarendon Press, 1997.

Clark, Stuart, ed. *Languages of Witchcraft: Narrative, Ideology and Meaning in Early Modern Culture.* New York: St. Martin's Press, 2001.

Del Rio, Martin. *Investigations into Magic.* Edited and translated by P. G. Maxwell-Stuart. Manchester: Manchester University Press, 2000.

Demos, John Putman. *Entertaining Satan: Witchcraft and the Culture of Early New England.* Oxford: Oxford University Press, 1982.

Gaskill, Malcolm. *Witchfinders: A Seventeenth-Century English Tragedy.* Cambridge, Mass.: Harvard University Press, 2005.

Gentilcore, David. *From Bishop to Witch: The System of the Sacred in Early Modern Terra d'Otranto.* Manchester: Manchester University Press, 1992.

Gibson, Marion. *Reading Witchcraft: Stories of Early English Witches.* London: Routledge, 1999.

———. *Early Modern Witches: Witchcraft Cases in Contemporary Writing.* London: Routledge, 2000.

Gibson, Marion, ed. *Witchcraft and Society in England and America, 1550–1750.* Ithaca, N.Y.: Cornell University Press, 2003.

Ginzburg, Carlo. *The Night Battles: Witchcraft and Agrarian Cults in the Sixteenth and Seventeenth Centuries.* Translated by John and Anne Tedeschi. Baltimore: Johns Hopkins University Press, 1983.

———. *Ecstasies: Deciphering the Witches' Sabbath.* Translated by Raymond Rosenthal. New York: Pantheon, 1991.

Godbeer, Richard. *The Devil's Dominion: Magic and Religion in Early New England.* Cambridge: Cambridge University Press, 1992.

———. *Escaping Salem: The Other Witch Hunt of 1692.* Oxford: Oxford University Press, 2005.

Goodare, Julian, ed. *The Scottish Witch-Hunt in Context.* Manchester: Manchester University Press, 2002.

Henningsen, Gustav. *The Witches' Advocate: Basque Witchcraft and the Spanish Inquisition.* Reno: University of Nevada Press, 1980.

Hester, Marianne. *Lewd Women and Wicked Witches: A Study of the Dynamics of Male Domination.* London: Routledge, 1992.

Hults, Linda C. *The Witch as Muse: Art, Gender, and Power in Early Modern Europe.* Philadelphia: University of Pennsylvania Press, 2005.

Karlsen, Carol F. *The Devil in the Shape of a Woman: Witchcraft in Colonial New England.* 1987. Reprint, New York: Norton, 1998.

Klaits, Joseph. *Servants of Satan: The Age of the Witch Hunts.* Bloomington: Indiana University Press, 1985.

Kors, Alan, and Edward Peters, eds. *Witchcraft in Europe 400–1700: A Documentary History.* 2nd ed. Philadelphia: University of Pennsylvania Press, 2001.

Kunze, Michael. *Highroad to the Stake: A Tale of Witchcraft.* Translated by William E. Yuill. Chicago: University of Chicago Press, 1987.

Larner, Christina. *Enemies of God: The Witch-Hunt in Scotland.* Baltimore: Johns Hopkins University Press, 1981.

———. *Witchcraft and Religion: The Politics of Popular Belief.* Edited by Alan Macfarlane. Oxford: Blackwell, 1984.

Lea, Henry Charles. *Materials Toward a History of Witchcraft.* Edited by Arthur C. Howland. 3 vols. Philadelphia: University of Pennsylvania Press, 1939.

Levack, Brian P. *The Witch-Hunt in Early Modern Europe.* 3rd ed. Harlow, England, and New York: Pearson Longman, 2006.

Macfarlane, Alan. *Witchcraft in Tudor and Stuart England: A Regional and Comparative Study.* London: Routledge, 1970.

Martin, Ruth. *Witchcraft and Inquisition in Venice, 1550–1650.* Oxford: Oxford University Press, 1989.

Maxwell-Stuart, P. G. *Satan's Conspiracy: Magic and Witchcraft in Sixteenth-Century Scotland.* East Lothian, Scotland: Tuckwell, 2001.

———. *Witchcraft in Europe and the New World, 1400–1800.* New York: Palgrave, 2001.

———. *Witch Hunters: Professional Prickers, Unwitchers, and Witch Finders of the Renaissance.* Stroud, England: Tempus, 2003.

———. *An Abundance of Witches: The Great Scottish Witch-Hunt.* Stroud, England: Tempus, 2005.

Midelfort, H. C. Erik. *Witch Hunting in Southwestern Germany, 1562–1684: The Social and Intellectual Foundations.* Stanford, Calif.: Stanford University Press, 1972.

Monter, E. William. *Witchcraft in France and Switzerland: The Borderlands During the Reformation.* Ithaca, N.Y.: Cornell University Press, 1976.

———. *Ritual, Myth, and Magic in Early Modern Europe.* Athens: Ohio University Press, 1983.

Normand, Lawrence, and Gareth Roberts. *Witchcraft in Early Modern Scotland: James VI's Demonology and the North Berwick Witches.* Exeter: University of Exeter Press, 2000.

Norton, Mary Beth. *In the Devil's Snare: The Salem Witchcraft Crisis of 1692*. New York: Knopf, 2002.

Oldridge, Darren, ed. *The Witchcraft Reader*. London: Routledge, 2002.

Pócs, Éva. *Between the Living and the Dead: A Perspective on Witches and Seers in the Early Modern Age*. Translated by Szilvia Rédey and Michael Webb. Budapest: Central European University Press, 1999.

Quaife, G. R. *Godly Zeal and Furious Rage: The Witch in Early Modern Europe*. New York: St. Martin's Press, 1987.

Reis, Elizabeth. *Damned Women: Sinners and Witches in Puritan New England*. Ithaca, N.Y.: Cornell University Press, 1997.

Roper, Lyndal. *Oedipus and the Devil: Witchcraft, Sexuality and Religion in Early Modern Europe*. London: Routledge, 1994.

———. *Witch Craze: Terror and Fantasy in Baroque Germany*. New Haven, Conn.: Yale University Press, 2004.

Rosen, Barbara, ed. *Witchcraft in England, 1558–1618*. Amherst: University of Massachusetts Press, 1991.

Rowlands, Alison. *Witchcraft Narratives in Germany: Rothenburg, 1561–1652*. Manchester: Manchester University Press, 2003.

Scarre, Geoffrey. *Witchcraft and Magic in Sixteenth- and Seventeenth-Century Europe*. 2nd ed. Atlantic Highlands, N.J.: Humanities Press, 2001.

Sharpe, James. *Instruments of Darkness: Witchcraft in Early Modern England*. Philadelphia: University of Pennsylvania Press, 1996.

———. *The Bewtiching of Ann Gunther: A Horrible and True Story of Deception, Witchcraft, Murder, and the King of England*. London: Routledge, 2001.

———. *Witchcraft in Early Modern England*. London: Longman, 2001.

Spee, Friedrich von. *Cautio Criminalis, or a Book on Witch Trials*. Translated by Marcus Hellyer. Charlottesville: University of Virginia Press, 2003.

Stephens, Walter. *Demon Lovers: Witchcraft, Sex, and the Crisis of Belief*. Chicago: University of Chicago Press, 2002.

Thomas, Keith. *Religion and the Decline of Magic*. New York: Scribner, 1971.

Trevor-Roper, H. R. *The European Witch-Craze of the Sixteenth and Seventeenth Centuries and Other Essays*. New York: Harper, 1969.

Weyer, Johann. *Witches, Devils, and Doctors in the Renaissance: Johann Weyer, De Praestigiis Daemonum*. Edited and translated by George Mora. Binghamton, N.Y.: Medieval and Renaissance Texts and Studies, 1991.

———. *On Witchcraft: An Abridged Translation of Johann Weyer's De praestigiis daemonum*. Edited by Benjamin G. Kohl and H. C. Erik Midelfort. Translated by John Shea. Ashville, N.C.: Pegasus Press, 1998.

Williams, Gerhild Scholz. *Defining Dominion: The Discourses of Magic and Witchcraft in Early Modern France and Germany*. Ann Arbor: University of Michigan Press, 1995.

Willis, Deborah. *Malevolent Nurture: Witch-Hunting and Maternal Power in Early Modern England*. Ithaca, N.Y.: Cornell University Press, 1995.

Zika, Charles. *Exorcising our Demons: Magic, Witchcraft and Visual Culture in Early Modern Europe*. Leiden: Brill, 2003.

Chapter Six

Almond, Philip C. *Demonic Possession and Exorcism in Early Modern England: Contemporary Texts and the Cultural Contexts*. Cambridge: Cambridge University Press, 2004.

Ankarloo, Bengt, and Stuart Clark, eds. *Witchcraft and Magic in Europe: The Eighteenth and Nineteenth Centuries*. Philadelphia: University of Pennsylvania Press, 1999.

Connor, James A. *Kepler's Witch: An Astronomer's Discovery of Cosmic Order Amid Religious War, Political Intrigue, and the Heresy Trial of his Mother*. San Francisco: HarperSanFrancisco, 2004.

Copenhaver, Brian. *Hermetica: The Greek Corpus Hermeticum and the Latin Asclepius in a New English Translation with Notes and Introduction*. Cambridge: Cambridge University Press, 1992.

Couliano, Ioan. *Eros and Magic in the Renaissance*. Chicago: University of Chicago Press, 1987.

Daston, Lorraine, and Katharine Park. *Wonders and the Order of Nature 1150–1750*. New York: Zone Books, 1998.

Davies, Owen. *Cunning-Folk: Popular Magic in English History*. London: Hambledon and London, 2003.

Davies, Owen, and Willem de Blécourt, eds. *Beyond the Witch Trials: Witchcraft and Magic in Enlightenment Europe*. Manchester: Manchester University Press, 2004.

Debus, Allen G. and Michael T. Walton, eds. *Reading the Book of Nature: The Other Side of the Scientific Revolution*. Sixteenth Century Essays and Studies 41. Kirksville, Mo.: Sixteenth Century Journal Publishers, 1998.

de León Jones, Karen Silvia. *Giordano Bruno and the Kabbalah: Prophets, Magicians, and Rabbis*. New Haven, Conn.: Yale University Press, 1997.

Eamon, William. *Science and the Secrets of Nature: Books of Secrets in Medieval and Early Modern Culture*. Princeton, N.J.: Princeton University Press, 1994.

Easlea, Brian. *Witch Hunting, Magic, and the New Philosophy: An Introduction to the Debates of the Scientific Revolution, 1450–1750*. Atlantic Highlands, N.J.: Humanities Press, 1980.

Ferber, Sarah. *Demonic Possession and Exorcism in Early Modern France*. London: Routledge, 2004.

Fix, Andrew. *Fallen Angels: Balthasar Bekker, Spirit Belief, and Confessionalism in the Seventeenth-Century Dutch Republic*. Dordrecht, Netherlands: Kluwer, 1999.

Gouk, Penelope. *Music, Science, and Natural Magic in Seventeenth-Century England*. New Haven, Conn.: Yale University Press, 1999.

Grafton, Anthony. *Cardano's Cosmos: The Worlds and Works of a Renaissance Astrologer*. Cambridge, Mass.: Harvard University Press, 1999.

Hanafi, Zakiya. *The Monster in the Machine: Magic, Medicine, and the Marvelous in the Time of the Scientific Revolution*. Durham, N.C.: Duke University Press, 2000.

Hsia, R. Po-chia. *The Myth of Ritual Murder: Jews and Magic in Reformation Germany*. New Haven, Conn.: Yale University Press, 1988.

Lehrich, Christopher I. *The Language of Demons and Angels: Cornelius Agrippa's Occult Philosophy*. Leiden: Brill, 2003.

Lindberg, David C., and Robert S. Westman, eds. *Reappraisals of the Scientific Revolution*. Cambridge: Cambridge University Press, 1990.

Maggi, Armando. *Satan's Rhetoric: A Study of Renaissance Demonology*. Chicago: University of Chicago Press, 2001.

———. *In the Company of Demons: Unnatural Beings, Love, and Identity in the Italian Renaissance*. Chicago: University of Chicago Press, 2006.

Maxwell-Stuart, P. G., ed. *The Occult in Early Modern Europe: A Documentary History*. New York: St. Martin's, 1999.

———. *Wizards: A History*. Stroud, England: Tempus, 2004.

Mebane, John S. *Renaissance Magic and the Return of the Golden Age: The Occult Tradition and Marlowe, Jonson, and Shakespeare*. Lincoln: University of Nebraska Press, 1989.

Merkel, Ingrid, and Allen G. Debus, eds. *Hermeticism and the Renaissance: Intellectual History and the Occult in Early Modern Europe*. Washington, D.C.: Folger Shakespeare Library, 1988.

Moran, Bruce T. *Distilling Knowledge: Alchemy, Chemistry, and the Scientific Revolution*. Cambridge, Mass.: Harvard University Press, 2005.

Ruggiero, Guido. *Binding Passions: Tales of Magic, Marriage and Power at the End of the Renaissance*. Oxford: Oxford University Press, 1993.

Ryan, W. F. *The Bathhouse at Midnight: A Historical Survey of Magic and Divination in Russia*. University Park: Pennsylvania State University Press, 1999.

Scribner, R. W. *Popular Culture and Popular Movements in Reformation Germany*. London: Hambledon Press, 1987.

———. *Religion and Culture in Germany (1400–1800)*. Edited by Lyndal Roper. Leiden: Brill, 2001.

Smith, Pamela H. *The Business of Alchemy: Science and Culture in the Holy Roman Empire*. Princeton, N.J.: Princeton University Press, 1994.

Thorndike, Lynn. *A History of Magic and Experimental Science*. Vols. 5–8. New York: Columbia University Press, 1941–58.

Walker, D. P. *Spiritual and Demonic Magic from Ficino to Campanella*. 1958. Reprint, University Park: Pennsylvania State University Press, 2000.

———. *Unclean Spirits: Possession and Exorcism in France and England in the Late Sixteenth and Early Seventeenth Centuries*. Philadelphia: University of Pennsylvania Press, 1981.

Walker, Timothy D. *Doctors, Folk Medicine and the Inquisition: The Repression of Magical Healing in Portugal during the Enlightenment*. Leiden: Brill, 2005.

Yates, Frances A. *Giordano Bruno and the Hermetic Tradition*. Chicago: University of Chicago Press, 1964.

————. *The Art of Memory*. Chicago: University of Chicago Press, 1966.

————. *The Rosicrucian Enlightenment*. London: Routledge, 1972.

————. *The Occult Philosophy of the Elizabethan Age*. London: Routledge, 1979.

Chapter Seven

Adler, Margot. *Drawing Down the Moon: Witches, Druids, Goddess-Worshippers, and Other Pagans in America Today*. Rev. ed. Boston: Beacon Press, 1986.

Ankarloo, Bengt, and Stuart Clark, eds. *Witchcraft and Magic in Europe: The Twentieth Century*. Philadelphia: University of Pennsylvania Press, 1999.

Bado-Fralick, Nikki. *Coming to the Edge of the Circle: A Wiccan Initiation Ritual*. Oxford: Oxford University Press, 2005.

Berger, Helen A. *A Community of Witches: Contemporary Neo-Paganism and Witchcraft in the United States*. Columbia, S.C.: University of South Carolina Press, 1999.

Berger, Helen A., ed. *Witchcraft and Magic: Contemporary North America*. Philadelphia: University of Pennsylvania Press, 2005.

Blavatsky, H. P. *Isis Unveiled: A Master-Key to the Mysteries of Ancient and Modern Science and Theology*. New York: J. W. Boulton; London: Quaritch, 1877.

Darnton, Robert. *Mesmerism and the End of the Enlightenment in France*. Cambridge, Mass.: Harvard University Press, 1968.

Davies, Owen. *Witchcraft, Magic, and Culture, 1736–1951*. Manchester, England: Manchester University Press, 1999.

Davies, Owen, and Willem de Blécourt, eds. *Witchcraft Continued: Popular Magic in Modern Europe*. Manchester: Manchester University Press, 2005.

Devlin, Judith. *The Superstitious Mind: French Peasants and the Supernatural in the Nineteenth Century*. New Haven, Conn.: Yale University Press, 1987.

Eller, Cynthia. *Living in the Lap of the Goddess: The Feminist Spirituality Movement in America*. Boston: Beacon Press, 1995.

Faivre, Antoine, and Jacob Needleman, eds. *Modern Esoteric Spirituality*. New York: Crossroads Publishing Company, 1992.

Favret-Saada, Jeanne. *Deadly Words: Witchcraft in the Bocage*. Translated by Catherine Cullen. Cambridge: Cambridge University Press, 1980.

Gardner, Gerald B. *Witchcraft Today*. London: Rider, 1954.

Gibbons, J. B. *Spirituality and the Occult: From the Renaissance to the Modern Age*. London: Routledge, 2001.

Greenwood, Susan. *Magic, Witchcraft and the Otherworld: An Anthropology*. Oxford: Berg, 2000.

Harvey, David Allen. *Beyond Enlightenment: Occultism and Politics in Modern France*. DeKalb: Northern Illinois University Press, 2005.

Hutton, Ronald. *The Triumph of the Moon: A History of Modern Pagan Witchcraft*. Oxford: Oxford University Press, 1999.

Jacob, Margaret C. *The Origins of Freemasonry: Facts and Fictions*. Philadelphia: University of Pennsylvania Press, 2006.

Kelly, Aidan. *Crafting the Art of Magic*. St. Paul, Minn.: Llewellyn, 1991.

Leland, Charles G. *Aradia, or the Gospel of the Witches*. 1899. Reprint, Custer, Wash.: Phoenix Publishing, 1996.

Lévi, Éliphas. *Transcendental Magic: Its Doctrine and Ritual*. Translated by Arthur Edward Waite. London: Rider, 1896.

Lewis, James R. *Magical Religion and Modern Witchcraft*. Albany: State University of New York Press, 1996.

Luhrmann, T. M. *Persuasions of the Witch's Craft: Ritual Magic in Contemporary England*. Cambridge, Mass.: Harvard University Press, 1989.

Magliocco, Sabina. *Witching Culture: Folklore and Neo-Paganism in America*. Philadelphia: University of Pennsylvania Press, 2004.

McCalman, Ian. *The Last Alchemist: Count Cagliostro, Master of Magic in the Age of Reason*. New York: HaperCollins, 2003.

Meyer, Brigit, and Peter Pels, eds. *Magic and Modernity: Interfaces of Revelation and Concealment*. Stanford, Calif.: Stanford University Press, 2003.

Michelet, Jules. *Satanism and Witchcraft: A Study in Medieval Superstition*. Translated by A. R. Allinson. New York: Walden Publications, 1939. Most recently reprinted as *Witchcraft, Sorcery, and Superstition*. Secaucus, N.J.: Carol Publishing Group, 1995.

Midelfort, H. C. Erik. *Exorcism and Enlightenment: Johann Joseph Gassner and the Demons of Eighteenth-Century Germany*. New Haven, Conn.: Yale University Press, 2005.

Murray, Margaret A. *The Witch-Cult in Western Europe: A Study in Anthropology*. Oxford: Clarendon Press, 1921.

———. *The God of the Witches*. London: Sampson Low, Marston, 1931.

———. *The Divine King of England: A Study in Anthropology*. London: Faber and Faber, 1954.

Owen, Alex. *The Darkened Room: Women, Power, and Spiritualism in Late Nineteenth Century England*. Philadelphia: University of Pennsylvania Press, 1990.

———. *The Place of Enchantment: British Occultism and the Culture of the Modern*. Chicago: University of Chicago Press, 2004.

Pearson, Jeanne, Richard Roberts, and Geoffrey Samuel, eds. *Nature Religions Today: Paganism in the Modern World*. Edinburgh: Edinburgh University Press, 1998.

Pike, Sarah M. *Earthly Bodies, Magical Selves: Contemporary Pagans and the Search for Community*. Berkeley: University of California Press, 2001.

Salomonsen, Jone. *Enchanted Feminism: The Reclaiming Witches of San Francisco*. London: Routledge, 2002.

Starhawk. *The Spiral Dance: A Rebirth of the Ancient Religion of the Great Goddess*. 20th Anniversary Edition. San Francisco: HarperSanFrancisco, 1999.

Styers, Randall. *Making Magic: Religion, Magic, and Science in the Modern World*. Oxford: Oxford University Press, 2004.

Tambiah, Stanley J. *Magic, Science, Religion, and the Scope of Rationality.* Cambridge: Cambridge University Press, 1990.

Treitel, Corinna. *A Science for the Soul: Occultism and the Genesis of the German Modern.* Baltimore: Johns Hopkins University Press, 2004.

Washington, Peter. *Madame Blavatsky's Baboon: Theosophy and the Emergence of the Western Guru.* London: Secker and Warburg, 1993.

Winter, Alison. *Mesmerized: Powers of Mind in Victorian England.* Chicago: University of Chicago Press, 1998.

Worobec, Christine D. *Possessed: Women, Witches, and Demons in Imperial Russia.* DeKalb: Northern Illinois University Press, 2001.

Index

About the Author

Michael D. Bailey is assistant professor of history at Iowa State University. He studied at Northwestern University as well as at the universities of Basel and Munich. He has previously taught the history of magic and witchcraft at the University of Cincinnati, Saint Louis University, and the University of Pennsylvania. His publications include *Battling Demons: Witchcraft, Heresy, and Reform in the Late Middle Ages* (2003) and *Historical Dictionary of Witchcraft* (2003). He is currently working on a book about superstition in late medieval Europe.